Higher and Degree Apprenticeships

This edited collection offers a comprehensive exploration of Higher and Degree Apprenticeships, bringing together perspectives from learners, employers, educators, coaches, providers, and policy influencers. It provides readers with real-world insights into the application, potential challenges, and successes of higher degree apprenticeships alongside the knowledge and tools needed to thrive within this sector.

Divided into three key sections, the book enables a holistic understanding of how Higher and Degree Apprenticeships function in practice. Part I focuses on the perspectives of key stakeholders, including the Learner, the Employer, the university training provider, the Learner Coach and compliance and regulatory bodies. Part II explores industry contexts, with chapters dedicated to health and social care, education, business and management, finance, and cyber security.

This is an essential resource for students, educators, employers, and policymakers, as well as a must-read for anyone seeking to deepen their understanding or succeed in this dynamic and evolving field.

Emily Beaumont is an Associate Professor of Enterprise and Entrepreneurship and Head of REF at the University of Gloucestershire, UK.

Stephanie Reynolds is the stream lead for the Chartered Manager Degree Apprenticeship, Lecturer, and Learner Coach at the University of Gloucestershire, UK.

Matthew Scott is a Senior Lecturer and Apprenticeship Co-Ordinator at the University of Gloucestershire, UK.

Clare Taylor is the Academic Course Leader for the Senior Leader Apprenticeship and Senior People Professional Apprenticeship at the University of Gloucestershire, UK.

Higher and Degree Apprenticeships

A 360-Degree, Multi-Perspective View

Edited by
Emily Beaumont,
Stephanie Reynolds,
Matthew Scott,
and Clare Taylor

Routledge
Taylor & Francis Group
LONDON AND NEW YORK

Cover image: Appleuzr via Getty Images

First published 2026
by Routledge
4 Park Square, Milton Park, Abingdon, Oxon OX14 4RN

and by Routledge
605 Third Avenue, New York, NY 10158

Routledge is an imprint of the Taylor & Francis Group, an informa business

British Library Cataloguing-in-Publication Data
A catalogue record for this book is available from the British Library

ISBN: 978-1-032-93838-7 (hbk)
ISBN: 978-1-032-93832-5 (pbk)
ISBN: 978-1-003-56784-4 (ebk)

DOI: 10.4324/9781003567844

Typeset in Optima
by SPi Technologies India Pvt Ltd (Straive)

Contents

Contributors

Jordan Allison is a Senior Lecturer in Computer Science in the School of Business, Computing and Social Sciences at the University of Gloucestershire, United Kingdom. He has experience as an Academic Course Leader for the Digital Technology Solutions Degree Apprenticeship, including achieving Tech Industry Gold Accreditation. Jordan has served as an Apprenticeship lead during Ofsted Inspections, recruited and coordinated a team of learner review coaches, and successfully led validation processes for collaborative partner apprenticeship courses.

Elizabeth Ashman has had a long and varied career ranging from a veterinary nurse and civil servant, through to an extended period working in the NHS as a clinical vascular scientist with career progression to Head of Vascular Services in an acute trust. Elizabeth has been able to further develop her capabilities and skillset through completing an MBA and SLA (level 7), for which she studied alongside her full-time work commitments. During this learning journey, Elizabeth paid focus to developing a network of contacts, who were enablers of extending her knowledge and tools for success. Elizabeth's assigned learner coach was critical in facilitating the drawing together of her knowledge gaps and aligning any learning experiences to her career aspirations. Consequentially, Elizabeth has further climbed the professional ladder and gone on to successfully deliver whole-organisation transformational and strategic change. This has brought about her heightened job satisfaction with immense personal and professional reward, as well as bringing added value for the associated organisations and their staff, and patient, outcomes.

Emily Beaumont is an Associate Professor of Enterprise and Entrepreneurship at the University of Gloucestershire, UK. Emily is a former President and current Director of Enterprise Educators UK (EEUK), a membership organisation that enables excellence in enterprise and entrepreneurship education by connecting and supporting enterprise and entrepreneurship educators across the UK. Emily is also an active member of the AGCAS (Association of Graduate Careers and Advisory Services) Enterprise and Entrepreneurship Task Group, Director and Vice President of ISBE (Institute for Small Business and Entrepreneurship), and Co-Chair of the Research in Enterprise and Entrepreneurship Education Special Interest Group, a collaboration between EEUK and ISBE.

Stavroula Bibila started her teaching career as a Further Education lecturer. Before making the transition into work-based learning and degree apprenticeships in 2018, she was a PhD student at Cardiff University and an ESRC visiting researcher at the European Centre for the Development of Vocational Training (CEDEFOP). As a post-doctoral researcher, she examined curriculum and assessment strategies for postgraduate work-based learning programmes in the NHS. She is a co-convenor for the Universities Association for Lifelong Learning (UALL) Work & Learning Network and a member of the Practitioner Advisory Group (PAG) to the Society for Education and Training (SET).

Dan Boon is Early Careers & Skills Development Lead at Gloucestershire County Council, a role he has held since 2016. With eight years' prior experience in the apprenticeship sector as a Trainer, Assessor, and Area Manager, Dan's career began in hospitality management in London and Gloucestershire. Passionate about training and development, he now supports community initiatives that enhance education, training, and employment opportunities for local residents.

Kieron Chadwick is a Senior Lecturer in Business at the University of Staffordshire, author and consultant qualified to doctorate level via the CMI Level 8 Diploma in Strategic Direction and Leadership. A first-generation university attendee, Kieron obtained a BA (Hons) in Business Management via the Chartered Manager Degree Apprenticeship (CMDA) and MSc in Management with Human Resources as a mature student. He is a Chartered Manager and Fellow (CMgr FCMI) of the Chartered Management Institute (CMI) and Fellow (FHEA) of AdvanceHE.

Helen Charlton is Associate Professor and Head of Executive Education at Newcastle Business School, leading business apprenticeships, executive CPD, and distance learning. With extensive expertise in Higher and Degree Apprenticeships, she bridges academic theory and professional practice. Helen's research interests include practice-based HRM, informed by senior human resources (HR) roles in the not-for-profit and arts sectors. A Senior Fellow of the HEA, Chartered CIPD member, and CMI Fellow, she co-convenes UVAC's HE Tripartite Professionals network to professionalise apprenticeship delivery.

Michelle Civile is a Senior Lecturer at the University of Exeter, specialising in work-based learning and Degree Apprenticeships. She leads on programme development and delivery for professional learners, ensuring strong links between academic theory and industry practice. With extensive experience in higher education and professional development, Michelle focuses on innovative pedagogies that support career progression and lifelong learning. She is committed to enhancing student experience through inclusive teaching and industry engagement.

Sophie Cole is a dedicated education pracademic and Department Head of Apprenticeships at Northumbria University, championing collaborative, creative cultures that make apprenticeships transformative and employer relationships reciprocal. She designed and leads the Academic Professional Higher Apprenticeship for early-career academics and NHS clinical educators, blending theory and practice to develop professional leaders. Her research explores higher education pedagogy, accountability, and fostering belonging. Sophie is also an independent End-Point Assessor and external examiner for the Academic Professional Apprenticeship nationally.

Fernando Correia is a Senior Lecturer in Sustainable Business for the Degree Apprenticeships and Executive Education programmes at the University of Exeter. Fernando has more than 20 years of professional and academic experience in sustainability-related fields. Having started his career as an ecologist and, later on, development work in the third sector, he started his research career with a PhD on the implementation of sustainable tourism in Protected Areas across Europe. Since then, he has worked in academia and consultancy in areas like the low-carbon economy, sustainable procurement, leadership for sustainability, sustainable tourism, well-being and ecosystem services, and skills for sustainability, amongst others.

Mandy Crawford-Lee is Chief Executive of the Universities Vocational Awards Council (UVAC), where she leads policy and operations, representing over 80 UK universities. With extensive experience in skills policy, strategic planning, and education reform, she has been instrumental in shaping national policy that expanded higher-level apprenticeships beyond Level 3 into professional and managerial pathways. Since joining UVAC in 2012, Mandy has championed degree apprenticeships and higher technical education, establishing UVAC as the leading authority on higher and degree apprenticeships in England.

Susan Dawson is Assistant Professor and Head of Apprenticeships in the Department of Architecture and Built Environment at Northumbria University's Faculty of Engineering and Environment. She leads on the development and delivery of apprenticeship programmes, ensuring strong collaboration between industry and academia. With expertise in built environment education, Susan is committed to embedding work-based learning into higher education curricula. She actively supports apprentices' professional development and fosters innovative approaches to teaching and industry engagement.

Julie Derbyshire is Associate Professor and Programme Leader of Nursing Apprenticeships at Northumbria University, where she also serves as Head of Apprenticeships in the Department for Nursing, Midwifery and Health, Faculty of Health and Life Sciences. Julie leads on the design and delivery of innovative nursing apprenticeship pathways that bridge academic study with clinical practice. Passionate about workforce development, she supports apprentices to thrive in health professions and promotes collaboration between universities and healthcare employers.

Peter Dickinson is employed at the Warwick Institute for Employment Research, and currently specialises in local labour market jobs and skills and their intersection with productivity and inclusive growth. Recently, Peter has led a number of research projects focusing on apprenticeships, including: the impact of the Apprenticeship Levy; the development of degree apprenticeships; and apprentice wage setting. He is also leading on research analysing the impact of new technology, and the green transition on jobs and skills.

Hilary Duckett is an internationally experienced academic who has held senior strategic and operational leadership roles. She is Director of the Senior Leader Apprenticeship at the University of Exeter. She has delivered several funded research projects, including a Management Knowledge Transfer Partnership and two international projects supporting women tech entrepreneurs (Philippines) and women into senior leadership roles (Nigeria).

Emily Erickson is employed at the Warwick Institute for Employment Research and has particular research interests in apprenticeships, the impact of new technology on jobs and skills and productivity, job quality and access, and migrant labour. Emily is particularly interested in how labour markets and public policy can shape local community development.

Marian Evans is a Senior Lecturer in Entrepreneurship and Enterprise at Leicester Castle Business School, De Montfort University. A former owner-manager and SME director, she remains active in business and brings extensive industry experience in apprenticeships and management training. Marian's teaching and research focus on entrepreneurial cognition, innovation, and higher degree apprenticeships. She has designed executive programmes, teaches across Senior Leader Apprenticeship, Master of Business Administration and Chartered Manager Degree Apprenticeship courses, and has published widely. Her current research explores pedagogy, innovation, start-up mindset and apprenticeship relationships.

Beverley Gibbs is Director of the Dyson Institute of Engineering and Technology and chairs the Engineering Professors' Council's Education, Employability and Skills Committee. An engineer by background and an apprenticeship alumna herself, she champions work-ready, industry-focused pedagogy in higher education. Beverley has led initiatives like Year in Industry degrees at the University of Sheffield and challenge-based learning at New Model Institute for Technology Engineering (NMITE) Hereford. She now leads the Dyson Institute, delivering engineering degree apprenticeships and employer-sponsored degrees, and is also an academic accreditor with the Institution of Engineering and Technology (IET).

Peter Goodwin is an Academic Mentor supporting the Senior Leader Degree Apprentices within the University of Exeter Business School. His role is to guide and facilitate understanding of the requirements of evidencing achievement against the Senior Leader Apprenticeship Standard.

Julian Grail is a Senior Lecturer in Enterprise with over 25 years' experience in senior business roles, including running and establishing companies. A self-described pracademic, he brings real-world insight into the classroom, making learning practical and engaging using creative teaching tools. He teaches subjects such as strategy, entrepreneurship, enterprise, and management consultancy. He is an apprenticeship Learner Coach and enjoys helping learners apply their academic knowledge to workplace practice. Julian mentors and advises startup and SME business owners across various sectors. He holds multiple postgraduate qualifications and is a Chartered Manager and Fellow of both the Chartered Management Institute and Higher Education Academy.

Rhidian Lewis has worked at the University of Bedfordshire, UK, since 2013. Initially, Rhidian worked within the Business School, where he was responsible for working with small and medium-sized businesses from across the local region to access support, guidance, and training opportunities. Since 2017, Rhidian has championed the opportunities that exist for employers and employees through the modern apprenticeships programme. Currently, Rhidian is the University of Bedfordshire's Lead for Apprenticeships, working across all faculties and disciplines to raise awareness of apprenticeships and the benefits that such development activities can bring.

Naowarat Lewis is an Associate Professor in Educational Technology at Anglia Ruskin University, UK. Her background in Applied Statistics, Information Technology and Information Science has formed a major part of her research and teaching activities. Her research investigations have led to the development of the 'Lewis Dynamic Model', which highlights tutor–learner engagement and achievement through the use and application of technology. Her dedication to enhancing students' learning experiences and employability skills through digital media and technology-based platforms has yielded significant improvements in student achievement.

Michael Matthews is a Senior Lecturer in Strategy at the University of Exeter Business School. He has expertise in strategic business planning and finance and supports learners through their project planning as part of the apprenticeship standard.

Paula McIver Nottingham is an experienced academic practitioner specialising in practice-based and work-integrated learning within higher education. She currently leads a professional doctorate at Middlesex University and was a co-programme leader for a standards-based degree apprenticeship. Paula is a co-convenor for the Universities Association for Lifelong Learning (UALL) Work & Learning Network and led a government-funded collaborative project for the Apprenticeship Workforce Development (AWD) programme that featured both on- and off-the job learning/training. Paula's professional interests include pedagogic research, degree apprenticeships, doctoral studies, professional practice/work-based learning, creative higher education, lifelong learning, and the use of digital technology for learning.

Julie Pepper is Programme Director of the Operations Manager Apprenticeship and the Chartered Manager Degree Apprenticeship (Amazon) at the University of Exeter. Also, she currently convenes a module on self-awareness, where she brings psychology research and Lego Serious Play into her teaching. A common thread through Julie's work is her interest in workplace psychology – women in risky leadership positions, rule breaking, healthy workplaces, and the careers that young people aspire to. Julie has published research on all of these topics.

Phil Power-Mason is Head of Strategic Management at the University of Hertfordshire Business School, overseeing executive education, apprenticeships, and diverse programmes. With extensive expertise in higher and degree apprenticeships, he bridges academic theory with professional practice, supported by his business partnerships. Phil's interests span educational leadership, governance, and policy, underpinned by public sector experience. He has held governance and consultancy roles in education and charities, holds a PhD in Management Studies, is a Senior Fellow of the HEA, and convenes national networks to advance tripartite collaboration.

Debbie Reel has more than twenty years' experience in higher education and is known for her purpose-driven approach to staff development and support for new educators. Starting in primary education, she has specialised since 2002 in adult learning and mentoring. As Academic Course Leader for two Level 7 professional development programmes, Debbie designs and delivers impactful learning, applying strong pedagogical principles that emphasise how we teach. She integrates entrepreneurial skills and coaching to foster growth, empowering the next generation of educators and leaders.

Stephanie Reynolds is a Lecturer, Learner Coach and Stream Lead for the Chartered Manager Degree Apprenticeship at the University of Gloucestershire. She has an extensive background in education from secondary teaching, right through to master's-level degree apprenticeships. Stephanie spent five years working on the Office for Students Uni Connect Programme, which highlighted the opportunities higher and degree apprenticeships can offer our most disadvantaged learners. Stephanie is also a member of the UCAS Media Advisory Board.

Victoria Rosamond works as a Senior Lecturer in Business and Management at the University of Derby, UK, and is the Programme Leader for the Chartered Manager Degree Apprenticeships (CMDA). With expertise in finance, marketing, and vocational education and having more than ten years of industry experience, Victoria works closely with the industrial partners and the Chartered Management Institute to design and deliver applied learning within degree apprenticeships. She works closely with the apprentices to conduct their professional reviews, guide them through business impact projects, and support them as they progress towards successful completion of their End Point Assessment (EPA). An active member of the University Vocational Awards Council (UVAC), she contributes to the structure and delivery of high-quality apprenticeship programmes across sectors.

Julia Russell is the Senior Advisor for Early Careers Resourcing and Programmes at Renishaw plc and speaks regularly with other businesses that employ apprentices. Julia is a member of the Apprentice Ambassador Network and Next Gen Makers and has been in her role since 2021. She was previously the Apprentice Lead in the business. Julia has worked at Renishaw since 2006, moving from an Assembly Operator position, into Human Resources as a Recruitment Administrator, and then (in 2009) started working with apprentices. The scope of her role has grown alongside an increase in the number of early careers programmes the company offers.

Adrienne Sharples is interim Head of the School of Applied Social Sciences at the University of Bedfordshire, UK. She trained as a podiatrist at the University of Salford and joined the National Health Service in 1989, where she practised for 25 years within in a variety of clinical podiatry and practice placement roles. After joining the University of Bedfordshire in 2014, Adrienne delivered apprenticeships for assistant practitioners and nursing associates, and became the school Apprenticeship Lead for a variety of apprenticeships in health and social care. She has also led on the curriculum development, implementation, and evaluation of a variety of apprenticeships in this field.

Peter Stephenson is a Lecturer in Leadership and Management on the Degree Apprenticeships programme at the University of Exeter. Coming from an entrepreneurial background, having started and successfully exited two ventures, he turned to academia in 2019, gaining an MBA and a PhD in the field of leadership. Peter is an active researcher and a reviewer for *Leadership* journal.

Clare Taylor is Senior Lecturer in Leadership and Human Resource Management at the University of Gloucestershire, UK. Clare has extensive experience of leading educational courses and is currently responsible for two master's-level higher degree apprenticeships – Senior Leader and Senior People. Clare has spent her 15-year-long academic career supporting professional learners in achieving their personal and professional goals through master's-level study. She also brings a wealth of real-life experience, having worked in industry for 12 years prior to a career change. These personal and professional work-based experiences enable her to offer a unique perspective on leading, managing, and enhancing higher degree apprenticeship programmes to meet the contemporary challenges of the world of work.

Ahmad Timsal works as a Lecturer of Business & Management at the University of Derby, UK. He has been associated with the academic sector for more than a decade. He has also worked in the corporate sector for several years as a Business Development Manager, with tech giants such as IBM. Dr. Ahmad completed his PhD from Lancaster University. At the University of Derby, he teaches on the Chartered Manager Degree Apprenticeship (CMDA) programme, combining academic insight with real-world business application. He provides tailored support to apprentices across a range of academic activities, including developing independent research skills, academic writing, critical analysis, and preparation for End-Point Assessment (EPA).

1 Introduction

Emily Beaumont,
Matthew Scott, Clare Taylor, and
Stephanie Reynolds

Higher (Levels 4, 5, 6, and 7) and Degree Apprenticeships (Levels 6 and 7) (H&DAs) are developing a solid reputation as the flagship apprenticeship programmes in England (Universities UK, 2021). Introduced in England in 2015, Degree Apprenticeships (DA) marked a pivotal shift in higher-level skills policy, offering an alternative, flexible route that combines paid employment with structured academic study. Designed to be both vocationally relevant and academically rigorous, these programmes differ from traditional higher education by being co-developed with employers through trailblazer groups (employer-led groups that develop new apprenticeship standards), ensuring curriculum content aligns closely with real workplace demands (Crawford-Lee & Moorwood, 2019). Their rapid growth reflects a wider response to the increasing need for work-ready graduates and the demand for higher-level skills, supporting the former and current government's ambition to close persistent skills gaps and boost productivity (Department for Education [DfE], 2024). As a result, Higher and DA have become a significant component of the UK's education and workforce development landscape. Recent figures highlight this: participation in Higher Apprenticeships rose by 4.75% from 261,300 in 2022/23 to 273,700 in 2023/2024 (DfE, 2025). This steady increase suggests that higher-level apprenticeships are now firmly embedded as a credible, work-based alternative to full-time university study, supporting the government's aim to address skills gaps in key sectors such as engineering, nursing, social work, policing, and leadership and management across all sectors (Universities UK, 2021; CMI, 2022).

Early data for the 2024/2025 academic year (covering August 2024 to January 2025) reinforces this upward trend. Higher Apprenticeship starts

DOI: 10.4324/9781003567844-1

have increased by 8.7% compared to the same period last year, reaching 76,970 (DfE, 2025). Starts at Level 6 and 7, which include DA, have risen even more sharply – up by 12.5% to 36,570. This now represents 18.1% of all apprenticeship starts so far this year, compared to 16.2% over the same period last year. This growth indicates that employers are increasingly confident in using DA to develop their future professional and managerial workforce, while learners see them as a valuable, debt-free route into graduate-level employment (Crawford-Lee & Wall, 2018).

H&DA give employers an effective way to attract new talent and widen access to skilled jobs (Crawford-Lee & Moorwood, 2019). Given their professional and technical focus, that often suits those already established in work, it is perhaps unsurprising that the DfE (2024) reports that H&DA are mainly taken up by people over the age of 25. In 2023/2024, only about 4,300 out of 92,840 Higher Apprenticeship leavers were aged 16–18, just 4.6% of the total. In contrast, 25.1% were aged 19–24, while the largest proportion; 69.1%, were aged 25 and over. Notably, the share of learners aged 25 and above grew by 1.4% from 2022/2023 to 2023/2024, indicating a steady trend of mature learners continuing to use these pathways to upskill or retrain. There are also positive signs that H&DA are an increasingly inclusive form of education with the number of apprentices from ethnic minority backgrounds increasing at a faster rate than the overall apprenticeship population. For example, starts for learners from ethnic minorities (excluding white minorities) grew from 12,760 in 2019/2020 to 23,560 in 2023/2024, an 84% increase (DfE, 2024). This suggests H&DA are helping to support greater ethnic diversity across higher-level skills routes.

There is also increasing participation of learners with learning difficulties and/or disabilities (LLDD). The total number of Higher Apprenticeship learners recorded as having an LLDD rose from 7,160 in 2019/2020 to 15,730 in 2023/2024, more than doubling over five years (DfE, 2024). For the current academic year so far (August 2024 to January 2025), 10,190 Higher Apprenticeship starts are already recorded for LLDD learners, indicating that this upward trend is likely to continue (DfE, 2025). This increase means that learners with an LLDD now represent a much larger share of the Higher Apprenticeship cohort than they did previously demonstrating that H&DA can offer accessible routes for learners with additional needs to progress in both education and employment, supporting national policy goals to extend opportunity and raise skill levels for all (UVAC, 2023).

Perhaps the most significant factor regarding the inclusivity of H&DA is that they offer learners a debt-free pathway to higher education. Unlike traditional university routes, apprentices earn while they learn, avoiding the burden of tuition fees and student loans (Yeboah, 2024). This makes them particularly attractive to learners from diverse backgrounds, mature students, and those who may otherwise be deterred by the cost of full-time study (Universities UK, 2021).

For universities and other higher education providers, H&DA represent a new way to engage with employers and co-create workforce solutions that respond to rapidly changing skills demands (UVAC, 2023) and meet regional needs. This approach allows institutions to diversify their student base, strengthen employer partnerships, and adapt provision to support local and regional economic priorities, all within an increasingly complex and shifting quality assurance and funding landscape (Crawford-Lee & Wall, 2018). Those teaching on apprenticeships, who we refer to as the 'Educators' in this book, also play a critical role, operating at the intersection of pedagogy, compliance, and industry relevance. They must navigate dual accountabilities to learners and employers, develop curricula that meet both academic and occupational standards (QAA, 2021), and balance innovation with regulatory demands from organisations such as the Office for Standards in Education, Children's Services and Skills (OFSTED), the Office for Students (OfS), the Education and Skills Funding Agency (ESFA), the Institute for Apprenticeships and Technical Education (IfATE), the Quality Assurance Agency (QAA) and any relevant Professional, Statutory and Regulatory Bodies (PSRBs). Alongside the Educators, Learner Coaches (also known as learning/workplace mentor, apprenticeship advisor and many other iterations) have emerged as vital figures in apprenticeship support and the tripartite relationship, offering pastoral care, academic mentoring, and professional development guidance that help apprentices succeed in both workplace and academic settings.

However, there is a fly in the H&DA ointment, following a recent announcement from the government. In June 2025, the government stated their future investment focus would be towards young people at the start of their working lives, rather than those already in work with higher levels of prior learning and qualifications. Consequently, from January 2026, the UK government will change how Level 7 apprenticeships are funded and will only continue to be government-funded for young people aged 16–21, and under 25 for care leavers and those with an Education, Health and Care Plan (EHCP).

Clearly, this will have a significant impact, not only on learner numbers and the learners themselves, but on employers, key sectors and public and private providers. Vivienne Stern MBE, Chief Executive of Universities UK said:

> The exemption for those aged 21 and under will leave so few students on these courses eligible for funding that many will become unviable at a time when Skills England's forecasts show we need more high-level skills in the economy.
>
> (2025)

About H&DA: A 360-degree multi-perspective view

This edited volume, *H&DA: A 360-Degree Multi-Perspective View*, is purposefully structured to offer a 360-degree, multi-perspective view of H&DA, foregrounding the experiences, challenges, and contributions of the full range of stakeholders involved. Chapters are organised around key roles within the apprenticeship ecosystem; learners, employers (public and private, both large and SME), educators, providers (public and private), Learner Coaches, and trailblazer groups. This approach enables a holistic understanding of how H&DA function in practice, capturing the relational and interdependent nature of H&DAs.

The Learner-focused chapters offer a rich exploration of the lived experiences of H&DA participants. Learners are portrayed as active decision-makers, often drawn to H&DA by the promise of a debt-free, career-focused alternative to traditional higher education. These chapters highlight the appeal of real-world experience and the opportunity to apply learning directly in the workplace, which enhances confidence and professional identity. They also explore how H&DA can support social mobility, while acknowledging persistent barriers such as structural inequalities and regional disparities. Personal narratives emphasise the importance of supportive employers, effective mentorship, and strong peer networks – especially for those balancing academic study with full-time work. By centring the Learner voice, these chapters challenge traditional assumptions about higher education and underscore the transformative potential of learning through work.

The Employer-focused chapters examine the critical role employers play in the success of H&DA. Drawing on experiences across sectors and organisation sizes, they reveal both the opportunities and challenges of employer engagement. While large employers often have the resources to navigate apprenticeship systems, they still face issues such as policy shifts and aligning academic content with business needs. SMEs, on the other hand, often struggle with administrative burdens but bring unique strengths like agility, community ties, and personalised mentoring. These chapters also explore employer perspectives on programme design, funding mechanisms, and the value of long-term partnerships with providers. A clear message emerges: meaningful employer involvement enhances not only business outcomes but also broader goals of inclusion and workforce development.

Chapters focused on educators delve into their evolving and multifaceted roles within H&DA. Educators operate at the intersection of pedagogy, policy, and partnership, co-designing curricula with employers and adapting teaching to meet occupational standards. These chapters highlight the pressures educators face, from regulatory compliance to balancing academic quality with learner support. The emergence of industry-informed academics: 'pracademics', is explored, along with the challenges they face in traditional academic structures. The chapters call for institutional reforms, including clearer workload models and more inclusive promotion pathways, to better support those delivering apprenticeship education.

The chapter on providers explores the strategic and structural challenges faced by Higher Education Institutions (HEIs) and Independent Training Providers (ITPs). Using Johnson et al.'s (2011) four lenses of strategy, it examines market dynamics, regulatory pressures, and the need for innovation. It warns against over-reliance on apprenticeships for income and advocates for strategic diversification and collaboration across sectors.

Chapters on the Learner Coach highlight their pivotal role in supporting apprentices. Framed as tripartite practitioners, coaches bridge the gap between academic, pastoral, and professional development. Through case studies, these chapters show how structured coaching enhances learner achievement, confidence, and reflective practice.

Finally, the chapter on trailblazers critiques the Employer-led development of apprenticeship standards. It reveals a dominance of large employers and underrepresentation of SMEs, particularly in generic occupations. This imbalance risks narrowing the relevance and legitimacy of standards. The chapter calls for more inclusive, transparent, and representative governance to ensure apprenticeship standards reflect the full spectrum of employer needs.

The book also considers H&DA from prominent discipline areas where they are particularly active, including Health and Social Care, Education, Engineering, Computing, and Business and Management. These disciplines reflect not only high levels of apprenticeship enrolment but also areas of critical national skills need, ensuring the content is relevant to both policy and practice. By combining diverse stakeholder voices with discipline-specific insights, the book offers a comprehensive picture of the opportunities and tensions within H&DAs. This structure ensures readers gain both breadth and depth of understanding, positioning the book as a valuable resource for improving policy, pedagogy, and practice across the apprenticeship landscape.

Looking ahead: Sustaining progress and navigating change

As this introduction has outlined, H&DAs represent a dynamic and evolving part of England's skills and education landscape. Their growth, diversity, and increasing inclusivity signal a shift in how higher-level learning is accessed, delivered, and valued. Yet, as the chapters ahead will show, this evolution is not without complexity. The recent policy changes to Level 7 funding underscore the fragility of progress and the need for sustained advocacy, evidence-informed practice, and inclusive policymaking.

This book brings together a wide range of voices; learners, employers, educators, coaches, providers, and policy influencers and explores the lived realities, strategic tensions, and transformative potential of H&DA. By presenting these perspectives side by side, we aim to foster a deeper understanding of the interdependencies that shape apprenticeship success and sustainability.

Whether you are a policymaker, practitioner, researcher, or stakeholder in the apprenticeship ecosystem, we invite you to engage critically with the insights offered in the chapters that follow. Together, they provide not only a panoramic view of H&DA but also a call to action: to protect and enhance these pathways so they continue to serve learners, employers, and society in meaningful and equitable ways.

References

Chartered Management Institute (CMI). (2022). *Apprenticeships: The Skills Solution*. https://www.managers.org.uk/knowledge-and-insights/research/apprenticeships-the-skills-solution/

Crawford-Lee, M., & Moorwood, S. (2019). Degree apprenticeships: Delivering quality and social mobility? *Higher Education, Skills and Work-Based Learning*, 9(2), 134–140. https://doi.org/10.1108/HESWBL-05-2019-123

Crawford-Lee, M. S., & Wall, T. (2018). Sustainability 2030: A policy perspective from the university vocational awards council. *Higher Education, Skills and Work-Based Learning*, 8(3), 233–242. https://doi.org/10.1108/HESWBL-03-2018-0037

Department for Education (DfE). (2024). *Apprenticeships in England: Academic Year 2023/24*. https://explore-education-statistics.service.gov.uk/find-statistics/apprenticeships

Department for Education (DfE). (2025). *Apprenticeships: Academic Year 2024/25* (August 2024 to January 2025). https://explore-education-statistics.service.gov.uk/data-tables/fast-track/7eeeff60-ea52-487c-aee3-08dd33ecd5dc

Johnson, G., Scholes, K. & Whittington, R. (2011). *Exploring Corporate Strategy: Text and Cases*. 9th edn. Pearson Education.

Quality Assurance Agency for Higher Education (QAA). (2021). *Advice and Guidance: Work-Based Learning*. https://www.qaa.ac.uk/docs/qaa/quality-code/advice-and-guidance-work-based-learning.pdf

Universities UK. (2021). The future of degree apprenticeships. https://www.universitiesuk.ac.uk/sites/default/files/field/downloads/2021-07/future-degree-apprenticeships.pdf

Universities UK. (2025, May 27). *Universities UK Responds to Level 7 Funding Announcement* [Media release]. Retrieved July 29, 2025, from https://www.universitiesuk.ac.uk/what-we-do/creating-voice-our-members/media-releases/universities-uk-responds-level-7-funding

University Vocational Awards Council (UVAC). (2023). *Universities Fear Government Reforms Will Stifle Employer Demand for H&DA*. https://uvac.ac.uk/universities-fear-government-reforms-will-stifle-employer-demand-for-higher-and-degree-apprenticeships/

Yeboah, J. (2024). Earn while you learn: Is a degree apprenticeship the right choice for you?, *The Guardian*, 11 September. https://www.theguardian.com/education/article/2024/sep/11/earn-while-you-learn-is-a-degree-apprenticeship-the-right-choice-for-you (Accessed: 23 July 2025).

2

The recontextualisation of apprenticeships in higher education in England

A discursive shift

Mandy Crawford-Lee

Introduction

The chapter is concerned with how the concepts of Higher and Degree Apprenticeships have been constructed within both apprenticeship and higher education (HE) discourse, particularly in light of the rapid growth of combined apprenticeship and degree programmes (Lester, 2024). It positions relevant public documents as 'texts' for empirical analysis, identifying and organising oppositions, alliances, and juxtapositions to show how each document operates within policy. In exploring the higher and degree apprenticeship discursive field, and understanding official texts as instances of social-cultural action, this chapter draws on both Bourdieu's description of a social field of forces and struggles (1988, 1998) as a structured arena of objective power relations and Foucault's description of discursive formation as 'practices that systematically form the objects of which they speak' (1972, p. 49), to recontextualise the description of higher and degree apprenticeships. Dowling's (2009) notion of 'conceptual spaces' and Bravenboer (2019) idea of 'discursive spaces' (as applied by Crawford-Lee, 2022) are used to identify oppositions and alliances.

DOI: 10.4324/9781003567844-2

The nexus

The connection between universities and apprenticeships emerged under New Labour (1997–2010) with a commitment to pilot honours and master's programmes founded on the principles of English apprenticeships, namely: employed status, technical expertise, and occupational competency (DBIS, 2009). Formal discussions regarding the lack of progression from apprenticeships to HE emerge in early 2010. This conversation, framed around equity and social mobility, culminated in a policy paper from the Lifelong Learning Network, which introduced the concept of a missing link in the apprenticeship system in England.

The debate about the limitations of the existing apprenticeship system in terms of scope, prestige and opportunity highlighted that the lack of progression from apprentices to HE was not due to UCAS tariff points, course articulation, or barriers to admission. Instead, it was suggested that:

> ...Higher apprenticeships are the missing link in the apprenticeship family...Without clear work-based progression pathways, leading in appropriate sectors to professional or para-professional accreditation, apprenticeships and advanced apprenticeships will always be seen as having a ceiling at level 3, only leading to technician occupations.
>
> (Hall et al., 2010)

By the time the Cameron–Clegg Coalition Government (2010–2015) formed, UK Government initiatives had long encouraged increasing university attendance (see DfEE, 1998; DfES, 2003). For some, such normalisation of HE following decades of expansion, reflected broader economic and social changes (Bathmaker, 2003). However, for others, it reinforced the belief that an academic degree had more value than vocational training. The mindset was particularly evident in the discussions surrounding the status of apprenticeships in England. A study by Wall and Perrin (2015) (cited in Crawford-Lee and Wall, 2018) highlighted misconceptions about the academic and vocational divide, particularly among the middle classes who perceived university degrees as inherently superior to apprenticeships, with the belief that '[...] choosing a path other than university is a mark of failure' (Bawden, 2011). This presented an early challenge in balancing the purpose of HE and apprenticeships.

Reflecting on this historical context requires interpretation on subject positioning and control of the discourse. In Foucauldian terms, the focus is not on 'what *people* say' but to the 'things said', considering the relationships that lend legitimacy and meaning to these statements (Bacchi and Bonham, 2014). In what Foucault calls 'rules of formation' these rules 'at a given period…define…the limits and forms of the sayable' (Foucault, 1991) and demonstrate not how political practice has determined the meaning and form of apprenticeship discourse but how – and in what form – political and policy practice contributes to apprenticeship discourse itself.

In February 2011, the arrival of higher-level apprenticeships was declared (Joslin, 2011) with the publication of the Specification of Apprenticeship Standards for England (SASE) (Employment and Training, 2011). For the first time, the criteria and specification for higher apprenticeships at Levels 4 and 5 (sub-degree level) were included. This was followed in March 2011 by the Government's 'Plans for Growth' which announced 10,000 new advanced and higher apprenticeship places and stated 'higher apprenticeships provide a good alternative to full-time HE for young people who want to develop a career through on-the-job training' (HM Treasury, 2011, p. 85).

In what can be described as the start of a long period of policy in 'motion' concerning apprenticeships and skills, the government made practical moves to address the lack of a higher apprenticeship route by launching a £25 million Higher Apprenticeship Fund (HAF) (NAS, 2011) in recognition that the gap might limit opportunities for social mobility. Findings indicated that half of all apprentices completing an advanced apprenticeship showed interest in progressing to a degree-level equivalent course (UKCES, 2010), but failed to do so.

Industries traditionally associated with apprenticeships were to be joined by sectors linked to the professions. The aim was that as higher apprenticeships expanded in scope, recognition and importance, the traditional division between academic disciplines and vocational skills training could be challenged and reduced (Crawford-Lee, 2012). From 2011, this vision became central to the narrative surrounding apprenticeships in HE in England. Apprenticeships were seen as the vocational option, while A levels followed by an honours degree, as the conventional linear route to employment, or post-graduate study. Just like apprenticeships, HE has been misconstrued in popular discourse, which reflects how: The change in the size and character of the publics who have an interest in higher education and exert an influence on higher education policy greatly influences the nature and content of the discussions about higher education; particularly, who takes part in them, and the decisions that flow out of them (Trow, 2007).

The alignment of non-technical apprenticeships with degree programmes, in terms of funding and delivery, was still a number of years away. However, putting apprenticeship standards on a statutory basis for the first time alongside the launch of the HAF (NAS, 2011) became watershed moments for the role of HE providers in apprenticeship development. This was significant, both for what these initiatives addressed and for what they failed to resolve.

The misalignment between SASE (DBIS, 2011) and HE qualifications further hindered university engagement at this time. Although professional bodies supported the principle of higher apprenticeships, their restricted qualification level meant they could not support progression to professionally qualified status (Williams and Hanson, 2010). This was despite research by the Professional Associations Research Network (PARN) noting that 70% of professional bodies surveyed considered higher apprenticeships to be a suitable programme for becoming fully qualified and professionally recognised (Williams and Hanson, 2010). The Wilson Review (2012) also recognised the importance of higher apprenticeships, advocating for stronger links between universities and employers. Yet, it paradoxically stated that while higher apprenticeships and professional qualifications, 'are not congruent with the requirements of an honours degree [they] are equal in rigour and esteem' (Wilson, 2012, p. 46).

The positioning

The statement that positioned higher apprenticeships as 'not congruent' but 'equal' obfuscated their status and, conceivably, consigned higher apprenticeships to the margins of university business. The advent of Level 6 and 7 apprenticeships with the inclusion of an honours degree would challenge the recurring notion that apprenticeships represent an 'alternative' to university; an idea which highlights the struggle amongst policymakers to articulate the relationship between practice-based discipline and work-based knowledge.

So, how has policy fluctuation positioned higher and degree apprenticeships within the HE discursive field? The concept of the HE discursive field can pull on both Bourdieu's description of a social field of forces (Bourdieu, 1988, 1998) and Foucault's description of discursive formation as 'practices that systematically form the objects of which they speak' (Foucault, 1972). Indeed, what are the truths of apprenticeships in England we are trying to seek? How have official texts, including some of those referenced in this chapter, operated by deploying technologies of truth (Simola et al., 1998) to (re)produce or be resistant to particular ideas about HE vis-à-vis apprenticeships?

The origin

A significant text is the Higher Apprenticeship Fund Prospectus (the Prospectus) created for the development of a 'new wave' of apprenticeships (NAS, 2011). The National Apprenticeship Service (NAS) acted as the author of this 'official text', with a foreword by the Minister of State for Further Education, Skills and Lifelong Learning and presented by the Executive Chair of the National Apprenticeship Service. The text constitutes a range of authoritative subjectivities (Simola et al., 1998) incorporating and excluding various voices, presenting itself as an expert-led, official narrative on apprenticeships in England. NAS, an institution of government central to planning and justifying policy reform, is positioned as articulating the official truth on apprenticeships in England.

Although the result of individual civil servant effort, the text gives the appearance of anonymity, 'of an official truth' (Simola et al., 1998) in which it may be assumed there are suggestions and indications of what is the 'true' knowledge about apprenticeships at the higher level, what a 'good' apprenticeship system is like and what kind of power is 'right' in the field of apprenticeships in HE. The text positions a variety of subjectivities, including 'employers, key partners, stakeholders and providers' (NAS, 2011), framing them as audiences who will be impacted by the intended HAF and its implications for their practice (Bravenboer, 2022). The failure to define 'providers' and the late mention of universities and HE providers in collaborative partnership bids subtly directs the discourse on apprenticeships, seemingly relegating HE providers to a secondary role, almost to the point of exclusion.

The limited mention of universities in the Prospectus had been described as 'indicative of a degree of ambivalence, in policy terms regarding the extent of university involvement with the higher apprenticeship initiative' (Bravenboer, 2016). The ambiguity extends further with the unclear reference to how 'universities are fully able to support Higher Apprenticeships' (NAS, 2011, p. 12) without specifying what this 'support' entails, thereby creating ambiguity and uncertainty in the policy's intent.

The Prospectus captured the tensions in framing strategic and policy direction with Bourdieu's work on practice and its relationship with 'habitus' giving a perspective on policy as a 'practice of power' (Bourdieu, 1977). The dominant discourse in 2011 described traditional forms of HE and vocational and technical education – including apprenticeships – as separate realms within the UK's education and skills system. In policy terms, it would appear inconsistent to promote a model for the development of new higher apprenticeships that by its very policy design principle limits, or at best misconstrues, university collaboration. Moreover, the Prospectus failed to consider the implications for university engagement when it overlooked the fact that most Professional, Statutory and Regulatory Bodies recognise professional status at Level 6 and above. The oversight meant the mainstay of university provision was always going to be at odds with the ambition of the Prospectus.

Modes and mapping

To illustrate how the Higher Apprenticeship Fund Prospectus operated within the apprenticeship and HE discursive field, the work of Dowling (2009) and Bravenboer (2009, 2012) on the recontextualisation of 'official' texts in HE is utilised. This framework provides insight into how the Prospectus is producing or resisting the purpose of apprenticeships in HE. The 'opening up' of what Dowling calls 'conceptual spaces' and Bravenboer terms 'discursive spaces' are applied to examine oppositions and alliances within the official text and relate at least two sets of bifurcated or binary variables.

Building on Dowling's schema, the 'Modes of Authority Action' in Table 2.1 reflect oppositions between open and closed authorship, as well as open and closed fields of practice. 'Modes of Authority Action' offer a valuable way to describe the techniques and strategies used to establish the rule of who is authorised to 'speak' (Bravenboer, 2009), and whether claims to authority are individualised or institutionalised.

Table 2.1 Modes of authority action (Dowling, 2009)

Author category	Field of practice	
	Open	Closed
Closed	Charismatic	Traditional
Open	Liberal	Bureaucratic

Authority strategies emerge from how an author derives their authority and the type of discursive space they create. The question here is: what role did the Higher Apprenticeship Fund Prospectus play in either the opening up or closing down of the discursive space in the development of apprenticeships in HE? By this measure, the Prospectus can be declared an example of 'closed discursive practice', the opposite of encouraging participation and building alliances. The identification of 'NAS' as the chief author (or authority) indicates a closed category of authorship. According to Dowling, 'the closure of authorship and practice...[is] achieved together in alliances and oppositions that both define membership and regulate the rules of the discourse' (2009). The Prospectus's description of the role and purpose of higher apprenticeships involves certain learning providers and stakeholders, intentionally or unintentionally marginalising or excluding others, specifically universities. The minimal references to universities and their loose characterisation as 'an academic preserve' (NAS, 2012) make the discursive field of practice 'closed'. This represents either 'traditional' or 'bureaucratic' modes of authority action by NAS.

At first glance, the Prospectus may appear bureaucratic given its branding and prefacing, but the authorship category is 'closed'. Therefore, as demonstrated by the Prospectus, the mode of authority action is 'traditional', a reflection of a particular habitus and the non-transferability of government.

As a governmental public body, NAS had the 'power' to determine what is, and what is not, described in the Prospectus, and what is and what is not procured. From the schema it is clear that 'the liberal' mode is constituted as opposite to the traditional form of authority: open category of author and open field of practice, where authority is relinquished by the author(s) and given over to the audience(s). In this exchange mode, the Prospectus positions NAS as an 'investor' with a desire to, in the context of the fiscal challenge, 'back' high-quality applications and 'kick-start activity' with a transfer of authority to the audience by way of an open invitation to those who have a 'sound business case and are able to clearly articulate the approach you will take and the benefits it will deliver' (NAS, 2012). While the Prospectus' frames self-evidencing and evaluating as a carefully authored and open field of practice, the authorial voice of government makes it clear that NAS retains the decision-making authority and power to decide 'what it is that we're willing to invest in, the basis on which we will invest, and the requirements on which projects will proceed if we invest' (NAS, 2012, p. 15).

The distribution of authorial or audience voices vis-à-vis the modes of authority action in the Prospectus (identified in the text as NAS, government, employers, apprentices, stakeholders and 'providers') reveals a critical moment in the construction of knowledge in the apprenticeships discourse in HE. In 2011, the coalition government did not see apprenticeships as a central concern for universities or an opportunity to be explored. The discursive effect was to separate the language and discourse of higher apprenticeships from those of HE.

While criticism emerged that the Prospectus' intention was 'off mission' (Bravenboer, 2016), the potential for the discourse on apprenticeships in HE to address misalignments with mainstream university qualifications was reflected in a second official text – the revised Specification of Apprenticeship Standards for England (SASE) (DBIS, 2013). This revision created fresh opportunities for universities (Bravenboer and Lester, 2016; Bravenboer and Workman, 2016).

Authorial and audience voices

A revised Specification of Apprenticeship Standards for England (SASE) was published in 2013 following discussions on the main barriers to the success of higher apprenticeship. The primary argument centred around the need for higher apprenticeships to stretch beyond technical and associate professional skill levels. Anderson et al. (2012) and Bravenboer (2016) identified that higher apprenticeships, limited by the Level 5 ceiling and lacking access to funding, were not aligned with qualifications. This exclusion also prevented the potential for degree-level provision (typically the main pillar of university business) that could open up access to the professions.

The official text constitutes a range of subjectivities (Simola et al., 1998) with multiple organisations identified as the 'author', including the Department for Education, the Department for Business, Innovation and Skills and the Skills Funding Agency. The authority of these 'authors' is based on the legal right to act, stemming from 'parliamentary sovereignty' and, when diffused to ministers, makes them semi-autonomous rule makers. While some subjectivities are named, others are inferred and positioned as audiences of this official text. These audiences are giving them official notice of intended government action that will impact their operational practice, including HE providers.

The 'apprentice' and 'employer' subjectivities are notably absent from direct mention. However, the text emphasises the need 'to develop clear work-based career routes to senior technician, managerial and professional job roles' and calls for stronger ladders of opportunity to widen access to HE. This is framed as the purpose of the official guidance, intended to 'complement' the change in legislation. Interestingly, the text does not position apprentices or employers as authorial voices or even as audiences – though this would soon change as both groups began to be recognised as 'customers' and 'purchasers' of apprenticeship training (Anderson and Crawford-Lee, 2016) with greater recognition of the role of HE in delivery of apprenticeships.

This official text employs the language of parliamentary practice to describe higher apprenticeships as 'rationally planned strategic governmental policy' (Bravenboer, 2009). This positions the text as an example of 'technologies of government' in so far as it 'operates to structure the field of action for others' (Simola et al., 1998). Enacted with the full force of 'the State', this official text serves as a disciplining mechanism that sets out, in legislative terms, what is included and excluded in the official definition of apprenticeships in England by type and size. The Westminster government is positioned as the principal authority authorised to define what HE is in the context of apprenticeship policy and what it must be. This has had the effect of slowing early university engagement (Anderson et al., 2012).

Reflections

(Re)contextualising higher and degree apprenticeships as a form of discourse in HE provides an opportunity to explore and reflect on their conceptual beginnings. Where once there was a more settled policy and ideological stance from the government, with a strong commitment from Westminster to the growth in higher-level skills – including higher and degree apprenticeships (IfATE, 2021; Whieldon, 2021) – since July 2024, the government has sought to reset the definition and purpose of apprenticeships in England. It may be the case that the potential of higher and degree apprenticeship growth will be reduced within a constrained 'vocational educational narrative' (Crawford-Lee, 2025). It would seem that for higher and degree apprenticeships delivered by HE, in England, we are about to enter a new discursive age.

References

Anderson, A., Bravenboer, D. and Hemsworth, D. (2012) 'The role of universities in higher apprenticeship development'. *Higher Education, Skills and Work-Based Learning*, 2 (3), pp. 240–255.

Anderson, A. and Crawford-Lee, M. (2016) 'The role of higher education in a world-class apprenticeship system'. In David Way (ed.), *A Race to The Top: Achieving Three Million More Apprenticeships by 2020*. Winchester: The Winchester University Press, pp. 446–455.

Bacchi, C. and Bonham, J. (2014) 'Reclaiming discursive practices as an analytic focus: Political implications'. *Foucault Studies*, 17, pp. 173–192.

Bathmaker, A.M. (2003) 'The expansion of higher education: A consideration of control, funding and quality'. In S. Bartlett and D. Burton (eds.), *Education Studies. Essential Issues*. London: Sage, pp. 169–189.

Bawden, T. (2011) 'Degree or apprenticeship: Which works best in the job market?' *Guardian* [online] 15 May. Available at: https://www.theguardian.com/money/2011/may/15/graduate-jobs-university-work-experience-apprenticeships. [Accessed: 28th February 2025].

Bourdieu, P. (1977) *Outline of a Theory of Practice* (R. Nice, Trans.). Cambridge: Cambridge University Press.

Bourdieu, P. (1988) *Homo Academicus*. Cambridge: Polity Press.

Bourdieu, P. (1998) *Practical Reason: On the Theory of Action*. Cambridge: Polity Press.

Bravenboer, D. (2016) 'Why co-design and delivery is a "no-brainer" for higher and degree apprenticeship policy'. *Higher Education, Skills and Work-Based Learning*, 6 (4), pp. 384–400.

Bravenboer, D. (2019) 'The creative disruption of degree apprenticeships in the UK'. In J. Talbot (ed.), *Global Perspectives on Work-Based Learning Initiatives*. IGI Global Scientific Publishing, pp. 57–83. https://doi.org/10.4018/978-1-5225-6977-0.ch003

Bravenboer, D. (2022) 'The official discourse of academic credit in England'. In: W. Turnbull and H. Woolf (eds.), *Widening Access to Higher Education in the UK: Developments and Approaches Using Credit Accumulation and Transfer*. Maidenhead: Berkshire Open University Press. pp. 63–79.

Bravenboer, D. and Lester, S. (2016) 'Towards an integrated approach to the recognition of professional competence and academic learning'. *Education + Training*, 58 (4), pp. 409–421.

Bravenboer, D. and Workman, B. (2016) 'Developing a transdisciplinary work-based learning curriculum: A model for recognising learning from work'. In M. Keppell S. Reushle and A. Antonio (eds.), *Open Learning and Formal Credentialing in Higher Education: Curriculum Models and Institutional Policies*. Hershey: IGI Global, pp. 144–167.

Bravenboer, D.W. (2009) *Commodification and the Official Discourse of Higher Education*. London: University of London, Institute of Education.

Bravenboer, D.W. (2012) 'The official discourse of fair access to higher education'. *Journal of Widening Participation and Lifelong Learning,* 14 (3), pp. 120–140.

Crawford-Lee, M. (2012) 'Championing higher apprenticeships'. *Higher Education, Skills and Work-Based Learning,* 2 (3), pp. 285–287.

Crawford-Lee, M. (2022) Gamekeeper Turned Poacher: Discursive Shifts in Apprenticeship Reform in England, 2011–2021. Thesis (DProf.). Middlesex University. London: Middlesex University.

Crawford-Lee, M. (2025) 'In anticipation...Level 7 apprenticeships – decision awaited'. Available at: https://uvac.ac.uk/in-anticipation-level-7-apprenticeships-decision-awaited/. [Accessed 31 March 2025].

Crawford-Lee, M. and Wall, T. (2018) 'Sustainability 2030: A policy perspective from the university vocational awards council'. *Higher Education, Skills and Work-Based Learning,* 8 (3), pp. 233–242.

Department for Business, Innovation and Skills (DBIS). (2009) *Higher Ambitions: The Future of Universities in a Knowledge Economy.* London: Stationery Office. Available at: https://www.ed.ac.uk/files/atoms/files/bis-higherambitions-summary-nov2009.pdf. [Accessed: 31 January 2025].

Department for Business, Innovation and Skills (DBIS). (2011) *Higher Apprenticeship Fund.* London: Stationery Office. Available at: https://www.gov.uk/government/news/19-000-new-higher-apprenticeships-to-deliver-skills-for-growth. [Accessed: 10 March 2025].

Department for Business, Innovation and Skills (DBIS). (2013) *Specification of Apprenticeship Standards for England.* London: Stationery Office.

Department for Education and Employment (DfEE). (1998) *Higher Education for the 21st Century – Response to the Dearing Report.* London: HMSO.

Department for Education and Skills (DfES) (2003) *The Future of Higher Education (White Paper).* London: HMSO.

Dowling, P. (2009) *Sociology as Method: Departures from the Forensics of Culture, Text and Knowledge.* Rotterdam: Sense Publishers.

Employment and Training (England) *the Apprenticeships (Specification of Apprenticeship Standards for England) Order* (2011), (SI 2011/219). Available at: https://www.legislation.gov.uk/uksi/2011/219/pdfs/uksi_20110219_en.pdf [Accessed: 3 March 2025].

Foucault, M. (1972) 'The discourse on language'. In *The Archaeology of knowledge and the Discourse on Language.* New York: Pantheon Books, pp. 215–237.

Foucault, M. (1991) 'Politics and the study of discourse'. In G. Burchell, C. Gordon and P. Miller (eds.), *The Foucault Effect: Studies in Governmentality.* Chicago: University of Chicago Press, pp. 53–72.

Hall, G., Joslin, H. and Ward, J. (2010) 'Developing higher apprenticeships in England'. *Lifelong Learning Networks National Forum Policy Paper* [online] May. Available at: https://www.heacademy.ac.uk/system/files/developing_higher_apprenticeships_in_england.pdf. [Accessed: 1 February 2025).

HM Treasury. (2011) *Plan for Growth.* London: HM Treasury and Department for Business Innovation and Skills.

Institute for Apprenticeships and Technical Education (IfATE). (2021) *Institute Backs Tough and Ambitious Targets for Degree Apprenticeships and Higher Technical Qualifications*. Available at: https://www.instituteforapprenticeships.org/about/newshub/news-events/institute-backs-tough-and-ambitious-targets-for-degree-apprenticeships-and-higher-technical-qualifications/. [Accessed: 14 February 2025].

Joslin, H. (2011) *Implementing Higher Apprenticeships – Learning from Practice*. London: University of Greenwich.

Lester, S. (2024) *Beyond Degree Apprenticeships: Conceptualising Integrated Professional Development*. Bolton: UVAC (conceptual paper).

National Apprenticeship Service (NAS). (2011) *Higher Apprenticeship Fund Prospectus*. Available at: www.apprenticeships.org.uk/highers [Accessed: 10 January 2025].

National Apprenticeship Service (NAS). (2012) *Meeting Employer Skills Needs: Consultation on Criteria for Higher Apprenticeships at Degree Levels*. Coventry: National Apprenticeship Service.

Simola, H., Heikkinen, S. and Silvonen, J. (1998) 'A catalogue of possibilities: Foucaultian history of truth and education of truth and education research'. In T.S. Popkewitz and M. Brennan (eds.), *Foucault's Challenge: Discourse, Knowledge and Power in Education*. New York: Teachers College Press, pp. 217–233.

Trow, M. (2007) 'Reflections on the transition from elite to mass to universal access: Forms and phases of higher education in modern societies since WWII'. In J.J.F. Forest and P.G. Altback (eds.), *International Handbook of Higher Education*. Dordrecht: Springer, pp. 243–280.

UKCES. (2010) *Progression from Vocational and Applied Learning to Higher Education across the UK: A Comparative Study by the University Vocational Awards Council* [online]. Available at: https://dera.ioe.ac.uk/1299/1/424657_progression%20to%20higher%20Ed.pdf. [Accessed: 13 March 2025].

Wall, T. and Perrin, D. (2015) *Slavoj Žižek: A Žižekian Gaze at Education*. London: Springer.

Whieldon, F. (2021) 'Universities could be incentivised to run degree apprenticeships, minister suggests'. *FEWEEK* online, 29 October. Available at: https://feweek.co.uk/universities-could-be-incentivised-to-run-degree-apprenticeships-minister-suggests/. [Accessed: 14 March 2025].

Williams, C. and Hanson, W. (2010) *Foundation Degrees: Barriers and Opportunities in the Professional Bodies Sector*. Bristol: PARN.

Wilson, T. (2012) *A Review of Business-University Collaboration: The Wilson Review*. London: DBIS.

PART

I

Key stakeholders

3

The Learner

From subject matter expert to organisational strategic change agent

Julian Grail and Elizabeth Ashman

Introduction

This chapter will review Elizabeth's (apprentice) learning journey as she completed a Senior Leader Apprenticeship (SLA) programme. Her coach, Julian, supported her, using a ladder to brilliance approach to transform Elizabeth from an experienced subject matter expert into a strategic change agent operating across a large public sector organisation. The ladder of brilliance consists of six steps:

Step 1 – Committing to undertaking learning and development.
Step 2 – Having a clear sense of a desired future professional self.
Step 3 – Having a mentor as a critical friend to provide a psychologically safe environment to facilitate personal and professional development.
Step 4 – Putting yourself out there.
Step 5 – Networking with people who can influence your career.
Step 6 – Stepping forward and saying yes to the big opportunities.

However, in some real-world journeys, learning and development is not always a linear process. Some steps occur simultaneously, others are revisited multiple times, and progress often requires reflection and iteration. Nonetheless, these steps provide a structured approach for apprentices to

DOI: 10.4324/9781003567844-4

navigate their career transformation effectively. Each section of this chapter is structured around the individual steps to brilliance, capturing perspectives from both the Learner and Learner Coach.

Step 1 – Committing to undertaking learning and development

The starting point for any growth journey is a commitment to learning and development (Tuttle & Critchlow, 2025). As the adage states, if we do the same thing, we invariably get the same result. Structured learning pathways, such as the SLA, offer a transformative programme that enables learners to broaden their professional horizons and reimagine their professional identity through intentional engagement with leadership, innovation, and interdisciplinary practice. In addition to providing formal leadership education, apprenticeships offer work-integrated learning, allowing learners to apply theoretical insights directly to their roles. The SLA is free to the Learner, with all of the related costs borne by the Employer. This accessibility removes financial barriers, allowing professionals from various backgrounds to invest in their leadership development.

Elizabeth's perspective (learner)

> Although my inherently curious nature has always provided the impetus for my continued learning, the SLA represented something far more profound. The fact the programme was fully funded was hugely inviting as it negated any personal financial burden. However, working in the operationally and financially challenged NHS, I did have large concerns surrounding my limited available study time and how this was likely to necessitate a trade-off between my depth and breadth of knowledge, and bring compromise to my overall learning. But through actively engaging in the programme and pursuing meaningful learning opportunities, it held promise to make me a better leader within my own department and far beyond. Such growth beyond my own area of expertise was highly appealing and motivational. Thus, having identified the SLA benefits which for me far outweighed any costs, I embarked on my learning journey.

An apprenticeship is much more than just academic learning. It also requires the acquisition of Knowledge, Skills, and Behaviours (KSBs) that are in line with professional body requirements, in this case the Chartered

Management Institute, whose aim is to raise the quality and standard of management in the workplace (CMI, 2025). This apprenticeship is based on a bespoke Masters in Business Administration (MBA) programme from the University of Gloucestershire. A fundamental component of the programme is that students learn and apply the acquired knowledge and skills within their workplace; with the alignment of teaching and assessment based on their own workplace. This makes teaching and learning relevant and personalised for each individual learner.

Step 2 – Having a clear sense of a desired future professional self

Lifelong learning and a commitment to continuing professional development (CPD) are central tenets of professionalism (Mlambo, Silén & McGrath, 2021), representing essential requirements for entry into, and continued membership, of professional bodies such as the CMI. Professional registration in healthcare is often mandatory, with CPD a vital mechanism for ensuring practitioners maintain a current and adaptable skill set aligned with the evolving demands of the healthcare landscape.

Elizabeth's perspective (learner)

> Prior to my SLA apprenticeship, my CPD activities were predominantly tied to my NHS role as a Senior Scientist, with a focus on maintaining clinical competencies and driving incremental improvements from a bottom-up, practice-based perspective. However, such framing of myself purely as a clinical professional resulted in a strong feeling of disconnect from any positions outside this role, which I felt was limiting my career progression.

Whilst a focus on maintaining status as a "Subject Matter Expert" ensures technical proficiency, it can inadvertently narrow the scope of CPD. This framing risks constraining the development of a professional identity, limiting it to purely technical expertise, and therefore limiting awareness of the broader organisational context in which the role is situated. Consequently, interdisciplinary collaboration, broader leadership development, and innovation opportunities can be overlooked, which are key elements necessary for meaningful career progression (Edmondson & Harvey, 2017). Over time, this narrow focus can result in frustration as career growth stagnates. To address this, CPD should be framed with a dual focus: supporting the current professional identity while fostering a vision of a desired future self. As Friedman and Phillips (2004, p. 365) note:

> Professional identity is not static; it evolves through engagement with diverse experiences, collaboration across boundaries, and the assumption of broader roles that extend beyond technical expertise.

Elizabeth's perspective (learner)

> Prior to the SLA commencing, all my leadership roles had been adopted informally with applied learning on the job only. And without doubt, this distinct lack of formal leadership training had resulted in a lack of knowledge about leadership approaches, skills and behaviours, in turn compromising my capabilities and effectiveness as a leader. Consequently, I had always felt daunted by the thought of shifting my professional identity from the well-defined and established clinician to the less familiar and ill-defined senior leader. Thus, the SLA programme provided me with an instrumental opportunity to formally develop my leadership skills and offered a true means of successfully transitioning from a clinician to effective senior change agent. Such formal training included, for example, carrying out leadership self-assessments and personal gap analysis. These broader development opportunities, beyond my clinical role, bought insight to my existing leadership skill set and my future desired state. And as a direct result of this process, the necessary developmental support was then provided through the university learning and teaching, and by my employer in the form of targeted shadowing opportunities and project assignments.

Step 3 – Having a coach and mentor as a critical friend to provide a psychologically safe environment to facilitate personal and professional development

Having a coach who fulfils also the role of mentor can play a vital role in career development by providing guidance, knowledge, and professional networking opportunities that can significantly enhance an individual's career trajectory. Studies highlight that mentorship fosters professional growth, improves job satisfaction and leadership development, and is essential in career transitions to help individuals navigate challenges and make informed career decisions (Dewasiri, Yadav, & Chandel, 2025). A crucial relationship during the SLA is that between the coach and the apprentice. The coach serves as a mentor, acting as the vital link between academic learning, workplace experience, and professional growth. Coaching, mentoring, and work-integrated learning ensure apprentices develop strategic, ethical, and competent leadership skills, which are aligned with business needs (Quew-Jones & Rowe, 2022). In today's evolving business landscape, leadership requires more than technical expertise; it demands adaptability, resilience, and critical thinking. The coach plays a vital role in nurturing these qualities, helping apprentices build confidence and navigate complexity in uncertain environments.

Julian's perspective (coach)

> At our first meeting, Elizabeth presented as a highly competent clinical professional, accustomed to working independently and at pace. She was confident in her ability to manage study alongside work. However, while I was certain she could pass the course, I was keen to ensure that she reflected deeply on her ability to develop the knowledge, skills, and behaviours (KSBs) necessary for meaningful career transformation. The SLA isn't just about academic success; when done well, it's about evolving into the next version of a professional self.

This perspective aligns with the Critical Friendship approach (Costa & Kallick, 1993), a coaching framework that fosters collaboration, trust, and constructive challenge. In this model, the coach provides structured support while encouraging apprentices to redefine their professional identity (Beaton, 2010).

The key elements of successful critical friendship in the ladder of brilliance approach can be encapsulated in the five P's:

Push – Challenging comfort zones

Leadership growth often begins when individuals are encouraged to venture beyond their habitual thinking and behavioural routines. Coaches play a vital role in constructively challenging learners, providing the professional push needed to take the first steps towards new roles, responsibilities, and mindsets both within and beyond their organisational context.

Pull – Inspiring change and curiosity

People tend to default to familiar and safe patterns. Effective coaching involves creating a developmental pull, inspiring learners to adopt fresh approaches, reframe challenges, and cultivate new habits that align with leadership effectiveness. This helps build a natural curiosity and openness to experiment with alternative perspectives.

Permission – Enabling courageous action

Taking meaningful developmental steps can feel risky. Coaches provide a psychologically safe space and give explicit or implicit permission for learners to explore, act, and reflect. This kind of permission is not about authority but about legitimising exploration, reducing fear, and reinforcing the Learner's agency.

Present – Expanding awareness

One of the most transformative aspects of coaching is helping learners shift their view from narrow, localised concerns to a broader organisational and strategic perspective. Coaches help learners bring themselves into the present moment, grounding them in both situational awareness and strategic foresight, often referred to as the executive lens.

Provide – Equipping the journey

Coaches offer both tangible and intangible forms of support. They provide resources, tools, networks, and developmental opportunities, while also serving as sounding boards and reflective partners. Their role includes helping learners identify and access the conditions necessary for their growth and leadership excellence.

Used flexibly and in combination, these Five P's help structure coaching and mentoring engagements in ways that are developmentally dynamic and contextually responsive. By fostering trust, reflective dialogue, and co-learning, coaches help create the conditions for innovative leadership development (Fletcher et al., 2016), echoing values of honesty, mutual respect, and shared inquiry (Schuck & Russell, 2005; Nilsson, 2013). Such an environment fosters self-directed learning, critical reflection, and professional autonomy – essential traits for senior leaders (Keller and Barabasch, 2022).

Elizabeth's perspective (learner)

> Beyond my motivation and dedication, I soon realised that my success depended on engaging with professionals integral to the process, particularly my coach. Initially, I was sceptical about the added value of this relationship, given my self-driven approach. However, through mutual investment in the coaching dynamic, it became central to my learning experience. By tailoring the programme to my strengths and areas for growth, my coach helped me optimise my learning and development. The trust we built enabled open, honest conversations and provided a psychologically safe space where I felt comfortable admitting mistakes and learning from them. Through this process, I gained clarity on my career aspirations and aligned my apprenticeship with long-term goals that had previously been undefined.

Julian's perspective (coach)

> To be a truly successful coach I moved beyond the transactional nature of the relationship – form filling and procedural guidance – towards a critical friendship, where personal and professional development happens in a safe space in which challenging conversations are possible. With Elizabeth, this meant recognising her drive for success while gently nudging her to own her leadership development. By providing strategic insights into the complexities of organisational life, academic guidance, practical coaching, and confidence to take leaps of faith, I helped her to clarify her long-term career goals and transition into a more defined professional identity.

Step 4 – Putting yourself out there

A key role of the coach is to encourage apprentices to step beyond their immediate professional roles and engage with broader organisational opportunities. Exposure to different departments, cross-functional projects, and networking opportunities enhances career development and strategic awareness (Fuller & Unwin, 2003). Actively seeking these experiences fosters adaptability, innovation, and a deeper understanding of organisational dynamics, equipping learners with the skills needed for leadership and professional growth (Eraut, 2011; Billett, 2011). By stepping outside their comfort zones, apprentices develop resilience, build essential relationships, and contribute to cross organisational collaboration; key factors for individual and business success.

Julian's perspective (coach)

> A pivotal step in Elizabeth's journey took place through strong coaching conversations about leveraging the academic assessments of the taught element of the apprenticeship to reach out to senior people within the organisation. This was framed around the apprenticeship, providing permission to meet with the finance director to talk about her finance assessment or the strategy director to talk about strategy. Like many learners, Elizabeth was initially hesitant, and it took more than one discussion underpinned with critical friend coaching pushes and permissions to take the initial leap. Once Elizabeth developed the confidence to do this for several of her assignments, she realised that she was visible to the executive team within her organisation. Something that would later provide crucial to her career development...

Elizabeth's perspective (learner)

> One example of moving beyond my comfort zone was the opportunity to coach employees as part of my first assessment – something which had been missing from my previous leadership experience(s). Recognising the impact of coaching on performance and organisational change, I was observed by an Executive Coach, who provided constructive feedback to refine my approach. This experience significantly enhanced my coaching skills, helping to drive transformational change across individuals, teams, and the organisation. This gave me the confidence that I had potential to be a different kind of leader.

Step 5 – Networking with people who can influence your career

Networking is a critical enabler of career success, yet its role in apprenticeships is often undervalued. While external networking is commonly associated with securing future job opportunities, internal networking – developing relationships within the workplace – is equally vital for career progression (Cross & Parker, 2010; Fuller & Unwin, 2003). Apprentices who actively engage with colleagues gain technical skills, workplace insights, and a deeper understanding of industry expectations (Billett, 2011). However, many apprentices underutilise networking due to a lack of confidence, workplace hierarchy, or an underestimation of its role in long-term career success (Evans, Unwin, Rainbird, & Hodkinson, 2007). A reason for this lack of confidence can be a lack of exposure to a different professional culture with its rituals, practices, and lexicon, which can be intimidating. Research indicates that those who build strong professional relationships are more likely to secure permanent employment, access advanced training, and progress into leadership roles (Guile & Young, 2003). Here, the coach is vital in helping apprentices establish meaningful connections that facilitate career development and manage the cultural immersion shock and these new rituals. Like all new things, the more it's practised, the easier it becomes until the new way of working becomes normalised.

Elizabeth's perspective (learner)

> I came to understand that my career progression was closely linked to my employer's evolving skill requirements. To advance professionally, it was essential to align my development with their strategic priorities. Thus, to broaden my expertise, I actively built relationships with key stakeholders. During my SLA, I developed an interest in business strategy and leadership but lacked theoretical and practical knowledge in the area. Instead of struggling alone, and encouraged by my coach, I reached out to the Director of Strategy, who generously provided guidance on my assignments. This experience not only deepened my understanding of strategy and change management through this new-found networking, but also broadened my perspective beyond my scientific background – sparking a developing interest in corporate leadership. Through my relationship with the Director of Strategy, I was invited to attend monthly executive board meetings, providing me with a firsthand view of strategic decision-making. Initially, I felt out of place, but I soon realised I understood the discussions – thanks to my academic learning and new experiences. I was also asked to provide feedback directly to the Chief Executive, making me feel valued and respected. This experience reaffirmed my transformation from a clinician to a strategic change agent, broadening my perspective and my role within the organisation.

Step 6 – Stepping forward and saying yes to the big opportunities.

The Ladder of Brilliance approach highlights that opportunities for career development are always available, but their value often goes unrecognised due to fear, uncertainty, or self-doubt. Research shows that early-career professionals frequently hesitate to take on new challenges due to a lack of confidence or fear of failure (Eraut, 2011). However, apprentices who push past these barriers and say "yes" to new experiences gain invaluable skills, industry exposure, and professional growth (Fuller & Unwin, 2017). Hands-on learning, particularly through real-world challenges, is significantly more effective than staying within one's comfort zone (Billett, 2011). By embracing opportunities, apprentices maximise the transformative potential of their training, positioning themselves for future leadership roles.

Elizabeth's perspective (learner)

> A pivotal opportunity came from my dissertation, which tackled a real business challenge within my organisation – a partially successful strategic change initiative. My research provided evidence-based recommendations to enhance its implementation, aligning both organisational policy and practice. Encouraged by my university supervisor, I presented my findings to the executive team, demonstrating my ability to apply academic research to real-world challenges. Recognising my new-found strategic expertise, my employer seconded me into the strategic leadership team, where I contributed to cross-divisional organisational change management. My academic work had evolved into applied practice, solidifying my transition from student to strategic change agent.

Final thoughts

Julian perspective (coach)

> Elizabeth's transformation during her SLA journey highlights the opportunity that apprenticeships can present. However, those opportunities must be embraced. Through a successful coaching relationship following the Ladder to Brilliance approach, Elizabeth has transformed into a highly successful senior change agent capable of transforming organisations. Not all

apprentice learners are willing to be transformed; and those who are, are not always willing to take a leap of faith. Elizabeth was brave enough to do both and this has been transformative.

Elizabeth's perspective (learner)

Balancing the demands of the SLA alongside my role as a Vascular Scientist was undoubtedly challenging. At times, I felt overwhelmed, but careful time management – such as ring-fencing dedicated study hours within my work schedule – helped me stay on track. Engaging with my SLA peers fostered a strong sense of camaraderie, enhancing both my well-being and course retention. The shared understanding of challenges, coupled with constructive feedback loops, provided a supportive learning environment that kept me motivated. Throughout my journey, I seized numerous invaluable opportunities – each one initially daunting, yet embraced with a willingness to learn, and adapt to the challenges presented. Investing time in key professional relationships – with peers, my coach, and senior leaders – proved transformative. Their support, encouragement, and guidance were instrumental in my growth. The 20% off-the-job training enabled me to gain hands-on experience in strategic change and leadership, accelerating my career progression from clinician to senior change agent. This journey has been life-changing, shaping my professional identity and opening doors I never imagined possible. The SLA offer an unparalleled opportunity for career transformation. I encourage anyone to embrace it – to climb the Ladder to Brilliance, achieve career success, and gain personal fulfilment – all without the financial burden of traditional higher education.

Conclusion

The Ladder of Brilliance approach highlights that large and small opportunities consistently arise for those who take proactive steps in their professional growth. However, fear, uncertainty, or self-doubt often obscures their true value. This was the case for Elizabeth, a mid-career professional who embarked on a senior leadership apprenticeship with trepidation about transitioning into a strategic role.

Research suggests that developing leaders frequently hesitate to seize new challenges due to a lack of confidence or a fear of failure (Eraut, 2011). Yet, those pushing past these apprehensions gain hands-on experience, high-level decision-making exposure, and industry networks (Fuller & Unwin, 2017). In Elizabeth's case, embracing challenging projects in her apprenticeship developed her strategic thinking and executive presence – key leadership competencies (Kouzes & Posner, 2017).

Studies on workplace learning emphasise that growth occurs most effectively when individuals engage with real-world strategic challenges rather than remaining in their comfort zones (Billett, 2011). This principle is particularly evident in senior leadership apprenticeships, where apprentices like Elizabeth gain opportunities to influence organizational change and develop emotional intelligence – critical for high-level leadership (Goleman, 1998).

By actively embracing leadership challenges, apprentices unlock the transformative power of training, gaining confidence and strategic insight in real time. Elizabeth's success illustrates that structured leadership apprenticeships and a proactive mindset drive exceptional professional growth.

References

Beaton, G. (2010). Why Professionalism Is Still Relevant. *SSRN Electronic Journal*. U of Melbourne Legal Studies Research Paper No. 445, Available at SSRN: https://ssrn.com/abstract=1545509; http://dx.doi.org/10.2139/ssrn.1545509

Billett, S. (2011). Purposes of Vocational Education. In *Vocational Education* (pp. 135–175). Springer, Dordrecht. https://doi.org/10.1007/978-94-007-1954-5_6

Chartered Management Institute. (2025). *Our Vision, Mission and Values*. https://www.managers.org.uk/about-cmi/vision-mission-and-values/ https://www.managers.org.uk/about-cmi/vision-mission-and-values/

Costa, A. L., & Kallick, B. (1993). Through the Lens of a Critical Friend. *Educational Leadership*, 51(2), 49.

Cross, R., & Parker, A. (2010). *The Hidden Power of Social Networks: Understanding How Work Really Gets Done in Organizations*. Harvard Business School Press.

Dewasiri, N., Yadav, M., & Chandel, A. (2025). The Role of Education and Training in Career Transitions. In M. Tunio (Ed.), *Applications of Career Transitions and Entrepreneurship* (pp. 387–410). IGI Global.

Edmondson, A. C., & Harvey, J. F. (2017). *Cross-Boundary Teaming for Innovation: Integrating Research on Teams and Knowledge in Organizations*. Harvard Business School.

Eraut, M. (2011). Informal Learning in the Workplace: Evidence on the Actual Value of Work-Based Learning (WBL). *Development and Learning in Organizations*, 25(5), 8–12.

Evans, K., Unwin, L., Rainbird, H., & Hodkinson, P. (2007). *Improving Workplace Learning*. Taylor & Francis.

Fletcher, T., Ní Chróinín, D., & O'Sullivan, M. (2016). A Layered Approach to Critical Friendship as a Means to Support Pedagogical Innovation in Pre-Service Teacher Education. *Studying Teacher Education*, 12(3), 302–319.

Fuller, A., & Unwin, L. (2017). Apprenticeship Quality and Social Mobility. In *Better Apprenticeships: Access, Quality and Labour Market Outcomes in the English Apprenticeship System* (pp. 9–36). London: The Sutton Trust.

Friedman, A., & Phillips, M. (2004). Continuing Professional Development: Developing a Vision. *Journal of Education and Work*, 17(3), 361–376.

Fuller, A., & Unwin, L. (2003). Learning as Apprentices in the Contemporary UK Workplace: Creating and Managing Expansive and Restrictive Participation. *Journal of Education and Work*, 16(4), 407–426.

Goleman, D. (1998). *Working with Emotional Intelligence*. Bloomsbury.

Guile, D., & Young, M. (2003). Transfer and Transition in Vocational Education: Some Theoretical Considerations. In T. Tuomi-Gröhn & Y. Engeström (Eds.), *Between School and Work: New Perspectives on Transfer and Boundary-Crossing* (pp. 63–82). Elsevier.

Keller, A., & Barabasch, A. (2022). Coaching to Support Apprentice's Ability to Manage their Own (Further) Competence Development: Results of a Case Study and their Implications. *Journal of Education and Work*, 35(8), 858–870. https://doi.org/10.1080/13639080.2022.2144167

Kouzes, J. M., & Posner, B. Z. (2017). *The Leadership Challenge* (7th ed.). Jossey-Bass.

Mlambo, M., Silén, C., & McGrath, C. (2021). Lifelong Learning and Nurses' Continuing Professional Development, a Metasynthesis of the Literature. *BMC Nursing*, 20, 62.

Nilsson, P. (2013). Developing a Scholarship of Teaching in Engineering: Supporting Reflective Practice through the Use of a Critical Friend. *Reflective Practice*, 14(2), 196–208.

Quew-Jones, R. J., & Rowe, L. (2022). Enhancing the Degree Apprenticeship Curriculum through Work-Based Manager and Mentor Intervention. *Journal of Work-Applied Management*, 14(2), 242–256.

Schuck, S., & Russell, T. (2005). Self-study, Critical Friendship, and the Complexities of Teacher Education. *Studying Teacher Education*, 1(2), 107–121.

Tuttle, L., & Critchlow, K. (2025). Beyond Compensation: Non-Monetary Factors Influencing Retention of Highly Skilled IT Professionals in the 21st Century Digital Age. *International Journal of Research in Human Resource Management*, 7(1), 122–127.

4

The Learner

Navigating the senior leader apprenticeship journey

Marian Evans

Introduction

This chapter explores the lived experiences of small and medium enterprises (SME) learners who have attended a Senior Leader Apprenticeship programme (SLA) in business management. The SLA provides opportunities for learners to complete an academic Postgraduate Diploma (PGDip), which can lead to further career progression opportunities and a Master's in Business Administration (MBA), including a professional pathway to Chartered Manager or Fellow. For those who are pursuing professional development or seeking a career step-up, funding provided by the Apprenticeship Levy has been a tempting offer. The programme invites those who can use their years of business experience, without the formal requirement of a degree entry route (CMI, n.d.). For some SME managers and leaders, the offer to acknowledge or validate their experience and expertise with a formal qualification as an 'in-service learner' (Cook et al., 2024) is a great opportunity.

Higher and Degree Apprenticeships (HDAs) were introduced to improve productivity, management, and leadership skills across the economy. Labour's Industrial Strategy Consultation (DBT, 2024) identifies that there are still weaknesses in these skills, particularly in small businesses. The two most popular Level 7 apprenticeships – Senior Leader and Accountancy and Taxation – represent 70% of the market (Richmond, 2025) with public sector services, including the NHS, education, and local councils frequently demonstrating the largest take-up of the current system for this level (Richmond, 2025). Therefore, if SMEs are to play a crucial role in the economy, why are they not more widely represented upskilling their managers and leaders via the SLA programme?

DOI: 10.4324/9781003567844-5

The purpose of this chapter is to explore *'How do SME learners manage their expectations of the SLA journey and what challenges do they experience?'* Findings from this study will provide a richer understanding of their reflections on the benefits, barriers, and challenges in a SME context.

Background

Existing HDA research literature identifies several common themes surrounding the SLA qualification; career aspirations (Mulkeen et al., 2017; Evans and Cloutier, 2023; Cook et al., 2024), off-the-job training (Fabian et al., 2022; Poole et al., 2023), work-study time habits (Poole et al., 2023; Cook et al., 2024), work–life balance and resilience (Poole et al., 2023; Cook et al., 2024), and the tripartite relationship (Taylor-Smith et al., 2023; Evans and Cloutier, 2025).

Outcomes from this literature demonstrate that, in terms of career aspirations, the SLA qualification is perceived as a valuable and effective way of supporting personal and professional development (Evans and Cloutier, 2023; Cook et al., 2024). Despite issues regarding structural barriers (Poole et al., 2023) or collaboration between learner and delivery (Taylor-Smith et al., 2023), senior leaders value their engagement with others across industry sectors, developing friendships that provide mutual support and motivation.

Several studies have examined the wider sphere of HDA challenges, for example, the expectations of off-the job-training as 'busy professionals' (Fabian et al., 2022) can be a major issue, so this time must be carefully managed. Senior leaders who are familiar with their job roles already have strategies for routines (Cook et al., 2024) and may be better placed to manage time constraints. The collaboration between all parties engaged in the tripartite relationship (Taylor-Smith et al., 2023; Evans and Cloutier, 2025) note that combining work and study time is a key tension. Many manage this pressure themselves (Taylor-Smith et al., 2023), while others show resilience and personal characteristics that enable them to successfully complete their studies (Cook et al., 2024). However, this creates a balancing act, juggling work/personal life pressures and educational commitments (Poole et al., 2023).

The literature also points out the challenges associated with the tripartite relationship (learners, training provider, and employer) and suggests that improving stakeholder collaboration would help to address these (Chadwick et al., 2024). Although some of these studies have focused on Level 7 challenges (for example, Evans and Cloutier, 2023; Poole et al., 2023; Cook et al., 2024), many do not specifically take an SME- or SLA-only business perspective. In addition to these insights, the work-based learning model of delivery, with divided responsibilities between employer and the training provider, presents further challenges (Mulkeen et al., 2017). Mentoring must be proactive in the workplace (Taylor-Smith et al., 2023) in order to support work-based application (Mulkeen et al., 2017; Evans and Cloutier, 2023). Furthermore, cross-boundary opportunities, including the collaboration and learning between learners outside of the sponsoring organisation, would also support this (Taylor-Smith et al., 2023).

Exploring how SME learners navigate their SLA journey will provide a new perspective, which may be different to apprentices from the public sector or larger, private sector organisations. Understanding this perspective will help to highlight effective practices and address any misunderstandings and concerns that are specific to SMEs.

The study

SLA learners in a post-92 UK university were invited to discuss their experience of the apprenticeship journey and reflect on the added value that the SLA brings to their personal and professional development. Private sector SME learners from 5 different cohorts were approached and a total of 8 took part. Table 4.1 below provides the socio-demographic characteristics of the participants. Most learners were near to concluding their knowledge award delivered by the university, so they had good understanding of the programme, its benefits and challenges and were able to make a valued contribution to the study. One learner had successfully completed the SLA apprenticeship certification and completed an MBA top-up, so was able to provide a useful alternative perspective.

Each learner took part in an interview conversation on MS Teams with the author, lasting between 30 and 45 minutes. During the conversation, learners were asked about apprenticeship benefits, challenges, and barriers and how they managed their expectations of the SLA journey. These interviews were recorded and the text transcript used for analysis, in order to provide insight of perceptions and differing perspectives. In the excerpts provided later on in this chapter, learners' names have been coded P1–P8 to protect their identity.

Table 4.1 The socio-demographic characteristics of the Learners

Participant	Role	Sector	Business size	Highest qualification at application	Gender	Age	Ethnicity
P1	Director of customer experience	Education services	Small<50	AS level	Female	25–34	White
P2	Innovation manager	Engineering consultancy	Large>250	Doctorate	Male	45–54	Asian or Asian British
P3	Head of sales	Education services	Medium<250	Hons Degree	Male	45–54	White
P4	Programme manager	Engineering consultancy	Large>250	Dip HE level 5	Female	45–54	White
P5	Senior software architect	IT	Micro<10	BSc Computing	Male	35–44	White
P6	IT Projects and change manager	Healthcare/ homecare	Medium-Large>250	BA Management	Male	35–44	White
P7	Accountant	Plumbing and heating	Medium<250	ACCA	Male	45–54	Asian or Asian British
P8	Company director	Manufacturing	Medium>50	BSc	Male	35–44	White

From the analysed transcripts, key topic areas were identified and coded into themes. This process allowed the author to identify common patterns and areas of interest discussed by the Learners. The thematic analysis approach is a common method of organising and presenting information that has been identified from interview data. Typically, a codebook is kept that allows the researcher to show codes and their description, with quotes from the Learner (Saldaña, 2013, pp. 24–25). This helps to bring to life key perspectives and thoughts for the reader.

From this study, four key themes emerged:

1) Perceptions of programme benefits
2) Balancing work and study time
3) Mixed-sector cohorts
4) Managing the tripartite relationship

In the following section, each theme is discussed and incorporates illustrative quotations to highlight learners' key discussion points and perspectives.

Key themes

1. Perceptions of programme benefits
   All learners found the journey challenging; however, it facilitated personal and professional growth. This included the desired expectation of 'levelling up' to be a competent senior leader and was regardless of their existing position in the organisation and level of expertise (Evans and Cloutier, 2023).

The 'in-service' learner approach was perceived to be valuable, for example:

> *...It's been relatively positive; I think it's a good methodology of achieving a qualification whilst working.*
>
> (P5)

> *...I think every day or most days I am able to use something that I've learnt on the programme very practically, yes, I found it very useful.*
>
> (P1)

Others demonstrated career progression as an outcome:

> *...I think the expectation was that I would get some useful knowledge and personal development out of it, but also, that it would make me more employable or help me advance up the company and I think both of those things have been proven to have happened since I finished the course. I've had a couple of promotions and had job offers from other places.*
>
> (P6)

Furthermore, all considered that their expectations had been met, and reflections illustrated the interrelatedness of day-to-day management and leadership skill development. As one learner stated:

> *...I wanted to provide myself with a high level of business knowledge that I don't have...to make sure that I personally feel more confident in these situations because we deal with a lot of blue-chip customers.*
>
> (P8)

The majority were motivated towards self-development, but surprisingly, prior to commencing, were not aware of the SLA programme:

> *...I came across it by chance...I was looking to do an MBA anyway and I was just going to do the traditional part-time route, and I was just going to self-fund it. But when I heard about the apprenticeship pot at head office and then I saw this and I was like, oh hang on a minute, you can do this and then a conversion to an MBA. I was like, that's a no brainer...so for me, it's a much cheaper way of doing it.*
>
> (P8)

This suggests that the SLA is not broadly advertised across SME sectors. As noted by one senior manager:

> *...None of the people I spoke to about it was aware they could access to the Level 7 course by the apprenticeship levy.*
>
> (P3)

When asked further about this, several intimated that this was due to differences between the public and private sector recruitment approaches, stating:

...with the public sector, they are all from technical backgrounds where you need to have a degree or you need to have some kind of professional membership...

(P8)

Another apprentice thought that it was because the levy process was poorly understood:

...I think that the apprenticeship scheme and the apprenticeship levy is just not understood, businesses are obviously paying vast amounts into the pot. And yeah, the understanding of the breadth of courses that are available from that pot of money and how to spend it and how to go about it I think is lacking.

(P3)

Others believed it was due to a perception of the term 'apprenticeship' in SMEs:

...You're kind of fighting against the perception of what is an apprentice and an apprentice as a school leaver...to be in the sector that an SME works in, traditionally you haven't needed to come in as an apprentice, so why would you start doing an apprenticeship [now]? Everybody knows what an MBA is. People don't know what a Level 7 apprenticeship is...people don't even know what a Post Grad Diploma is.

(P4)

This highlights that a perception of an apprenticeship is still an issue and that the notion of 'Level 7' is poorly understood. As the MBA Top-Up apprentice commented:

...The reason why I was keen to do the top-up was that I felt that even though the SLA programme was a Level 7 and equivalent to a Master's level, I felt that I would constantly be explaining to people that I was a Level 7...It's a Master's equivalent. No. I've not got a Master's, it's a Master's equivalent!

(P3)

These comments may help to explain the poor SME take-up, although another learner thought this was because experience in SMEs was seen to be more valuable than qualifications:

> *...The private sector is more interested in getting experience in through the door with people who've already got the experience and the work experience, more interested in that than the qualification...Is there more of an expectation for the private sector to deliver quicker and so they don't want to wait two years for somebody to be in a position to do it?*
>
> (P6)

It may be SMEs have a limited opportunity to explore long-term career trajectories (Fabian et al., 2022), but these insightful comments do highlight issues around apprenticeship terminology and recruitment that may influence take-up.

2. Balancing work and study time
   A range of concerns associated with apprenticeship's regulatory requirements and study commitments were observed, where adjustments and interventions made to working patterns were an ongoing challenge (Poole et al., 2023). Meeting the 20% off-the-job time – where the Learner is provided time within normal working hours, for the purpose of achieving the Knowledge, Skills and Behaviours of the apprenticeship (Department for Education, 2023) – was difficult. Although plans were put in place, these were frequently disrupted by day-day work challenges. Individuals soon learnt to self-manage challenges, developing different strategies to cope with catching up on study time. One learner noted:

> *...It's hard, it's definitely challenging to fit in around work.*
>
> (P8)

Another took a more pragmatic stance:

> *...Yes, I think that the challenge is the work life, social, academic work balance, isn't it? It's always going to be the challenge.*
>
> (P6)

For the smaller SMEs, this was a critical issue when off-the-job time was problematic:

> *...but the problem I have is I go right; I'll spend Friday doing this. Yeah, and then Friday comes and I've got a choice to make, I can either do some work for a client and charge them £1000 per day or I can do work on the uni work like I'm supposed to, as part of my apprenticeship and the business won't earn £1000 in that day, and it's really hard to go yeah, I'll do the uni work.*
>
> (P5)

Another thought that the terminology gave the wrong message:

> *...possibly off-the-job is the wrong term to use for it...it sort of makes it sound like it's, Oh! We're having to agree to one of our staff doing a four-day week! Because in my experience, it just wasn't like that, it was doing stuff that was of immediate value and of immediate relevance.*
>
> (P3)

The work–study time dichotomy is a well-noted outcome of research (see Mulkeen et al., 2017; Poole et al., 2023), but appears to be more critical in smaller SMEs, where time off is less negotiable.

3. Mixed sector cohorts
   Findings highlighted SMEs' perception of the benefits of learning in mixed cohorts, that is, bringing together culturally different sectors. Engagement with different apprentices and acquiring a range of knowledge and experience in a university context was a positive outcome:

> *...Actually, being in a room with other people from different companies and different backgrounds is the most useful thing particularly for me, I've never worked in the public sector and a lot of people from that course were. So, it was interesting just to hear their points of view and their experiences.*
>
> (P5)

But for others an imbalance in cohort make-up between public and private sectors elicited a more mixed response:

> *...It depends on who you're targeting...you might have someone who's already an MD on the course who has been doing the senior leader role in a business for a long time...this course is just furthering them as a leader. Whereas your management graduates...they might not have any leadership experience or business experience...I think there are very different spectrums that you're working with...whilst that's really interesting, it didn't help me specifically in my learning.*
>
> (P1)

For others it was insightful:

> *...I think it holds a valuable lesson for some of us who come from bigger organisations and perhaps feel a bit more secure than others, where there isn't uncertainty around the corner and you can see that the SMEs are actually learning this, they have a more personal stake and they have a business, they want to enhance it using the tools... there's more urgency... you can see the tension in those people as opposed to someone coming from the public sector...*
>
> (P2)

These examples suggest that mixed cohorts provide opportunities to share and discuss different points of view, but for learning to be effective, there must be a variety of sectors and experience represented in the cohort.

4. Managing the tripartite relationship
   The tripartite relationship between employer mentors, learners, and the university received mixed responses from the participants. These regular meetings are designed to support work-based learning and encourage self-reflection and for some medium SMEs, it worked well.

> *...Yes, me and him, yeah...it's the perfect team...we have an almost identical work ethic, he's got a lot more experience in manufacturing and exposure to stuff over the years, so he's ideal for that...*
>
> (P8)

Other smaller businesses struggled to find time for conversations, especially where it was not perceived to add value. This highlights how employers and providers must work together on mentor interventions (Evans and Cloutier,

2025) and provide supportive collaboration (Taylor-Smith et al., 2023), particularly for small or micro businesses where it appeared to work the least effectively.

> *...It's really difficult to explain to people how it works, why it's important...if I were to say what's the barrier it's how you communicate internally about what you're doing, and being given tools and support to help...*
>
> (P1)

> *...Our business has a mentor...we've got two or three that we contact when we need help about things. I was like, I could do that, but they'd have to charge me...then it became about funding a problem...*
>
> (P5)

Additionally, the mandated elements of the apprenticeship were perceived to be bureaucratic. This suggests that for SMEs, some of the additional coursework, such as off-the-job activity logging, was a struggle to integrate and manage effectively. For smaller businesses, it was also another stress point:

> *...He comes to all my quarterly catch ups...he's like, this is bureaucracy...What value is he getting? What additional value is he getting from me going through this course and why should he invest his time into it? And I think in a profit-making business, I think that's a really big factor.*
>
> (P1)

> *...When I started the course, I hadn't realised that's it's going to be so much bureaucracy...to complete other assignments and other portfolio work as well, that is a bit challenging.*
>
> (P7)

However, an important element of the tripartite relationship was identified as collaboration across cohorts and communities of practice (Taylor-Smith et al., 2023). Examples below support an emergent theme of peer support:

> *...I met some of the cohort members on an informal basis over lunch and even later on it the day and there are so may nuggets of information and knowledge that you get from them; it enhances the experience.*
>
> (P2)

> *...That WhatsApp group is still in use, they finished two years ago and they're still all talking to each other and they're you know, sending. I'm still part of that WhatsApp group and yeah, there's a real sense of cohesion there.*
>
> (P1)

Notably, findings indicate that this tripartite relationship is important for personal and professional learning development and would be a fruitful area for future research, as it crosses contextual networks and boundaries and learning as a social practice.

Conclusion and ways forward

This chapter set out to explore the question *'How do SME learners manage their expectations of the SLA journey and what challenges do they experience?'* The experiences and challenges identified in this chapter are likely to be common to other HDAs, but this study has highlighted several critical insights that indicate differences in practice for SMEs.

Firstly, and positively, the SLA aligns with SME expectations by creating value, enabling managers to be more confident in their role, in readiness for strategic decision-making and senior leadership responsibilities.

Secondly, and more critically, there appears to be a challenge in making the provision for SMEs more accessible, compared to public and larger private sector organisations. The fact that all learners were unaware of the qualification and had found it by chance or by word of mouth is a concern.

Thirdly, the traditional definition of an 'apprentice' is still closely associated with lower qualification levels in an SME context, and a lack of SLA visibility does not help to address this issue. Indeed, with the removal of most Level 7 funding following the government's recent announcements, this perception is likely to continue or deepen.

Fourthly, there are still tensions in the tripartite relationship, particularly around mentoring. Adoption of a different delivery model for SMEs, for example, accredited employer-nominated mentors who can step in and bridge the gap for small businesses to ensure success might be a solution. Proactive mentors are significant facilitators for supporting the work–study balance, therefore improving understanding of the requirements would add value.

Finally, future HDA investigations must address the level of awareness for collaboration between *all* stakeholders in an SME context, with a particular focus on the impact of support networks and peer collaboration for learning and reflective practice. The private sector, especially SMEs, provide economic wealth and value. The question remains, however: How will the Labour government's modern Industrial Strategy and approach towards HDAs enhance this going forward?

Suggested further reading

Dawson, S. and Osborne, A. (2020). Reshaping built environment higher education: The impact of degree apprenticeships in England. *International Journal of Construction Education and Research*, 16(2) 102–116. https://doi.org/10.1108/HESWBL-02-2024-0058

Garnett, J. and Reynier, P. (2025). The degree apprenticeship experience: perceptions of apprentices and their employers. *Higher Education, Skills and Work-Based Learning*, 15(2) 441–451. https://doi.org/10.1108/HESWBL-02-2024-0058

Richmond, T. (2025). A level of uncertainty: How to resolve the debate over the future of level 7 apprenticeships, Briefing paper January 2025, Social Market Foundation. Retrieved from www.smf.co.uk/wp-content/uploads/2025/01/A-level-of-uncertainty-Jan-2025.pdfJanuary2025

References

Chadwick, K., Dimungu Hewage, D. and Hazzam, J. (2024). Barriers to effective higher and degree-level apprenticeships: A systematic literature review and future research agenda. *Higher Education, Skills and Work-Based Learning*, 15 (3): 595–611. https://doi.org/10.1108/HESWBL-07-2024-0208

Chartered Management Institute (CMI). (n.d.). *Senior Leader Apprenticeship*. https://www.managers.org.uk/education-and-learning/apprenticeships/level-7/

Cook, F., Sims, S., Brindley, J. and Poole, R. (2024). Level 7-degree apprenticeships – a story of challenge, resilience and success. *Research in Post-Compulsory Education*, 29(2), 191–219. https://doi.org/10.1080/13596748.2024.2330778

Department for Business & Trade (DBT). (2024). Open consultation - Invest 2035: The UK's modern industrial strategy. Updated 24 November 2024, Retrieved from www.gov.uk/government/consultations/invest-2035-the-uks-modern-industrial-strategy/invest-2035-the-uks-modern-industrial-strategy

Department for Education. (2023). *Apprenticeship Off-the-Job Training*. https://assets.publishing.service.gov.uk/media/6530efdb92895c000ddcba2b/2023_10_OTJT_Guide_v5_-_23_24_Rules_v1.0.pdf

Evans, M. and Cloutier, L.M. (2023). Integrating higher degree education with practice: Exploring the value proposition of executive MBA apprenticeships. *Higher Education, Skills and Work-Based Learning,* 13(2), 283–298. https://doi.org/10.1108/HESWBL-10-2022-0207

Evans, M. and Cloutier, L.M. (2025). Examining perceptions of the tripartite relationship in higher degree apprenticeship programmes. *Education + Training,* 67(2), 236–257. https://doi.org/10.1108/ET-01-2024-0011

Fabian, K., Taylor-Smith, E., Smith, S., Meharg, D. and Varey, A. (2022). An exploration of degree apprentice perspectives: A Q methodology study. *Studies in Higher Education*, 47(7), 1397–1409. https://doi.org/10.1080/03075079.2021.1897094

Mulkeen, J., Hussein, A.A. Leigh, J. and Ward, P. (2017). Degree and higher-level apprenticeships: An empirical investigation of stakeholder perceptions and of challenges and opportunities. *Studies in Higher Education,* 44(2), 333–346. http://dx.doi.org/10.2139/ssrn.3015407

Poole R., Cook, F, Sims, S. and Brindley, J. (2023). Challenges, barriers and strategies for engaging in level 7 apprenticeship studies. *Journal of Education and Work,* 36/2, 153–168. https://doi.org/10.1080/13639080.2023.2167953

Saldaña, J. (2013). *The Coding Manual for Qualitative Researchers*. London: SAGE.

Taylor-Smith, E., Smith, S. and Fabian, K. (2023). Apprentices' perspectives of the tripartite collaboration at the heart of degree apprenticeships: A longitudinal study. *Journal of Workplace Learning,* 35(8), 779–795. https://doi.org/10.1108/JWL-01-2023-0007

5 The Learner

A first-hand perspective of the degree apprenticeship journey

Clare Taylor

From curiosity to commitment: Deciding to pursue a Degree Apprenticeship

This chapter centres on a case study examining the experience of a second year BSc. (Hons) Chartered Surveyor Degree Apprentice (CDSA) working for a large UK property organisation. Our apprentice started this unique educational and career pathway after discovering the idea of the degree apprenticeship (DA) on a university website and social media feeds.

Choosing a five-year apprenticeship over a traditional three-year university degree was a carefully considered decision. Whilst the commitment of five years seemed initially daunting, our apprentice highlights a crucial advantage:

> *So, if you do a three-year degree starting at 18 and then spend another two years getting your Royal Institution of Chartered Surveyor's certification, you'll qualify at about the same time as someone who did an apprenticeship – but the apprentice will already have five years of real-world experience under their belt.*

Ullibarriarana-Garate et al. (2023) believe that young people have a lack of work experience, and this limits their access to employment opportunities. The dual benefit of academic achievement combined with hands-on expertise increases the quality, quantity and scale of impact DA graduates make.

DOI: 10.4324/9781003567844-6

This can be a particularly valuable career accelerator with Jones et al. (2022) finding in their study that many apprentices experienced career progression during the apprenticeship, and as such were some way along career pathways rather than starting in 'entry-level' graduate roles upon completion. Career advancements are usually coupled with pay rises and pay for DA graduate rises more rapidly than that of a non-DA graduate, demonstrating how valuable this practical workplace experience is to their employers (Nawaz et al., 2022).

With often high levels of debt associated with a traditional degree, the average being £44,940, (NUS, 2024), parents are starting to warm' to this non-traditional approach (Nawaz et al., 2022) which in turn is influencing their child's perception. But whilst there has been significant growth in the number of DAs on offer, there remain challenges making them accessible to all (UCAS, n.d.). Sinead Trudgill, Director of Learning and Development at Network Rail, believes individuals are 'choosing apprenticeships above going to university because of the financial impact traditional study will have on their families' (CIPD, 2025). The apprenticeship financial model offers learners an opportunity to avoid the debt associated with a traditional degree (Taylor-Smith et al., 2023). Our apprentice agrees with this sentiment:

> *This structure felt like a safer, more financially viable route compared to the traditional university pathway…I am able to start saving money earlier, for example for a house in the future, but also some more financial freedom to enjoy travel and adventure.*

But for a young person from a lower socioeconomic background the data suggests it's still far from an easy alternative to accessing a great career (Sutton Trust, 2025). While the DA model is often presented as a route to social mobility, the persistence of low uptake among disadvantaged groups suggests systemic barriers such as lack of targeted outreach, patchy employer engagement, and limited regional provision remain largely unresolved (Commission, 2020; FE Week, 2025). Stakeholders must reflect on whether enough is being done to ensure equitable access and to tackle deep-rooted inequalities.

Once the decision had been made to pursue a degree apprenticeship, instead of the more traditional degree approach, our apprentice notes:

> *I did a bit of research and then ended up completing some work experience with a residential estate agency, which helped me understand what surveyors do.*
>
> *Whilst I wasn't carrying out the same type of work e.g. red book valuations and Level 3 building surveys, there were chartered surveyors involved in the sale process of a property such as mortgage valuers, building surveyors who I could speak to and from whom I could gain insights.*

Success on a Higher or Degree Apprenticeship is more assured when the apprentice demonstrates higher levels of self-efficacy. As with our apprentice, Quew-Jones and Rowe (2022) found that apprentices who spend time early in the application process undertaking research about the profession and the sector meant that, once on the DA programme, they were more assured of their success as their initiative and persistence increased. But 1 in 3 apprentices from a lower socioeconomic background are currently receiving no support with their application, resulting in only 5% of degree apprentices, for instance, having been eligible for free school meals (Sutton Trust, 2025).

DAs are first and foremost a job (Lillis and Bravenboer, 2020), but job adverts for DAs show a surprising vagueness in what the Learner will be doing in the role once hired and so candidates may misconceive what the role involves, resulting in mismatched expectations and employee disengagement (Fabian et al., 2022b). It could even mean that potential apprentices may be prevented from embarking on the right educational path towards a rewarding career, due to incorrect, or even a total absence of, information (QA Ltd, 2019). In the case of our apprentice this was less of a problem as their prior work experience confirmed their interest in this sector and potential aptitude for the role by helping them to understand the actual work they would undertake.

> *Knowing about the industry and the specific career aspirations associated with the industry does help me to apply myself and strive towards that goal. In my case my aspiration is to become a qualified Chartered Surveyor, so I am working hard to gain as much hands on experience as possible across a wide range of areas. It is important to know about the progression path in the job so that you know what you are working towards.*

Our apprentice also highlights:

> *During my interview, I spoke with an apprentice who shared their experience. That really helped me understand what to expect and help me make a final decision on the apprenticeship.*

This exchange is something our apprentice acknowledged was not always available to prospective candidates and went on to suggest that anyone interested in a DA asks to speak with an apprentice directly, wherever possible. Opportunities to better understand the organisation, the nature of the work to be carried out, and the Knowledge, Skills and Behaviours needed to perform in the job, result in a more effective and inclusive recruitment and selection process (CIPD, 2015) and therefore higher chance for the organisation of recruiting the most appropriate candidate (Fabian et al., 2022b).

Securing the role: The application process

Finding a DA with an organisation involved our apprentice completing extensive independent research, as learning providers generally do not recommend specific employers. Our apprentice actively sought out apprenticeship vacancies and even graduate opportunities advertised online through job portals and company-specific webpages. Our apprentice also engaged in extensive networking, reflecting the strategic cultivation of social capital (Tomlinson, 2017), which is increasingly recognised as essential for navigating non-linear career pathways such as apprenticeships.

> *I looked around for apprenticeship roles and even reached out to companies advertising graduate roles, to ask if they'd consider taking a degree apprentice.*

Furthermore, our apprentice advises potential applicants to:

> *Carefully research programs and employers, ensuring the apprenticeship aligns with your career aspirations and learning preferences.*

DAs admission criteria echo the traditional qualifications sought by universities with an emphasis on pre-university subject-based qualifications (Fabian et al., 2022b). In this case, our apprentice was already in receipt of their A level results and knew that they met the minimum entry requirements ahead of the application to the role. Nonetheless the process was highly competitive. It included a formal recruitment process involving an application, online interview, and an in-person assessment and presentation to secure the much sought-after role.

Our apprentice stresses the importance of resilience during the application process. Gorb et al. (2023) note that the degree apprenticeship market is highly competitive. Our apprentice echoes this, acknowledging the challenges of waiting for responses and navigating demanding recruitment processes, while also emphasising the importance and value of persistence.

This proactive approach paid off and after approximately six months our apprentice secured a DA role. The job and the DA commenced one month apart. The timing of this was fortuitous, but with hindsight our apprentice reflects that:

> *Starting both at the same time can be a bit overwhelming. I found it helpful to settle into work for a month before taking on the university workload. In fact, starting even three months before university begins can be even more beneficial to establish yourself in the team and adjust to working life.*
>
> *Higher degree apprentices often have little, or no, work experience having joined fresh from school, so a gradual transition can be especially helpful.*

A broad yet balanced curriculum: Bridging theory and practice

Our apprentice's Chartered Surveyor Degree Apprenticeship (CSDA) curriculum is broad and multidisciplinary, encompassing modules on valuation, sustainable crop production, animal production, estate management law, and business management. This mirrors the complexity of real-world problems which often require transdisciplinary solutions (Taylor-Smith et al., 2023).

The year-round delivery of modules, including dedicated off-the-job study periods, offers an apprentice a dynamic and engaging educational experience. Our apprentice particularly values the blend of academic and practical components, which reflects Evans and Cloutier's (2023) argument that effective apprenticeship provision must move beyond theoretical instruction to incorporate applied, practice-based learning.

Some modules align directly with our apprentice's day-to-day tasks such as valuations, whilst others provide wider foundational knowledge. Apprentices on this CSDA come from a wide variety of organisations with client responsibilities ranging from land to property to construction. This holistic approach not only enriches their professional competence but also prepares them for sustained career progression within the industry. Andrea Gordon, CIPD Fellow and Director from Peabody Housing Association (CIPD, 2025), shares that, in her experience, apprentices are staying longer and working their way up through the organisation into senior roles. Exposure to disciplines outside a apprentice's immediate field helps foster a more comprehensive understanding of the sector, with Nawaz et al. (2022) confirming that organisations overwhelmingly believe DAs are a catalyst for growing talent and encouraging career progression.

Our apprentice shares their passion for this broad learning approach:

> *The variety keeps it interesting. I might not be an agronomist, but knowing about crops and soil helps when assessing agricultural property value.*

The value of real-time learning

One of our apprentice's favourite aspects of the apprenticeship is the immediate application of theoretical knowledge:

> *With a standard university degree, you might learn something in your first year and not apply it until years later. Here, I can take what I've learned straight back to work.*

This seamless integration of study and work deepens understanding and enhances retention. Apprentices see their professional identities evolve as they experience growth both academically and through 'embodied action' via the realisation of their academic learning within the workplace. In effect, the workplace becomes a 'credited place of learning' beyond the boundaries of traditional degree study programmes (Fabian et al., 2022b) and is positioned as an equally important and legitimate source of learning and knowledge generation for the apprentice (Lillis and Bravenboer, 2020).

One example shared by our apprentice involves being taught how to assess and prepare compensation claims as part of the Compensation and Utilities module:

> *Back in the workplace, it was great to have learned how compensation claims are prepared so that I can assess claims submitted to infrastructure undertakers straightway as part of my job and make suitable recommendations to them as our clients.*

As demonstrated above, DAs allow apprentices to contribute meaningfully to their organisations, even in the early stages of their careers, with the DAs serving as a vital pipeline for growing talents (Nawaz et al., 2022). This work-based knowledge exchange empowers the apprentice, builds self-efficacy and leads them, as is the case with our apprentice, to be even 'braver' by sharing their tacit knowledge (Quew-Jones and Rowe, 2022). Lillis and Bravenboer (2020) go even further to suggest that DAs 'creatively disrupt' the relationship between higher education and the workplace.

Our apprentice agrees:

> *Yes, I believe off-the-job learning helps build confidence. In my opinion, confidence comes with knowledge – being familiar with a topic makes you feel more assured and less anxious.*
>
> *When the subject aligns with workplace scenarios, it allows you to explore and practice situations before encountering them in real life, helping you feel more prepared and confident.*

This also increases the possibility of an apprentice successfully contributing to, or leading, real-world projects that benefit their employer. It ensures the apprentice's value to the organisation (Nawaz et al., 2022). Indeed, Ulliabaraiarana-Garate et al. (2023) go on to state that organisations participating in apprenticeships achieve overall 'better innovation performance'. Our apprentice found themself assigned clients early in their apprenticeship with their own portfolio of work to complete and associated targets. Karen Handley, Head of Early Careers at Virgin Media 02, concurs that apprentices deploy fresh thinking quickly as they are in a real role the whole time, with their capability increasing consistently (CIPD, 2025).

Facing the challenges: Time management and support

For our apprentice, time management emerges as one of the primary challenges of the apprenticeship. Balancing a full-time job with academic responsibilities can be very challenging and complex as our apprentice, like many others, had limited prior experience of higher education and must juggle work, personal and social commitments (Ullibarriarana-Garate, 2023). Our apprentice points out that:

> *This requires effective planning and strong organisational skills so creating a consistent study routine and breaking down assignments into manageable tasks are critical strategies for success.*

Our apprentice also acknowledges the importance of support from their employer by accommodating study-related needs:

> *My line manager has been great. They offer guidance on my approach and allow flexibility in my workplace schedule when assignment deadlines are approaching.*

Organisations that recognise the importance of social capital reduce work strain on apprentices. Social capital has four elements: enhancing the flow of information, influencing individuals with decision-making power (e.g. putting in a good word), offering necessary or desirable social credentials, and reinforcing an individual's identity and recognition with a given group (Lin, 1999). Organisations that play an active part in the 'triadic' learning endeavour (Lillis and Bravenboer, 2020) to support social capital means that their apprentices have a better chance of success. Conversely, lack of social capital can lead to outcomes such as emotional exhaustion, job dissatisfaction, anxiety and negative interest (Ullibarriarana-Garate, 2023).

Our apprentice shares:

> *The company is keen to invest in the education of younger talent, likely because they see us as the future of the business. This investment is empowering – it shows they're willing to spend money on your growth.*

> *Unlike school, where attendance is mandatory, in the workplace you choose to be there, so more effort is put into training. It's also job-specific, meaning it directly benefits your daily work.*
>
> *Support for my study and development is a major motivator – without it, I'd likely feel less valued and driven.*

Our apprentice's organisation fosters a supportive environment, providing practical advice and guidance from other experienced professionals (Quew-Jones and Rowe, 2022) with Ullibarriarana-Garate (2023) concurring that leadership and mentorship are seen as essential in the well-being of undergraduates. For our apprentice, previous apprentices act as a form of community of practice and offer crucial opportunities for reflection (Fabian et al., 2021).

Regular meetings with both the Employer and university are key to ensuring our apprentice stays on track. Research, however, indicates, that this ideal 'triadic' relationship is not consistently realised in practice, with some apprentices reporting a lack of joined-up communication between employer and university (Fabian et al., 2022a). Without clear alignment, apprentices risk falling between institutional cracks, undermining the very work-integrated learning that DAs are designed to deliver. Our apprentice has protected weekly time to help bridge any potential gap – in the form of a catch-up hour every Friday – dedicated to any apprenticeship related questions. Opportunities for the Employer to support the apprentice's well-being, monitor progress, remove any doubts about studying at this level and explore the balance between job demands back in their workplace are critical to ongoing success (Ullibarriarana-Garate, 2023). Even UCAS (n.d.) warns young people considering this approach that they need to be prepared for the rigours of working and studying for a degree at the same time. More importantly, the expert mentorship of an apprentice can help to increase the focus and value of learning and overall experience, when work can frequently take priority (Evans and Cloutier 2023). In our apprentice's case, the manager also completed an apprenticeship and so understands, and is particularly supportive of, the process, challenges and workload involved acting as a mediator to prioritise and balance studies and workplace pressures.

In only a short period of time, our apprentice has been able to recognise their growth and achievement on the DA. Their progress has been acknowledged through both formal assessments and informal feedback:

> *Getting a good grade on assignments in a field I'd never studied before felt like a big achievement.*

As the apprentice grows academically, their self-confidence is enhanced, transforming their personal and professional identities (Fabian et al., 2021). To then successfully apply their knowledge and skills in the workplace bolsters their confidence and earns them recognition from their employer. The apprentice is an *aligned student-worker*, and this ongoing validation reinforces their commitment to the organisation through a sense of belonging and provides important recognition of the value they contribute (Fabian et al., 2021). Our apprentice shares:

> *The sense of accomplishment I get from applying classroom knowledge directly to the workplace has been particularly rewarding. For example, learning at university how to carry out a valuation and being able to apply this knowledge using the exact same methodology was satisfying.*
>
> *It reinforces the fact that what you learn on a degree apprenticeship is, most of the time, directly beneficial to your job. This gives you further motivation to learn more and more.*

The importance of peer support

The degree is delivered via block weekly teaching approximately every four to six weeks off site, where our apprentice stays in university accommodation. A significant benefit of the block teaching format, completely away from the workplace, is the opportunity to build personal and professional networks:

> *There are 40 of us in my cohort, all from different sectors of the industry. You've got a network for life, people you can call up for advice or collaborate with in the future.*

These connections provide not only future networking opportunities and valuable career resources but also academic support. Beyond professional networking, our apprentice expresses the enjoyment of forming lasting friendships, sharing challenges, and celebrating milestones together. This notion of relatedness, or feeling connected to others (Ullibarriarana-Garate, 2024), is essential for human growth, development and overall well-being and ultimately leads to higher levels of apprentice engagement. As Eun (2018) states, such interactions play a crucial role in facilitating knowledge internalisation through mediation by a more knowledgeable person. However, it is worth noting that opportunities to build robust peer networks are not evenly distributed. Apprentices based in remote regions, those in smaller cohorts or those who struggled to get regular release from employment, may have fewer chances to develop such connections, potentially limiting their access to valuable peer learning and sector insights (Social Mobility Commission, 2020; Taylor-Smith et al., 2023).

Final thoughts: A path worth taking?

Our apprentice's experience of commencing the CDSA two years ago has, so far, been overwhelmingly positive. The integration of academic development, practical experience and the building of strong professional networks reinforces the value of the DA model for them. The journey has been fruitful, enjoyable, and rewarding. High levels of motivation stem from the immediate application of learning to real-world tasks, which not only enhances their productivity but also strengthens their sense of professional identity. In our apprentice's own words, they remain enthusiastic and confident in the path they have chosen:

> *It's a lot of work, but it's incredibly rewarding. I'd recommend it to anyone who's eager to learn and grow on the job.*

There are some practical steps for anyone deciding whether to pursue a DA:

Preparation

- Take the time to thoroughly understand the role, its expectations, and the structure of the DA programme.
- Engage with organisations, professionals, and fellow apprentices to build a well-rounded understanding of what the role entails and how to succeed within it.

Securing the role

- Be prepared, resilient, and persistent.
- Recognise the process is highly competitive and can be lengthy.
- Seek the opportunity to join the workplace ahead of the commencement of the apprenticeship.

On programme

- Foster peer networks to enhance social cohesion through the apprenticeship journey.
- Develop your time management skills to effectively balance academic study, workplace responsibilities, and personal commitments.
- Use your manager and/or workplace mentor to help mediate tensions between study and workplace pressures.

But the complexity of the 'triadic' learning endeavour (Lillis and Bravenboer, 2020) exposes many areas of challenge for those involved in apprenticeships. As the UK seeks to scale DAs, there must be sustained attention to ensuring quality, consistency of support, and genuine employer commitment. Without these safeguards, the transformative potential highlighted in this case risks becoming the exception rather than the norm.

For employers, securing apprentices with the appropriate motivations and resilience, while simultaneously providing the necessary support space and autonomy to learn and develop – amidst the pressures of workplace demands – is critical to achieving successful outcomes (Powers and Watt, 2021).

For apprentices, engaging with wider support services to identify the right apprenticeship and successfully navigate the recruitment process is essential. Additionally, drawing on peer networks to support learning and progress, alongside collaborating with employer mentors to mediate the challenges of balancing workplace responsibilities with academic study, are key strategies for success (Eun, 2018).

Finally, for the training provider, designing a programme that aligns with the evolving needs of organisations and the wider sector and adapts as the world of work continues to change. If training providers can master these 'complex brokerage skills' between the workplace and education (Taylor-Smith et al., 2023), then apprentices are better positioned to become active contributors within their organisations.

For anyone considering embarking on a DA, some final words of encouragement from our apprentice:

> *If you like being hands-on and seeing how things come together, this is for you. It's rewarding to apply what you're learning in real time. But be prepared to manage your time and stay committed.*

References

CIPD. (2015). *A head for hiring – Behavioural science of recruitment and selection*. https://www.cipd.org/globalassets/media/knowledge/knowledge-hub/reports/a-head-for-hiring_2015-behavioural-science-of-recruitment-and-selection_tcm18-9557.pdf

CIPD. (2025, February 8). Are apprenticeships the forgotten key to building talent pipelines? [audio podcast]. *Soundcloud*. https://soundcloud.com/cipd/are-apprenticeships-the-forgotten-key-to-building-talent-pipelines

Eun, B. (2018). The zone of proximal development as an overarching concept: Aframework for synthesizing Vygotsky's theories. *Educational Philosophy and Theory*, 51 (1), 18–30. https://doi.org/10.1080/00131857.2017.1421941

Evans, M., & Cloutier, L. (2023). Integrating higher degree education with practice: exploring the value proposition of executive MBA apprenticeships. *Higher Education, Skills and Work-Based Learning*, 13 (2), 283–298. https://doi.org/10.1108/HESWBL-10-2022-0207

Fabian, K., Taylor-Smith, E., Smith, S., Meharg, D., & Varey, A. (2021). An exploration of degree apprentice perspectives: A Q methodology study. *Studies in Higher Education*, 47 (7), 1397–1409. https://doi.org/10.1080/03075079.2021.1897094

Fabian, K., Taylor-Smith, E., Smith, S., Meharg, D., & Varey, A. (2022a). An exploration of degree apprentice perspectives: A Q methodology study. *Studies in Higher Education*, 47 (7), 1397–1407. https://doi.org/10.1080/03075079.2021.1897094

Fabian, K., Taylor-Smith, E., Smith, S., & Bratton, A. (2022b). Signalling new opportunities? An analysis of UK job adverts for degree apprenticeships. *Higher Education, Skills and Work-Based Learning*, 13 (2), 299–314. https://doi.org/10.1108/HESWBL-02-2022-0037

FE Week. (2025, March 25). *Apprenticeships reform could weaken social mobility impact*. https://feweek.co.uk/apprenticeships-reform-could-weaken-social-mobility-impact/

Gorb, L., Blyfield, S., & Marchant, C. (2023, February 7). *Why degree apprenticeships are win-win students, universities and employers*. https://www.ucas.com/corporate/news-and-key-documents/news/why-degree-apprenticeships-are-win-win-students-universities-and-employers#:~:text=Since%20the%20introduction%20of%20degree,all%20at%20the%20same%20time.

Jones, K., Christie, F., & Brophy, S. (2022). Getting in, getting on, going further: Exploring the role of employers in the degree apprentice to graduate transition. *British Education Research Journal*, 49, 93–109. https://doi.org/10.1002/berj.3831

Lillis, F., & Bravenboer, D. (2020). The best practice in work-integrated pedagogy in a post-viral future. *Higher Education, Skills and Work-Based Learning*, 10 (5), 727–739. https://doi.org/10.1108/HESWBL-04-2020-0071

Lin, N. (1999). Building a network theory of social capital. *Connections*, 22 (1), 28–51.

National Union of Students UK. (2024, March 21). *English maintenance loan system discourages working class students – new report*. Retrieved from [https://www.nus.org.uk/sutton-trust-report-response] (https://www.nus.org.uk/sutton-trust-report-response)

Nawaz, R., Edifor, E., Holland, S., Cao, Q., & Liu, L. (2022). The impact of Degree Apprenticeships: analysis, insights and policy recommendations. *Transforming Government: People, Process and Policy*, 17 (3), 372–386. https://doi.org/10.1108/TG-07-2022-0105

Powers, T., & Watt, H. (2021). Understanding why apprentices consider dropping out: Longitudinal prediction of apprentices' workplace interest and anxiety. *Empirical Research in Vocational Education and Training*, 13 (9). https://doi.org/10.1186/s40461-020-00106-8

QA Ltd. (2019). The social mobility impact of apprenticeships. https://www.qa.com/media/13940/qa-the-social-mobility-impact-of-apprenticeships-full-report.pdf

Quew-Jones, R., & Rowe, L. (2022). Enhancing the degree apprenticeship curriculum through work-based manager and mentor intervention. *Journal of Work-Applied Management*, 14 (2), 242–256. https://doi.org/10.1108/JWAM-03-2022-0015

Social Mobility Commission. (2020). *Apprenticeships and social mobility fulfilling potential*. https://assets.publishing.service.gov.uk/media/5ef1bb3dd3bf7f6c053a28a4/Apprenticeships_and_social_mobility_report.pdf

Sutton Trust. (2025, July 11). *Apprenticeships are a powerful tool for social mobility*. https://www.suttontrust.com/news-opinion/all-news-opinion/apprenticeships-are-a-powerful-tool-for-social-mobility/

Taylor-Smith, E., Smith, S., & Fabian, K. (2023). Apprentices' perspectives of the tripartite collaboration at the heart of degree apprenticeships: A longitudinal study. *Journal of Workplace Learning*, 35 (8), 779–795. https://doi.org/10.1108/JWL-01-2023-0007

Tomlinson, M. (2017). Forms of graduate capital and their relationship to graduate employability. *Education + Training*, 59 (4), 338–352. https://doi.org/10.1108/ET-05-2016-0090

UCAS. (n.d.). *Degree apprenticeships*. https://www.ucas.com/apprenticeships/degree-apprenticeships

Ullibarriarana-Garate, A., Agirre-Aramnuru, I., & Mesonero-De, M. (2023). Understanding the characteristics of work that foster workplace wellbeing in an apprenticeship programme and their effects on apprentices' employability. Exploring the gender moderation effect. *Higher Education, Skills and Work-Based Learning*, 13 (5), 886–910. https://doi.org/10.1108/HESWBL-12-2022-0268

Ullibarriarana-Garate, A., Agirre-Aramnuru, I., & Mesonero-De, M., & Sanchez-Urien, N. (2024). Higher education apprenticeship. Analyzing the impact and essential conditions of workplace resources on apprentices' career satisfaction. *Journal of Infrastructure, Policy and Development*, 8 (13), 9040. https://doi.org/10.24294/jipd.v8i13.9040

6

The Employer
Issues and challenges faced by SMEs as the Employer in the CMDA

Ahmad Timsal and Victoria Rosamond

Introduction

Degree apprenticeship (DA) programmes are gaining significant traction as effective pathways for higher education and workforce development. A crucial factor in their ongoing success is the strong collaboration forged between industry and higher education institutions (HEIs), often referred to as the 'training providers'. This collaboration helps to align training with industry needs, foster strong employment outcomes for graduates, and contribute to ongoing innovation and skills delivery (Wade, 2023).

Small and medium-sized enterprises (SMEs) are crucial partners in the expansion and diversification of DA programme employers. While their involvement remains limited due to structural and financial challenges, targeted policy interventions, institutional flexibility, and enhanced brokerage mechanisms can substantially increase their participation. Empowering SMEs to co-create and deliver apprenticeships will not only broaden the skills landscape but also foster more inclusive and locally rooted workforce development.

It is therefore important to first understand that this critical, yet sensitive partnership between the employers and the training providers rests on three core pillars of activity:

DOI: 10.4324/9781003567844-7

1. **Collaboration within the design and development of apprenticeship standards**: This process typically brings together trailblazer groups (see Chapter 14) composed of industry representatives alongside training providers and regulators (Institute for Apprenticeships and Technical Education, 2023b). This collaborative approach helps to align curricula with current occupational requirements, ensuring the training is relevant and current while retaining its strong theoretical foundation. According to UCAS (2023), degree apprenticeships that are co-designed with employers show higher completion rates and greater learner satisfaction, reflecting their ability to produce workplace-ready graduates.

   Such collaborative industry partnerships do not end once delivery commences; instead, they remain a key feature of ongoing quality assurance and improvement. Industry stakeholders contribute to performance reviews, workplace assessments, and mechanisms for continuous reflection, ensuring the training evolves alongside industry needs and maintains high standards of delivery.
2. **Sustained Employer engagement**: The Employer has a significant part to play in fostering a healthy relationship between three key stakeholders: the apprentice, the training provider, and the Employer organisation itself. A healthy relationship in a degree apprenticeship programme is collaborative, transparent, supportive, and growth-focused. It should reflect mutual respect and aligned goals among the apprentice, employer, and academic institution.

   In this relationship, the employers are responsible for providing workplace mentoring, allocating time for apprentices to pursue their academic studies, and offering access to live projects and workplace scenarios. The research by the Higher Education Policy Institute highlights that greater employer involvement correlates with higher retention and progression rates for apprentices (Patel, 2025).

   Nevertheless, SMEs sometimes face barriers related to resources or administrative capacity, which can make their participation more challenging. In the Apprenticeships Evaluation Employer Survey of 2023 conducted by the UK Government's Department for Education (DfE), it was reported that SMEs often lack dedicated Human Resources (HR) or apprenticeship coordinators, making it harder to navigate the complexities of degree apprenticeships (Department for Education, 2024). Similarly, research from the Chartered Institute of Personnel and

Development (CIPD) has shown that upfront costs, including mentoring time, equipment, and release for study, are harder for SMEs to absorb (CIPD, 2019).

A 2019 House of Commons Education Committee report also found that SMEs were often confused by the rules, paperwork, and funding processes associated with degree apprenticeships (House of Commons, 2019). This underscores the necessity for policy mechanisms and support structures that enable all employers, regardless of their size, to contribute effectively.

3. **Strategic partnerships and long-term benefits**: Sustained, strategic collaborations enable degree apprenticeships to become a permanent fixture within education and training. This strengthens the institution's ability to respond to regional skills gaps, foster innovation, and contribute to policy goals related to workforce development (Wade, 2023). Furthermore, these partnerships raise the profile of both the participating training providers and the employers, thereby strengthening their reputation and securing ongoing investment in developing future talent.

The COVID-19 pandemic caused complex challenges across the apprenticeship landscape, particularly for the SMEs. Several apprentices, particularly those working in the sectors and industries most adversely affected by the pandemic, were made redundant or furloughed or experienced breaks in learning (Doherty & Cullinane, 2020). This turbulence significantly impaired the ability of SMEs (already resource-constrained) to deliver on-the-job training, mentorship, and structured support. According to Mesma (2025), post-pandemic, the businesses were financially and psychologically strained – reducing their capacity for structured apprenticeship support.

This case study is aimed at exploring and highlighting the HEI perspective on how SMEs can be encouraged to collaborate and engage more effectively in degree apprenticeship programmes, particularly the CMDA. Through a series of discussions with internal training providers within the University of Derby, this chapter identifies the key challenges and barriers that SMEs face. The recognition and understanding of such issues can enable training providers, policymakers, and other key stakeholders within degree apprenticeships to develop more effective strategies, guidance, and support mechanisms that foster greater SME engagement, ease their participation, and ultimately contribute to the delivery of high-calibre training and education for apprentices.

Contextual details

Established in 2015 by the Leadership and Management Employer Trailblazer Group in collaboration with the Institute for Apprenticeships and Technical Education (IfATE), the Level 6 Chartered Manager Degree Apprenticeship (CMDA) was designed to address critical skills gaps within the workforce (IfATE, 2023a). Among the key employers involved in the initial development of CMDA are BAE Systems, Nestlé UK, HMRC, Lloyds Banking Group, BT Group, Santander and the BBC. These employers collaborated with professional bodies such as the Chartered Management Institute (CMI) and also with higher education institutions to ensure the CMDA addressed real-world workforce needs, especially around leadership, strategic thinking, and operational management (CMI, 2023; IfATE, 2023a).

This innovative programme prepares professional managers to make a measurable contribution to their organisations' sustained success, whether by leading people, managing projects, overseeing operations, or delivering services. The CMDA is applicable across all sectors and is designed to accommodate organisations of varying sizes.

The CMDA offers a work-based route towards developing professionally competent, chartered managers. The programme comprises two main components:

- **Work-based learning**: Apprentices remain in employment while developing their skills through on-the-job training and ongoing professional support.
- **Academic component**: This involves delivery by a higher education institution – in this case, the University of Derby – and culminates in the award of a relevant undergraduate degree. All modules are carefully mapped to the Knowledge, Skills, and Behaviours (KSBs) for chartered managers, as defined by the Chartered Management Institute (CMI).

The CMDA is delivered through a blend of delivery methods such as face-to-face teaching sessions, online seminars, and other asynchronous activities designed to enable apprentices to balance their workplace responsibilities with their studies. Upon successful completion of their degree, apprentices gain a Chartered Management Institute (CMI) Level 5 Diploma in Management and Leadership (if course is supported by the CMI) alongside their degree award. Importantly, they also become eligible for Chartered Manager Status, a nationally recognised standard of excellence in leadership and management practice.

Expectations, challenges and constraints: SMEs as collaborators within degree apprenticeships

SMEs represent a significant portion of the UK economy and hold considerable potential as partners in the delivery of degree apprenticeship programmes. Despite their scale and relevance, SMEs remain underrepresented in degree apprenticeship participation, primarily due to structural, systemic, and financial constraints.

SMEs have the potential to offer distinct value in degree apprenticeships as they operate in niche markets, which offer apprentices the opportunity to learn unique skills and gain sector-specific knowledge, something which is not always available in larger firms. Similarly, SME engagement supports regional upskilling agendas and contributes to local economies by addressing skill shortages. More recently, it has been seen that the involvement of SMEs within apprenticeship programmes provides more accessible, community-based opportunities, particularly in rural or underserved areas (IfATE, 2023b).

The University of Derby has been actively partnering with SMEs alongside larger organisations to deliver a wide-ranging degree apprenticeship programme aimed at strengthening regional skills in key sectors. The SME portfolio within the CMDA programme has expanded to sectors like local startups in technology, digital marketing and software development, local construction companies, schools and childcare providers, and, more recently, local accountancy firms, consultancies, and insurance firms. In 2024, the university secured substantial funding to support the development and expansion of degree apprenticeships, addressing skills gaps in key shortage areas within Derbyshire and Nottinghamshire (University of Derby, 2024). In addition to new programmes, the funding is being utilised to increase the awareness and participation of SMEs in apprenticeships, specifically guiding them with regard to various processes around the apprenticeship levy, co-investment, and how to best utilise these funds.

Post-pandemic, the recovery for SMEs as collaborative partners within degree apprenticeships has not been very smooth. The next section highlights some of the issues and challenges that SMEs are facing as employers within DAs and what effort (if any) can be made by the training providers to support this relationship in a relatively complex economic environment.

Bridging the gap between theory and practice

The main attraction of degree apprenticeships for any employer, particularly SMEs, is the *flexibility* and *customisability* of these programmes. The ability to co-design module specifications, assessment schemes, and other academic activities is a key feature of these degree apprenticeships. It helps align curricula with workplace needs, ensuring that apprentices acquire both the theoretical knowledge and practical skills valued by their sector. SMEs also customise and shape the apprentice's day-to-day tasks to align directly with the company's real-world projects. This ensures apprentices gain hands-on experience that is highly relevant to the business, not just generic training. In this collaborative manner, the career progression of the apprentice can be built around the SME's needs. For example, the assessments for most of the modules require the apprentice to evaluate various contextual realities surrounding their respective organisations and then discuss the relevant issues and challenges.

However, the challenge is that not all SMEs are able to provide apprentices with the full range of desirable practical skills, particularly when they lack formal departments or specialised teams to oversee certain aspects of their operations. This limitation can create a gap between theory and practice, making it more challenging for apprentices to apply their academic learning in a real-world context and fully develop the competencies they need for their future roles.

For example, an apprentice placed with a small engineering firm in Derbyshire studies a module on 'Sales and Marketing' as part of their CMDA programme. However, due to the company's limited focus on online channels and absence of a marketing department, the apprentice has had little or no opportunity to apply concepts like search engine optimisation (SEO) or social media strategy in practice. This creates a mismatch between the university-taught curriculum and the hands-on experience available in the workplace. Consequently, upon completing their apprenticeship, these apprentices will be less proficient in some industry-specific practices, affecting both their confidence and readiness for employment.

Resource constraints

In usual circumstances, SMEs are able to offer a good level of support to the apprentices; however, depending on their size and structure, coupled with the current business landscape, some of them face a real challenge in releasing apprentices for study or structured training.

SMEs typically operate with lean teams. In the last three academic years (2021–2024), there have been several issues where SMEs have reported that losing an apprentice for one or two days per week feels like losing a key worker, as staff availability has become tighter, especially in hospitality, retail, care, and construction. The resource limitation may manifest in reduced workplace mentoring, limited training opportunities, a lack of sufficient oversight, and additional pressure from covering colleagues' annual leave. It then impacts the off-the-job hours (OTJ) that apprentices get, and subsequently undermines the apprentice's ability to progress and complete their programme of study. Consequently, retention and completion rates are directly affected, as apprentices may become disengaged, experience difficulty in developing required competencies, or discontinue their training altogether.

Such a situation also impacts SMEs' sustained engagement as employers within degree apprenticeships, one of the key pillars of employer partnership with degree apprenticeships. When resource limitations hinder an apprentice's progression or lead to dropout, SMEs may view the programme as inefficient or burdensome. The time, cost, and effort invested may not yield the expected return, particularly for smaller organisations with limited capacity to absorb training disruptions. Over time, this can erode confidence in the apprenticeship model, discouraging continued participation and reducing the likelihood of future investment in developing apprentices. Therefore, some SMEs share that investing time and resources in such structured training (despite long-term benefits) feels unaffordable and unrealistic in the short term.

One of the ways in which a training provider can try and resolve this issue is through block teaching. For example, the CMDA programme at the University of Derby is delivered in a block delivery format, i.e., three-day blocks of face-to-face teaching spread across a ten-week term, supported by online learning, webinars, and other hybrid academic activities. This has enabled the apprentice to stay embedded in the workplace while still meeting academic obligations.

Complications surrounding the Apprenticeship Levy

The Apprenticeship Levy was introduced in 2017 in the UK as a policy measure designed to enable employers to invest directly in training and developing their workforce (Department for Education, 2017). However, this funding mechanism has presented a range of complications and implementation challenges, particularly for SMEs.

One key challenge lies in navigating the complex regulations and administrative processes that govern levy payments, transfer mechanisms, and funding drawdowns. Large firms, with greater financial resources and human capital, are typically able to manage these processes more effectively, while many SMEs struggle to keep abreast of policy updates, funding criteria, and compliance requirements (Learning and Work Institute, 2023). SMEs often report difficulty navigating the administrative demands of apprenticeship schemes and express concerns over the time and resource commitment required, particularly in relation to meeting off-the-job training requirements and maintaining adequate supervision (CIPD, 2022). Evidence suggests that non-levy-paying SMEs are disproportionately underrepresented in degree apprenticeship uptake, in part due to a lack of awareness and support mechanisms to access co-investment funding (Department for Education, 2023). Moreover, research indicates that SMEs are more likely to experience disengagement with apprenticeship schemes when confronted with bureaucratic hurdles, which in turn impacts overall retention and completion rates (Ofsted, 2023).

This policy complexity usually results in the under-utilisation of levy funds by those who may most benefit from them, thereby inhibiting their ability to provide training and upskilling opportunities for their staff. Similarly, the non-levy-paying SMEs must access funds through the Apprenticeship Service, a system some find difficult to navigate. The employers are required to register, reserve funds, and track usage through digital systems that require time and confidence with government portals. Some SMEs reported abandoning apprenticeship plans altogether due to perceived complexity.

Furthermore, the rigidity of the funding framework within which the levy operates, for example, the policy points around eligible training providers, delivery models, and funding bands, can undermine its adaptability to the unique operational needs and financial pressures faced by many small businesses. Consequently, the Apprenticeship Levy, while well-intentioned, may inadvertently contribute to ongoing skills gaps and a less equitable distribution of training opportunities across firms of different sizes. However, despite this porosity, some non-levy-paying SMEs have used apprenticeship levy transfer effectively.

Recommendations

Despite the clear value of degree apprenticeships in addressing skills gaps and supporting workforce development, many SMEs continue to face significant barriers to participation, as discussed above. However, these barriers are not insurmountable. A proactive, partnership-led approach can make a substantial difference in enabling SMEs to access and benefit from apprenticeship opportunities.

1. **Provide targeted guidance on levy funding and co-investment**: a fundamental step in increasing SME engagement is demystifying the complexities of apprenticeship funding. Many SMEs are unaware of how the Apprenticeship Levy works or believe they are excluded from its benefits because they do not meet the payroll threshold required to pay into the levy themselves. Universities should take a proactive role in providing SMEs with tailored guidance on key aspects of the apprenticeship system, including the mechanics of levy funding, co-investment opportunities (such as the 95% government contribution), eligibility requirements, and navigating the Digital Apprenticeship Service (DAS) for registration and utilisation.
2. **Facilitate levy transfer through strategic matchmaking**: Recognising that many SMEs are unable to access levy funding directly, the University of Derby has implemented a practical model to support employers through levy transfer schemes. In the last academic year, the university facilitated access to apprenticeships for SMEs by assisting with levy gifting and co-investment processes, acting as a broker between SMEs and large levy-paying organisations, and using their industry networks to identify surplus levy funds and match them with eligible small businesses.

This approach is not only a compliance mechanism; it is also a strategic tool to widen participation. Training providers should formalise these networks and establish levy transfer partnerships as a core part of their employer engagement strategy.

3. **Promote digital literacy and system navigation**: For many SMEs, one of the most daunting aspects of apprenticeship participation is the requirement to engage with digital platforms such as the Digital Apprenticeship Service (DAS). While these systems are essential for managing apprenticeship funding and reporting, they can be inaccessible or confusing

for businesses with limited IT infrastructure or experience. To counter this challenge, providers should offer hands-on workshops and one-to-one digital onboarding, plain-language guidance documents and toolkits, and ongoing support staff who can act as 'navigators' for SMEs as they use the system.

This kind of digital mentoring enables SMEs to become confident and independent users of the systems on which apprenticeship success depends.

4. **Build SME awareness through events and outreach**: Raising awareness remains one of the most powerful tools to boost SME participation. Many small businesses are simply unaware of the opportunities available through degree apprenticeships, or wrongly assume that such programmes are only for large corporations. Training providers need to invest in regular outreach events, both virtual and in-person, targeted specifically at SMEs, networking sessions that bring together small businesses, training providers, and levy-paying organisations, and case study campaigns that showcase successful SME apprenticeships and the benefits they deliver. These activities not only inform but also inspire, showing SMEs what is possible when the right support is in place.

Such measures can ensure that support for SMEs is not ad hoc, but rather part of a sustained and scalable model of inclusive apprenticeship delivery.

Looking ahead – 2026 and beyond

The apprenticeship standards are being revised in the UK. The CMDA programme is being transformed into Leadership and Management Professional Apprenticeship (see Chapter 17). These new standards are more strategic, future-focused, and innovation-driven, i.e. stronger emphasis on digital transformation, ethical leadership, and sustainability. The revised curriculum will focus more on real-world business projects, allowing apprentices to apply learning directly to SME challenges (e.g. digitalisation, sustainability planning, or new product strategy). The Knowledge, Skills and Behaviours embedded within this new apprenticeship programme will help SMEs become more agile, responsible, and digitally competent – all of which are key to thriving in today's economy.

References

CIPD (2019). Addressing employer underinvestment in training. *Chartered Institute of Personnel and Development*. Available at: https://www.cipd.org/globalassets/media/comms/news/addressing-employer-underinvestment-in-training_tcm18-61265.pdf (Accessed: 17 June 2025).

CIPD (2022). Employer views on skills policy in the UK. *Chartered Institute of Personnel and Development*. Available at: https://www.cipd.org/globalassets/media/knowledge/knowledge-hub/reports/employer-skills-survey-1_tcm18-110268.pdf (Accessed: 21 June 2025).

CMI (2023). *Chartered Manager Degree Apprenticeship | Level 6*. Chartered Management Institute. Available at: https://www.managers.org.uk/education-and-learning/apprenticeships/level-6/ (Accessed: 21 June 2025).

Department for Education (2017) *New levy to double annual investment in home-grown skills*. London: Department for Education. Published 6 April 2017. Available at: https://www.gov.uk/government/news/new-levy-to-double-annual-investment-in-home-grown-skills

Department for Education (2023). Employer skills survey 2022. *GOV.UK*. Available at: https://www.gov.uk/government/collections/employer-skills-survey-2022 (Accessed: 1 July 2025).

Department of Education (2024). *Apprenticeship Evaluation 2023: Employer Survey*. Available at: https://assets.publishing.service.gov.uk/media/66e991a0c069f68b7681bc93/Apprenticeship_Evaluation_2023_Employer_Survey_Technical_Report.pdf (Accessed: 21 June 2025).

Doherty, K. and Cullinane, C. (2020). COVID-19 impacts: Apprenticeships. *The Sutton Trust*. Available at: https://www.suttontrust.com/our-research/covid-19-impacts-apprenticeships (Accessed: 13 May 2025).

House of Commons (2019). *The Apprenticeships Ladder of Opportunity: Quality Not Quantity Sixth Report of Session 2017–19 HC 344*. Available at: https://publications.parliament.uk/pa/cm201719/cmselect/cmeduc/344/344.pdf (Accessed: 11 June 2025).

IfATE. (2023a). Chartered manager (degree). *Institute for Apprenticeships and Technical Education*. Available at: https://skillsengland.education.gov.uk/apprenticeships/st0272-v1-1 (Accessed: 21 June 2025).

IfATE. (2023b). The big conversation: Research report. *Institute for Apprenticeships and Technical Education*. Available at: https://skillsengland.education.gov.uk/media/7304/ifate-big-conversation-report-final.pdf (Accessed: 21 April 2025).

Learning and Work Institute (2023). Impact Report 2020–21. *National Learning and Work Institute*. Available at: https://learningandwork.org.uk/wp-content/uploads/2023/01/Impact-Report-2020-21.pdf (Accessed: 14 July 2025).

Mesma (2025). SME engagement in apprenticeships isn't just a UK problem. *FE News*. Available at: https://www.fenews.co.uk/exclusive/sme-engagement-in-apprenticeships-isnt-just-a-uk-problem/ (Accessed: 13 May 2025).

Ofsted (2023). Thematic reviews of alternative provision in local areas. *GOV.UK*. Available at: https://www.gov.uk/government/publications/thematic-reviews-of-alternative-provision-in-local-areas/thematic-reviews-of-alternative-provision-in-local-areas (Accessed: 21 June 2025).

Patel, J. (2025). Degree Apprenticeships in England: What can we learn from the experiences of apprentices, employers, and education and training providers? *Higher Education Policy Institute*. Available at: https://www.hepi.ac.uk/2025/01/30/degree-apprenticeships-in-england-what-can-we-learn-from-the-experiences-of-apprentices-employers-and-education-and-training-providers/ (Accessed: 13 May 2025).

UCAS (2023). *Apprenticeships Boosted under Plans to Broaden UCAS*. Available at: https://www.ucas.com/corporate/news-and-key-documents/news/apprenticeships-boosted-under-plans-broaden-ucas (Accessed: 11 May 2025).

University of Derby (2024). £1.2m degree apprenticeship funding set to help close skills gaps in the East Midlands. Available at: https://www.derby.ac.uk/news/2024/12m-degree-apprenticeship-funding-set-to-help-close-skills-gaps-in-the-east-midlands (Accessed: 3 June, 2025).

Wade, G. (2023). 10 ways we can boost degree apprenticeships. *Universities UK*. Available at: https://www.universitiesuk.ac.uk/what-we-do/policy-and-research/publications/10-ways-we-can-boost-degree (Accessed: 21 April 2025).

7

The Employer

Supporting apprenticeships through Levy Transfers at a County Council

Dan Boon and Stephanie Reynolds

Introduction

Gloucestershire County Council (GCC) has long been a committed advocate for apprenticeships, championing their value long before the Apprenticeship Levy was introduced in 2017. Driven by a strong focus on workforce development and social mobility, GCC has strategically utilised its apprenticeship levy fund to invest in both existing staff and new recruits. At any given time, GCC can have between 300 and 400 staff undertaking apprenticeship programmes ranging from Level 2 up to Level 7. Apprenticeship training is viewed not only as a tool for attracting talent into the organisation, but also as a means of retaining and retraining their workforce. Central to GCC's strategy is the principle of "growing our own" which ensures staff have access to lifelong learning opportunities and enables the organisation to address evolving skills needs from within. By making apprenticeships a central component of workforce planning, GCC have fostered a culture of continuous professional development.

A key component of GCC's approach is its active use of the Apprenticeship Levy Transfer system. This mechanism allows GCC to support small and medium-sized businesses across Gloucestershire that may otherwise struggle with the financial commitment required for apprenticeship training. By transferring levy funds to local businesses, GCC helps expand access high-quality training and development opportunities, contributing to a stronger more resilient regional economy.

DOI: 10.4324/9781003567844-8

This chapter explores GCC's strategic use of the Levy Transfer system, its impact on local businesses and individuals, and the broader implications for workforce planning in the region. Through two case studies, best-practice examples, and strategic insights, it illustrates how public sector organisations can harness apprenticeships to drive meaningful and lasting change.

The Apprenticeship Levy transfer fund and Gloucestershire County Councils commitment

When the Apprenticeship Levy transfer facility was introduced, GCC saw it as an opportunity to support the wider Gloucestershire community. Initially, their focus was on funding entry level apprenticeships in Adult Social Care and Early Years, two sectors facing significant recruitment and retention challenges. However, since 2021 GCC has broadened its support to include higher and degree apprenticeships (Levels 4, 5, 6 & 7), enabling career progression in key areas such as social work, business management, and public health. This strategic expansion reflects GCC's commitment to building a resilient and skilled local workforce. By investing in advanced apprenticeship pathways, the Council not only addresses immediate sector needs but also empowers individuals to grow professionally within their chosen fields.

Implementing the Levy Transfers

GCC was one of the earliest adopters of the Apprenticeship Levy Transfer scheme in the county. Since its inception, GCC has actively promoted the initiative to local businesses, clearly communicating that they can access levy funding without any repayment obligations. This proactive approach has enabled a wide range of organisations to benefit from apprenticeship training that might otherwise financially be out of reach. To date, GCC has transferred over £1 million in levy funds to support sectors critical to the local economy, including health and social care, childcare, engineering and hospitality. This investment reflects GCC's broader commitment to strengthening Gloucestershire's workforce by expanding access to high-quality training and development opportunities across the region.

Engaging with employers and training providers

To maximise the impact of levy transfers, GCC has cultivated strong partnerships with training providers such as the University of Gloucestershire and Gloucestershire Engineering Training (GET). These providers are actively involved in discussions with local businesses, helping to raise awareness of available levy funding and encouraging its use to upskill their workforce and attract new talent. To simplify access, GCC has established a presence on the national Levy Pledge website where Gloucestershire-based businesses can learn more about the apprenticeship levy and apply for funding. The application process is designed to be straightforward, with clear eligibility criteria based on location, apprenticeship level, and sector priorities. In addition to digital engagement, GCC conducts targeted outreach through employer forums, webinars, and networking events. These efforts ensure that businesses understand how levy transfers work and how they can benefit from them, reinforcing GCC's commitment to inclusive workforce development across the region.

Criteria for Levy Transfers

GCC has established clear criteria for approving levy transfer applications to ensure the sustainability and strategic impact of its funding. Key considerations include:

- The Employer must be based in Gloucestershire.
- The apprenticeship must be from Level 2 to Level 7.
- The request should involve a reasonable number of apprenticeships to maintain the viability of the fund.

Whilst these criteria guide the approval process, GCC also encourages recipient businesses to engage in wider workforce development initiatives. These may include offering work experience to school and college students, participating in T-Level partnerships, or collaborating with GCC's employment and skills hub. This holistic approach promotes a wider commitment to workforce development across the region, extending the benefits of apprenticeships into the broader education and employment ecosystem.

The impact of Levy Transfers

The impact of the Levy Transfer scheme has been significant, delivering clear benefits to employers, apprentices, and the local economy. Many small businesses have gained access to apprenticeship opportunities that would have otherwise been financially out of reach, enabling them to strengthen their workforce capabilities For sectors such as hospitality, construction, and retail – sectors that often face challenges with staff retention and skills development – the scheme has been transformative. By removing financial barriers, GCC has empowered SMEs to offer structured career development pathways. This not only enhances employee loyalty and productivity but also contributes to long-term workforce resilience across the region.

In summer 2019, Gloucestershire Engineering Training (GET), a not-for-profit non-levy training provider, accessed Levy Transfer funds from GCC to support the development of an existing employee. This funding helped cover the costs of a Level 3 Maintenance and Operations Engineering Technician (MOET) apprenticeship, which the employee successfully completed before progressing to a Level 4 Higher National Certificate (HNC) in Engineering. GET described the apprentice as having become 'an incredibly valuable and dependable member' of their team, with his achievements recognised externally when he won the Enginuity Awards' Apprentice of the Year 2022. Reflecting on the impact of the scheme, GET noted that the funding allowed us to develop this young person into our own Maintenance lead and delivery instructor', exemplifying their commitment to 'growing our own'. They now regularly showcase this employee to their wider employer network as a testament to the transformative potential of apprenticeships and their mission of Growing Engineering Talent.

Dingley's Promise, a charity dedicated to supporting children from birth to five years with special educational needs and disabilities (SEND), has used GCC's apprenticeship levy pledge to strengthen its workforce and expand its services. The charity, which offers early years education, holiday playschemes, and family support, learned about the levy pledge through its apprenticeship provider, Shaping Lives. They described the support as 'vital', enabling both apprentices and senior staff to upskill – something they 'would not have been able to offer so widely without the levy pledge'. The application process was described as 'straightforward', with excellent guidance from Shaping Lives' Business Development Manager. The impact has been felt across their centres, where staff at all levels are encouraged to 'grow our own', a philosophy rooted in the charity's own leadership journey, many of whom began as apprentices themselves. Apprentices are mentored to develop not only early years skills but also expertise in supporting children with SEND, including writing support plans and participating in multi-agency meetings. The charity noted that even if apprentices move on, they leave 'qualified and knowledgeable on how to best support children with SEND'. Staff undertaking qualifications together have fostered a culture of reflection and peer support, and the ability to recruit apprentices from the outset has helped Dingley's Promise fill vacancies efficiently as they expand their services.

Developing key sectors

GCC has strategically directed Apprenticeship Levy Transfer funding to address persistent skills shortages in key sectors such as social care and early years education. These areas are particularly vulnerable due to a combination of factors: high staff turnover, demanding workloads, relatively low pay, and limited career progression opportunities, all of which make recruitment and retention challenging. Apprenticeships offer a sustainable solution by creating structured pathways into these professions, equipping individuals with the necessary skills while allowing them to earn and learn. By investing in these sectors, GCC not only helps to build a more stable and qualified workforce but also ensures that essential services – those that support the most vulnerable members of the community – remain robust, responsive, and well-staffed. This approach ultimately strengthens the social infrastructure of the region and contributes to long-term community well-being.

Enhancing social mobility

Gloucestershire County Council's investment of levy transfer funds has played a vital role in supporting individuals from disadvantaged backgrounds across the region, opening doors to education and career progression that might otherwise have remained closed. Many of the apprentices funded through this initiative are the first in their families to access higher education, underscoring the transformative potential of apprenticeships in promoting social mobility. These programmes not only provide practical skills and qualifications but also instil confidence and a sense of purpose in learners who may have faced barriers to traditional academic routes. One particularly powerful example involves a young apprentice from an underprivileged background who, through levy-funded support, was able to complete a degree apprenticeship in social work. Without this financial assistance, pursuing higher education would have been out of reach. Today, that individual is a fully qualified social worker, actively contributing to the well-being of the community – a testament to how targeted investment in apprenticeships can change lives and strengthen public services.

Overcoming challenges

1. Despite the successes of GCC's Levy Transfer initiative, several challenges have emerged – particularly around employer awareness and persistent misconceptions about apprenticeships. Many businesses remain unfamiliar with the scheme or are unsure of how apprenticeships can benefit their operations. To address this, GCC has launched targeted educational campaigns, leveraging platforms such as LinkedIn, employer forums, and partnerships with training providers to raise awareness and promote the advantages of levy transfers.
2. One common misunderstanding involves off-the-job training, which some employers perceive as disruptive or unrelated to workplace productivity. GCC has worked to clarify that this training often takes place within the workplace itself and is designed to directly enhance business performance by equipping apprentices with relevant, practical skills.
3. Another challenge has been the rigidity of traditional recruitment cycles. Unlike many organisations that operate on fixed intake periods, GCC has adopted a flexible recruitment strategy, allowing apprentices to join programmes throughout the year. This approach ensures greater accessibility for school leavers and individuals seeking career changes, and, helps employers respond more dynamically to staffing needs.
4. Ensuring that transferred levy funds are used effectively is also a priority. GCC maintains close relationships with recipient employers, tracking apprentice progress and offering ongoing support. Regular tripartite feedback loops – bringing together employers, training providers, and apprentices – help to monitor outcomes and maintain high success rates, reinforcing the value of the initiative across the region.

The future of levy transfers at Gloucestershire County Council

GCC continues to refine its approach to Apprenticeship Levy Transfers, with a strong focus on expanding outreach and simplifying the application process to ensure that more employers can access funding with ease. As changes to the national Apprenticeship Levy system are anticipated, GCC remains committed to adapting its strategy to ensure that available funds are used effectively to support workforce development across the county. A key priority moving forward is aligning levy transfer investments with long-term workforce planning. This means going beyond simply filling current vacancies to proactively developing talent pipelines for roles that are expected to be in high demand in the future – such as healthcare professionals, legal experts, and environmental specialists. By anticipating future skills needs and investing in training today, GCC aims to build a resilient, future-ready workforce that can meet the evolving demands of the region.

Conclusion

Gloucestershire County Council's strategic use of Apprenticeship Levy Transfers offers a compelling example of how local authorities can lead inclusive, future-focused workforce development. By embedding apprenticeships into its organisational culture and extending support to small and medium-sized enterprises across the region, GCC has demonstrated that targeted investment in skills can yield wide-reaching benefits from strengthening critical sectors like social care and early years education to enhancing social mobility and economic resilience.

The chapter has shown that success lies not only in the volume of funding distributed, but also in the thoughtful design and implementation of the scheme: clear eligibility criteria, strong partnerships with training providers, and proactive employer engagement have all contributed to its effectiveness. The integration of real-world examples from organisations such as Gloucestershire Engineering Training and Dingley's Promise illustrates the tangible impact of levy transfers on individual learners, organisational capacity, and community wellbeing.

As GCC looks ahead, its commitment to refining processes, expanding outreach, and aligning investments with long-term workforce planning positions it as a leader in apprenticeship innovation. In an evolving skills landscape, the council's approach serves as a model for how public sector organisations can harness apprenticeships not only to meet immediate labour market needs, but also to shape a more equitable and sustainable future.

8

The Employer
The role of the Employer in overcoming challenges in apprenticeship provision

Julia Russell

The role of the Employer

Whether looking to set up a new apprenticeship programme or expand an existing one, employers will need to complete a number of steps to achieve this.

First, they must secure buy-in and approval from the business. Then the appropriate apprenticeship standard will be identified that best meets the business needs and desired outcomes. A provider, be it a college, university, or apprentice training facility, will then need to be sourced and engaged. In-house stakeholders who will run and support the apprenticeship will be identified and given any necessary training. Once the network is in place, recruitment to populate the programme can begin.

The recruitment process varies between employers but can and does often include: the initial application, an assessment centre, and an interview. They are often done either at the employers' site or virtually, and the whole process can be rigorous and sometimes lengthy. Different tasks done as part of the assessment centre can include group exercises, skills assessments, and an interview, which gives candidates opportunities to show different strengths. Recruitment for school leavers into apprenticeship is often launched simultaneously with National Apprenticeship Week, maximising awareness and exposure, but also competition between employers for the best candidates.

DOI: 10.4324/9781003567844-9

After the selection and onboarding processes are complete, the new cohort can start their apprenticeship journey. They will develop their job skills and learning through exposure to business areas and existing employees, who will educate and train apprentices on how to perform specific tasks and roles. The Employer will provide training, a safe environment, and opportunities in the workplace that allows the apprentice to develop and then meet the Knowledges, Skills and Behaviours required of their apprenticeship standard.

Training and development activities in work will give the apprentice context for what they learn with their provider. In turn, what they learn with their provider can be immediately applied in the workplace. After all the on-programme learning is complete, and the apprentice successfully passes their End Point Assessment (EPA), they can move to the next stage of their career, which will hopefully be a new role with their employer.

What has been set out here is a broad, over-arching summary of how an apprenticeship works in a business. On the face of it, it seems clear-cut and achievable. However, we must remember that, in reality, things are never this straightforward. There are many components that make up an apprenticeship. Many influences and stakeholders, many regulations and considerations. When we start to look at apprenticeships in a real business setting, and at apprentices as individuals, we start to see that the clear-cut model cannot be applied to all. There are as many apprenticeships as there are apprentices undertaking them. There are many potential complications and variations that can arise at all stages of the apprenticeship lifecycle. This is where the challenge for employers begins.

The challenges faced

One of the biggest frustrations that employers will face are the myths and misunderstandings surrounding apprenticeships. We've all heard them: apprenticeships are for people who aren't academic; it's not as good as going to university; it's a lesser option; you don't get the same qualification as if you went to university; they are for trade jobs; they are for other peoples' children.

The decision on what route to take at the start of a career journey is often shaped by the opinions of teachers, parents, and friends. There is often a lack of knowledge amongst these influencers about the apprenticeship option because of these myths and misunderstandings. This can potentially have a negative influence on someone's opinion of an apprenticeship as being a valid career choice and the right path for them: it can even stop people from starting to consider an apprenticeship at all.

For those who do decide to forge ahead and investigate the apprenticeship route, the sheer volume of information online, or knowing where to look to find information in the first place, is itself a barrier. Making sense of what is available, what the qualifications mean, and which employers to apply to, can be overwhelming. How can anyone know they are making the right choices without accessing the right guidance and advice?

Further barriers could include the individual's own concerns and needs. For example, someone may want to achieve a higher-level qualification but might not be able to wait the time necessary to complete a degree apprenticeship before they can start earning a salary; they might need a job and a salary straight away. Research undertaken by The Sutton Trust and UCAS in 2023 found that 24% of student respondents to their research survey did not pursue an apprenticeship because they could not afford to do so (UCAS, 2023). Similarly, not everyone has the same support when it comes to writing a CV or preparing for employment, or even the encouragement to find a job in the first place. The same research found that 1 in 3 apprenticeship applicants from a lower socio-economic background received no support with their application (UCAS, 2023).

Transport could also be a factor if an individual is not able to travel to a workplace for an interview or for any subsequent job they secure because they don't have transport of their own or the means of finding any. Public transport in even semi-rural areas is an ongoing challenge for residents. We also can't assume that everyone has access to a smartphone or laptop, or the means of affording the electricity needed to charge such devices. Digital poverty can put accessing online applications and assessments out of reach, and is as much of a barrier as not being able to physically travel somewhere.

Or it might just be that they will always have that niggling concern that all their friends are going to university, and they are worried they will be left out. After all, going into a job, which is what an apprenticeship is after all, is obviously not the same as going to university for three or four years as an undergraduate.

Employers are missing out on good candidates before any applications have even been made, and potential talent that could thrive on an apprenticeship is not given the opportunity to try.

The potential challenges don't end there. Employers are having to be increasingly focused on the pastoral care requirements of the new starters who do successfully make it onto an apprenticeship programme. An increasing number of apprentices in England are from the 16 to 24 age group, usually referred to as Gen Z. This is a generation that comes with a set of expectations influenced in no small part by their experiences of the COVID-19 pandemic and the post-pandemic world, and how they were caught up in it while at key stages in their education. Employers will know that work experience may well be lacking in cohorts of this age group, and time has to be spent on basic work-readiness training such as being on time, the appropriate use of personal devices, turning cameras on in virtual meetings, and a lack of social skills required to navigate onsite work placements (Travers, 2024). They are also a generation experiencing a crisis in their mental health challenges, with ever-decreasing levels of services and support to help them manage it all (Connor, 2024; Fonagy, 2025).

In addition to these external challenges, a business could also face obstacles from within.

A line manager's role is a busy one, with a focus on delivering products and services, and meeting business goals and targets. Having enough time and resource to train and manage an apprentice may be at odds with these other objectives. Releasing apprentices from the day-to-day tasks to attend learning and development opportunities is likely to be a challenge for any manager, even if those opportunities are necessary for the apprentice to achieve the requirements of their apprenticeship, and especially if they are in addition to any attendance to the training provider the apprentice is already undertaking. What appears to be an absence of support is simply a decision to prioritise one obligation over another; the result, however, is often a lack of engagement from the business, and in turn from the apprentices themselves. When the needs of the business and the apprentices are in conflict, it becomes a challenge for providers and early careers teams to deliver development programmes.

Employers may also find there are a lack of necessary stakeholders in place to support apprentices. A successful programme will require line managers, mentors, buddies, and people to champion apprentices in a business. The uncertainty about apprenticeships seen in external sources can be found inside a business too. People who have managed apprentices, or who were even apprentices themselves at one time, often use their own experiences when setting expectations for current apprentices, even though the requirements of a modern apprenticeship are different from those of previous decades.

Getting people to consider apprenticeships, make applications, attend work, and then be successfully supported once in a role are factors an employer only has so much control over. However, things can be done to mitigate some of the obstacles faced.

Having noted some of the challenges an employer will experience, it is worth remembering two things. First, the challenges are not going away. To ignore them would be to do potential harm to any apprenticeship programme, and also to any apprentices in a business. Second, challenges can be overcome. Solutions can , and indeed must, be found, and the problem solving required is just one part of apprenticeship provision as an employer. Challenges should not be the reason employers choose not to run apprenticeship programmes. Instead, they should be the reason why employers do run such schemes. Turning the challenges into opportunities is essential to ensuring a quality programme is offered and apprentices are set up for success.

Employers can't control or change all the challenges. They must therefore consider what they can do, what they do have control and influence over, and what actions they can take.

Overcoming the challenges

In a business, apprenticeship programmes are built on two foundations: the employer's reason for having a programme, and the people who will contribute to running it. These two key elements are fundamental to achieving successful programmes and for setting apprentices up to succeed.

Apprenticeships must have a point; they have to achieve an end goal. If the business decision-makers can understand the purpose and see the value of having an apprenticeship programme, they will be more likely to support it; within this context, having buy-in from the CEO and senior leaders is a must. Aligning to a business' people strategy, which will cover recruitment, succession planning, and talent development and retention, is a good place to start when making a business case for an apprenticeship programme. A business depends on its people to function. Products or services sold may be what generates profit, but skilled people design, develop, make, and sell those products and deliver those services; without a workforce of individuals, there is no business. Investing in and developing current and new talent is a key part of any business strategy that can be met in part by an apprenticeship programme.

Apprenticeships will mean a workforce has up-to-date skills and knowledge, which are maintained as each new generation of apprentices comes into the business. This ensures that the employees futureproof the business with their ongoing topping up of knowledge, skills, and professional behaviours. Apprentices can implement what they are learning straight away into their roles; they don't have to wait several years before they can apply what they have learnt as would be the case if they were graduates. Employers get instant return on their investment.

Over time, employers may be able to evolve, diversify, and grow their programmes due to an increased appreciation and understanding in the business of apprenticeships and in response to business needs. Any business is made up of several sectors: For example, the main business could be engineering, but there are going to be other departments, such as software, marketing, and HR, that could take apprentices on standards such as Software Developer, Marketing Executive, and HR Support. Apprenticeships may not work for all areas of a business, but they will probably work for some; thinking about programmes beyond the main business area could yield great success in talent development and retention.

Expanding the different areas in which a business can offer apprenticeships can also include expanding the range of people who can be an apprentice. While external recruitment is a great way to bring new talent into a business, it is important to remember that existing employees can also undertake apprenticeships. Upskilling and developing existing staff, whether done in conjunction with external recruitment or not, is a brilliant way to reinforce the knowledge and skills of a workforce. It sends a message that development is valued, and no one is excluded from career progression.

For those employers who pay into the apprentice levy, the reason for having an apprenticeship programme must go beyond just wanting to spend the levy funds, although this is an important area of consideration. It makes sense to utilise this funding source to develop existing employees and attract new ones. An employer can invest their levy in their own apprenticeships or transfer some of it to other businesses so that they can offer apprenticeship opportunities too. These other businesses could be in the employer's supply chain or customer base, so investing in them becomes a win for all.

Apprenticeship provision can become part of an employer's identity and culture. It supports strategy, and meets business needs and Corporate Social Responsibility policies and commitments. Apprenticeships futureproof the business through its workforce and encourage a culture and mindset that favours development and inclusion. All this makes a business more competitive as a preferred choice of employer for new and existing employees.

The role stakeholders play

Once the reason for having an apprenticeship programme has been established, stakeholders can be found who will support the running of the programme and the apprentices undertaking it. The right stakeholders are fundamental to enabling successful outcomes.

There must be subject matter experts who understand the legislation, compliance, and funding of apprenticeships, and who can navigate the changing landscape of apprenticeships that come over time, often with each new government and budget. The subject matter experts will work with the business to identify the right standard required for a scheme and source the best provider who can deliver training. Using their knowledge and expertise, they will help managers interpret elements of an apprenticeship such as off-the-job training, and ensure the business is giving apprentices the right opportunities to complete their learning and successfully complete End Point Assessment (EPA). They may be involved with recruitment and onboarding, designing, and delivering development curriculums, and can also influence other matters such as salary frameworks.

Line managers will look after the day-to-day work and the on-the-job training of apprentices in their placements. It is important managers have a good understanding of the requirements of the apprenticeship, what evidence needs to be gathered and how they can support the apprentice in reaching their EPA. Managers provide the real work experience that apprentices need so they can embed their knowledge and skills and develop their professional behaviours. We often hear that apprenticeships are a great way to develop existing staff as they can start their managerial experience by having apprentices report to them. However, given the additional needs of apprentices that come just by them being on an apprenticeship programme, more experienced line managers should be found who can draw on their expertise of organising work and supporting team members where there may be stressful and challenging times.

The same goes for those employees who will work alongside the apprentices and show them how to do tasks and jobs. The existing workforce means there is a ready-made pool of expertise that can be tapped into, across all sectors of a business, to help train and support apprentices.

Of course, there is more to the provision of apprenticeships than funding rules, placements, and work tasks that an employer must be mindful of. The transition from full-time education into what could be the apprentice's first job, coupled with greater mental health challenges than ever seen in young people, has put well-being and pastoral care at the forefront of apprenticeship provision by employers. Stakeholders must understand generational behaviours and expectations. Many apprentices have little or no work experience and are not 'work-ready' when they join an employer on their first day in their new job. No one has told them what to do or how to do it, and employers are increasingly finding they must spend time with their new apprentices to help them through this transition period, which can be overwhelming and damaging to the confidence of the apprentice. As well as the managers and colleagues already mentioned, a support system of mentors and buddies is a good way to help an apprentice embed, and eventually thrive, on their programme. Having Mental Health First Aiders, employee assistance programmes, and the space and safety to speak out and ask for help and support as needed, will reassure apprentices and allow them to flourish.

Having the right people in the right roles who support and understand the requirements of apprenticeships is vitally important, and training and communication of relevant information to the stakeholders is paramount. All stakeholders will play their part in the apprenticeship provision in a business. All need to be role models and apprentice ambassadors who understand the purpose of the apprenticeship programme and who support and demonstrate a development mindset and culture.

The stakeholders will also genuinely care for the individual apprentices' success and well-being, advocating for them, giving their time and patience, celebrating their successes and supporting them when things don't go well. Seeing an apprentice grow in confidence while on their programme and then watching their subsequent career progression, especially when they become apprentice stakeholders themselves, becomes a source of great pride for those involved in running apprenticeship programmes.

Why overcoming the challenges matters

We have looked at some of the challenges employers face and possible solutions to them. But why does overcoming the challenges matter? It takes resilience and time and resource to make an apprenticeship programme work successfully. Why should an employer attempt to tackle the challenges?

There are two responses to those questions. The first is that an employers' business will benefit greatly from having an apprenticeship programme in place. Apprentices add value in a variety of ways that only serve to strengthen and protect the future success of a business (Truman, 2025) Second, as stakeholders in the education and development of our nation's young people, it's simply the right thing to do.

Employers can spread the word about apprenticeships, flying the flag for them, and move to end the myths and misunderstanding. They can educate and inform the people who influence and shape career decisions by building relationships with local schools, college and communities through outreach work. Employers can showcase their apprentices and their successes by getting accreditation for their programmes, promoting National Apprentice Week, and sharing good news stories on websites, social media platforms, and through internal communication formats. Engaging with other, like-minded organisations to ensure knowledge and best practices are kept up to date, while engaging in the early careers community, is a fantastic way to build successful, quality programmes.

Inclusion should also be a key driver and is something employers have the power to deliver. Offering apprenticeships demonstrates that an employer recognises and supports alternative routes into work beyond university. By offering more opportunities to more people, including existing employees, a business can look to strengthen its workforce through diversity and inclusion. Apprenticeships mean there can still be engagement with people for whom university is not an option. Employers means employment; this benefits local communities and can provide social mobility nationally too.

Gen Z will account for 20% of the UK workforce in 2025 (Sommerville, 2024) and employers must provide the opportunities and support needed to help them succeed in the workplace. Think outside the box in terms of development and training that goes beyond just a work placement and day-to-day tasks. Topics such as financial well-being, imposter syndrome, resilience, office etiquette and a whole range of subjects can be delivered as part of a development curriculum that runs alongside an apprenticeship. And this investment in development doesn't end once an apprenticeship is completed. Post-scheme development will ensure that people not only stay in the business but also become the next generation of invested apprentice stakeholders.

Employers who deliver apprenticeship provision will face challenges; there is always work to be done and improvements to be made. The journey isn't always easy but the delivery of a successful, quality programme is worth the effort, for the Employer, its workforce, and community.

Ultimately, employers are ambassadors who have a responsibility that goes beyond profits and strategy goals. They have a responsibility to current and future apprentices who are our future leaders, decision-makers, influencers, workforce, and citizens. Living up to that responsibility is the real role of the Employer.

References

Connor, Jeanine. 2024. 'The big issue: The truth about generation anxiety'. https://www.bacp.co.uk/bacp-journals/therapy-today/2024/articles-july-august/the-big-issue/

Fonagy, Pete. 2025. 'Understanding the crisis in young people's mental health'. https://www.health.org.uk/features-and-opinion/blogs/understanding-the-crisis-in-young-people-s-mental-health

Sommerville, Robert. 2024. 'Gen Z is joining the workforce: What UK employers need to know', *LinkedIn*. https://www.linkedin.com/pulse/gen-z-joining-workforce-what-uk-employers-need-know-sommerville-9kqee

The Sutton Trust & UCAS. 2023. 'Where next? What influences the choices of would-be apprentices?' *The Sutton Trust*. https://www.suttontrust.com/wp-content/uploads/2023/07/Where-next-What-influences-the-choices-of-would-be-apprentices.pdf

Travers, Mark. 2024. '5 reasons why Gen Z is struggling in the workplace - by a psychologist', *Forbes*. https://www.forbes.com/sites/traversmark/2024/12/26/5-reasons-why-gen-z-is-struggling-in-the-workplace-by-a-psychologist/

Truman, Matthew. 2025. '8 Benefits of apprenticeships for employers', *Whyychange*. https://www.whyychange.com/benefits-of-apprenticeships-for-employers/

9

The Educator

Leading Higher and Degree Apprenticeships through the lens of curriculum design

Stavroula Bibila and Paula McIver Nottingham

Introduction

Apprenticeships in England have a long history, evolving from nineteenth-century craft models into modern standards-based programmes. Historically focused on practical workplace training within specific occupations, apprenticeships saw significant decline during the late twentieth century (Linford, 2016; Mirza-Davis, 2015) due to economic shifts and the dissolution of statutory training bodies. In response, a series of policy interventions from the 1990s onwards sought to revive apprenticeships (Clarke & Winch, 2013 ; Winch et al., 2024).

A major turning point came with the Richard Review (2012), which led to the development of Higher and Degree Apprenticeships in 2015. These new standards-based programmes were shaped by employer-led trailblazer groups and structured around Knowledge, Skills and Behaviours (KSBs). While this shift clarified occupational expectations, the limited involvement of educators in standard design raised concerns about curriculum coherence and educational quality (Richmond & Regan, 2022).

In this chapter we view apprenticeships as a form of education, based in the workplace, during which apprentices develop skills and abilities 'by testing and applying theoretical knowledge and methods directly to the practical world of work' (Richard, 2012, p. 31). In this process, the role of the Educator is twofold: (1) Providing apprentices from all socio-economic backgrounds and of all ages with access to theoretical and specialised

DOI: 10.4324/9781003567844-10

knowledge frameworks, aligning in this way with the social realist goal for social justice. (2) Designing and offering a curriculum that systematically combines different types of knowledge (e.g. theoretical, experiential, local, official) with higher level skills and transversal abilities, enabling apprentices to advance in their careers.

Social realism, social justice, and social mobility

There are several curriculum approaches for educators to consider when positioning their practices. Social realism is a broad school of thought in curriculum theory heavily influenced by the sociology of Basil Bernstein (1999, 2000, 2003). It emerged from Moore and Muller's (1999) critique of the anti-epistemological stance underpinning the New Sociology of Education (NSOE), as well as Young's (2008) belief in the reality and causal powers of knowledge as a social fact. Young's concept of 'knowledge of the powerful' was later combined with Wheelahan's (2007) notion of 'powerful knowledge'. Wheelahan critiqued competency-based vocational education and training programmes that denied students from disadvantaged socio-economic backgrounds access to theoretical knowledge and the structuring principles of academic disciplines. In the context of Higher and Degree Apprenticeships, these students are more likely to be older apprentices with no previous qualifications, those with English language needs, or working-class young people often lacking both 'technical' and cultural capital to successfully navigate routes to upward mobility (Wattam, 2024).

The pairing of Young's and Wheelahan's concepts highlighted an important distinction between two views of the curriculum: one as a system of social and power relations with a specific history, and the other as a complex body of specialist knowledge. According to Young (2014), the latter encourages students to provide powerful scientific explanations and alternative interpretations or to 'imagine moral and aesthetic alternatives' (Young & Muller, 2013, p. 245) by exploring the gap between independent meanings and their material bases. This gap is what Bernstein (2000, pp. 29–30) sees as the site of alternative possibilities - the site of the unthinkable and the not-yet-thought.

Young's views were influential in shaping Ofsted's (2019a, 2019b) approach, shifting their focus onto the curriculum and 'what' learners are learning on their programme, including higher and degree apprenticeships.

However, the role of disciplinary subjects in the curriculum has been a point of division between the 'philosophical' and 'sociological' camps of social realism. In the former camp, Muller explains that Morrow's (2009) notion of epistemological access in Higher Education suggests that students should be inducted 'into a facility with the warrants of logical argument' (Muller, 2014, p. 263) which is not constrained by specific disciplinary frameworks or curriculum subjects. To reconcile these differing views, both camps of social realists drew from analytical philosophy (Winch, 2010a, 2010b, 2013), though this shift carries the risk of moving the focus away from knowledge or the curriculum as social facts and towards the individual as an active agent capable of influencing the world's structure.

Table 9.1 presents a social realist view on knowledge and knowledgeable action by offering a summary of the contrasting approaches to curriculum development, education and key philosophical influences.

New educators may not be fully aware of the theoretical debates surrounding knowledge differentiation and organisation in the curriculum and the workplace. They may not have yet considered the relationship between

Table 9.1 Approaches to knowledge and knowledgeable action

Approach 1	Approach 2	Approach 3
Rationalist	Practice-based	Relational
Dualism	Personalism	Expertise
Disembodied	Embodied	Distinct but connected
'Know-that' severed from 'know-how' 'Know-that' as a cognitive operation	'Know-that' reduced to 'know-how' 'Know that' is a kind of 'know how'	'Know-that' and 'know-how' analytically distinct and related
Fact-based curriculum Hirst's Foundationalism Elitist – liberal education	Outcomes-based curriculum Technical-instrumentalism Pseudo-progressive education	Powerful knowledge-based curriculum Education for explanatory power, discovery and dealing with structural complexity
Descartes	Wittgenstein, Polanyi, McIntyre	Ryle
Stanley, Williamson, Chomsky	Dreyfus	McDowell, Brandom, Winch

Source: Adapted from Young & Muller, 2010

'formal' and 'epistemic' (Wheelahan, 2012; Muller, 2014) access; the former almost synonymous with apprentices obtaining certification and providers reporting apprenticeship completions, and the latter linked to 'powerful' or 'valuable' knowledge (Hordern, 2014, 2017) reaching privileged and disadvantaged apprentices equitably. All educators, however, are likely to have noticed divisions between learning that takes place on- and off-the-job, as well as differences in learning opportunities offered within and across different workplaces. No matter how well-managed and co-ordinated these divisions and differences are, they can act as a source of inequality of opportunity and outcome, particularly for occupations that require expert instruction and higher skills (Brockmann, Clarke, & Winch, 2010).

When discussing the pursuit of social justice and social mobility through higher and degree apprenticeships we cannot avoid acknowledging wider sociological realities. For example, structural economic inequalities and a stratified secondary education system (Ball, 2021; Reay, 2017) or the divisions between 'powerful' and 'less powerful' demographic characteristics and progression routes into the 'better' apprenticeships who offer graduates higher earnings in higher-paid industries (Fuller et al., 2017; Battiston et al., 2020; Cullinane & Doherty, 2020; Cavaglia, McNally, & Ventura, 2022). Social justice and social mobility have multiple complex and interrelated facets, including a curricular one. In the case studies that follow we share examples of educators adopting a curriculum-driven, knowledge-centred, and work-integrated approach to planning and facilitating apprentices' 'powerful' knowledge, occupational skill and transversal ability development.

Practical insights from the role of university-based educators

Apprenticeship policy has influenced how educators think about and deliver successful apprenticeship models. We could dismiss the 2022 EDSK report (Richmond & Regan, 2022) for its misleading claims about degree apprenticeships and its failure to recognise the role of universities in meeting the demand for higher-level skills training (Pullen, 2024). We do, nonetheless, acknowledge the report's calls for mandatory academic or research input in occupational route panels (or what these may be replaced with in the current wave of reforms) and for managing the risk of employer groups designing unsuitable apprenticeship standards. This is an important issue for policymakers to consider as educators can protect and enhance the quality of higher and degree apprenticeships and can create curricular progression opportunities within and across occupational pathways. We demonstrate these points in the three case studies of this chapter.

CASE 1: Turning a 'generic' job role into meaningful training programmes

This first case study exemplifies how educators transform the broadly defined Senior Leader Apprenticeship (SLA) standard—criticised by Richmond and Regan (2022) as lacking a genuine occupational focus—into a meaningful training programme for highly skilled strategists. In fact, and contrary to the EDSK report's claims, the reverse is also possible; well-designed apprenticeship standards for widely recognised occupational profiles can be reduced to vague and generic programmes by inexperienced educators!

In Bernstein's (2000) 'pedagogic device', all types of knowledge (e.g. theoretical, practical, expressive, official or local) undergo two transformations from their original production fields (e.g. universities, research labs, art studios): One in becoming official re-contextualised knowledge (e.g. apprenticeship standards, curricula and training schemes), and one in becoming re-produced knowledge, that is, formally taught and assessed knowledge through interactions apprentices have with lecturers, mentors, line managers and end point assessors.

In Chapter 13 of this book give an insightful account of the making of professional knowledge using coaching principles. These established processes for reproducing knowledge can help senior leader apprentices create and navigate an individualised learning programme not only focusing on applying theory to their current professional activity but also accounting for their career plans and aspirations. Horizon scanning in this context can involve apprentices proactively identifying emerging trends in their industries and opportunities in the labour market that match their skills. The overall curriculum at the University of Exeter (2023) draws on disciplinary and professional expertise from across and beyond the Department of Management. Teaching and learning on this programme operate both in the intellectual field of strategic leadership and in the field of senior management practice. In helping apprentices to recognise contexts to which taught theories can apply and discerning between those to which they may not, it is common practice for educators in most universities to involve distinguished guest speakers. These sessions expose apprentices to concrete strategic plans and tactical responses from various, often unfamiliar to most, contexts, including international diplomacy, tech startups, and even military strategies and warfare!

Richmond and Regan's (2022) genericism refer to a curriculum that is disconnected from any social context. Professional practices are no longer linked to a theoretical or disciplinary basis and apprentices' identities as senior leaders are constructed solely in and through the markets. Wheelahan (2015, p. 3) warns of the consequences of such an approach which has not been accepted by educators:

> The new principle governing the way knowledge is classified is oriented outwards, but to markets and not to a field of practice, and this severs the link between the regions and disciplines and changes the relationship between knower and knowledge. The knowledge and capacities 'that matter' are oriented to the market, and to the market's demands and accountabilities because markets endure while knowledge and occupations change.

Minton and Lowe (2019) explain how university-based educators approach the 'mapping' of the KSBs to the overall degree apprenticeship curriculum; The knowledge component of the apprenticeship standard is directly tied to theoretical learning, while skills and behaviours reflect the practical aspect of that learning within a specific professional or organisational context. Expanding this practice, the SLA Arts & Culture programme leader adapted the curriculum (University of Wolverhampton, 2022) for apprentices in the creative and cultural industries. A senior leader in the industry herself, she has developed an extended national network of key strategic 'learning' partners, including organisations such as the Birmingham Museums, the Midland Arts Centre, Punch Records, Compton Verney, Morris Hargreaves McIntyre and We Are Frilly. Their input is systematically embedded in sector-specific modules (Goodwin, 2021a, 2021b), mentoring sessions and workshops providing apprentices with the opportunity to cross-fertilise knowledge with leaders beyond their workplace. Knowledge and skill development in this case is not constrained by university requirements or employer processes, but it is led by sector requirements and informed by cultural leaders, apprentices and employers. Apprentices become critically aware of how the process of developing professional expertise simultaneously works within and against sector rules, values, norms, and definitions before gaining legitimacy (Addis & Winch, 2017). Parallels can be drawn by educators and apprentices between the processes of developing expertise and gaining acknowledgement as a senior leader in the cultural sector. These are critical curriculum re-contextualisation processes for a discipline less 'democratic' than sciences (Snow, 1961; Maton, 2007) and a sector in which cultural capital largely determines not only who leads it and who engages with its activities and places (Arts Council England, 2020), but also who can make valid judgements about its 'products' (O'Brien & Ianni, 2023). The success of this approach is evident in the programme acting as a gateway for those with less opportunity to gain leadership roles accessing the education and training enabling them to have the confidence to apply and progress onto more senior roles.

CASE 2: Combining experiential knowledge with 'social realist' principles

The role of educators in enhancing the quality of higher and degree apprenticeships is multifaceted. It involves negotiating the apprenticeship's occupational goals with employers and apprentices, and 'translating' and organising these into sequenced in-classroom theoretical instruction, academic mentoring and workplace learning.

The design and wording of the apprenticeship standard can facilitate or hinder this process, particularly when it comes to 'translating' what apprentices will be able to do (skills) and what they need to know (theoretical knowledge) in doing what they should as professionals. Take, for example, the conceptual ambiguity of different types of knowledge in the Chartered Manager Degree Apprenticeship standard (Ifate, 2023).

- 'Project Management Knowledge: Know how a project moves through planning, design […] evaluation. […]' instead of Knowledge of project lifecycles.
- "Understand risk management models". Operational Strategy Knowledge: "Know how to manage change in the organisation" instead of 'Knowledge of change management models' or 'Knowledge of change implementation processes'.

If not addressed by educators, such ambiguities can lead to the design of apprenticeship programmes, courses, or modules lacking specialised theoretical knowledge or strong links between KSBs and the competences they support.

In negotiating apprenticeship occupational goals, educators must consider both the apprentice's workplace role and the pacing of the academic programme. Within the BSc. (Hons) Professional Practice in Business-to-Business Sales Degree Apprenticeship (Middlesex University, 2025), educators fostered a collaborative approach between academic staff specialising in work-integrated experiential methodology and disciplinary sales content from an external partner. Nottingham and Mao (2023) acknowledge that organisational and practice-based theory (i.e. inductive model), grounded in experiential tradition (Dewey, 1938), use communities of practice to support stakeholder interactions in degree apprenticeships. This notion of learning by doing, and knowledge application by situated learning, can be empowering for apprentices with varied professional experience and an extensive empirical base on which to draw from. It could, however, have its limitations for learners who may lack a grasp of the context or technical concepts (Clarke & Winch, 2013, pp. 9–10). While it is tempting to design apprenticeship programmes, courses, or modules solely through skills and competences, by integrating key theoretical propositions and making explicit theoretical structures, educators can create impactful pedagogies that encompass 'powerful knowledge' and 'personalised' know-how.

Clarke and Winch (2013) are critical of apprenticeships that prioritise an atomised notion of skills as physical attributes to be developed through completing workplace-specific tasks. This narrow view of workplace know-how overlooks the social and historical context of occupations and may hinder apprentices' development of key attributes like problem solving and transferable abilities, limiting opportunities to create a curriculum for social mobility. Educators that support iterative rounds of planning (Bibila & Nottingham, 2020) and implementing work-based projects (Nottingham & Bibila, 2020), on the contrary, allow apprentices to practice a range of transversal abilities leading to a form of self-knowledge which has more general application in one's career (Winch & Addis, 2022, p. 7). In further combining experiential knowledge with 'social realist' principles, educators can integrate in the work-based project framework (University of Exeter, 2024) discipline-specific knowledge from the syllabus of a professional qualification (e.g. The Association of Project Management Project Fundamentals Qualification). By integrating guest sessions with expert technical input and active learning of project management techniques (Onuoha, 2025a, 2025b), educators can allow for differentiated instruction, ensuring the needs of novice and advanced apprentices are met on the same course.

CASE 3: Building relationships through work-based learning

Apprenticeship educators in fast-evolving industries must adapt curricula to integrate both interdisciplinary knowledge and competencies while meeting workforce development needs (Hordern, 2014). Hordern (2017) refers to this as 'valuable' occupational or professional knowledge, offering educators a useful lens to apply social realist perspectives to professional practice. This process often involves recontextualising specialised and cross-disciplinary knowledge to suit the demands of specific occupations that build relationships essential for integrated workplace learning.

An example of using an intuitive approach to present 'valuable' knowledge (Hordern, 2017) in the curriculum is found in the Level 6 Creative Digital Design Professional (Integrated Degree) apprenticeship developed by Riley (2021). After working with the Trailblazer group to support funding level validation, and having engaged with employer stakeholders, the Educator planned a curriculum that balances 'valuable' knowledge, applied skills, and personalised 'know-how'. This curriculum approach is facilitated by the design and wording of the apprenticeship standard (Ifate, 2025) which clearly differentiates between specialised and non-specialised knowledge and outlines apprentices' task to engage with both, including abstract conceptualisations and theoretical approaches in the discipline (e.g. 'being aware of all the principal design disciplines including the different perspectives, approaches or schools of thought and theories that underpin them').

The apprenticeship standard further highlights the need for creative digital design professionals to understand and navigate both aesthetic and disciplinary criteria that define what is 'valued' and what is 'new' in their field (e.g. 'they keep abreast of industry developments, creative trends and innovations, knowing what's emerging'). In guiding the Educator, the standard emphasises the importance of learning through pragmatic experimentation and professional inquiry as part of developing professional expertise (e.g. 'Select, refine, adapt and apply industry standard contemporary creative digital design technologies, and working with data to develop creative design solutions'). The latter aspect is crucial if apprentices are to develop complex skills and transferable transversal abilities that can apply across employers, job roles and sectors, or for those who have 'ambitions to carve a distinctive and high-quality niche in their area of expertise' (Winch & Addis, 2022).

Based on employer research and consultations, Riley (2021) emphasises the importance of niche areas or workplace-specific skills and attributes as the basic learning framework for apprentices, advocating for an educational approach that integrates academic considerations with employer stakeholder input. The creative digital design professional apprenticeship standard encourages the Educator and the Employer to foster apprentices' ability to exercise what Winch and Addis (2022) call 'workplace autonomy' (e.g. 'lead and manage end to end creative digital design projects in line with governance policies, meeting deadlines and managing client expectations for different environments'). This, together with the broader purpose of the occupation and the curricular intention for the apprentice to 'provide compelling digitally enabled design solutions to internal and/or external clients, across a range of sectors and for a range of different contexts', calls for specific pedagogic approaches in re-contextualising and re-producing knowledge. For example, workplace coaching, peer learning sets and specialist workshops led by industry experts (Middlesex University, 2024).

The approach followed is similar to Evans et al.'s (2010) 'workplace knowledges' focusing on inter-professional learning that can capture work-based interactions and promote effective learning. Their research highlights how both subject-based and work-based elements of the curriculum work together across various subjects and occupations. Evans et al. (2010, p. 250) emphasise that 'putting knowledge to work to meet educational, sectoral, organizational and learner needs depends on the quality of the relationships built between supply and demand, not on whether the programme is supply-led or demand-led'. Building these relationships through workplace learning requires educators to engage with stakeholders such as educational institutions, professional bodies, employers and employer organisations.

Concluding remarks and way forward

Educators who lead higher and degree apprenticeships navigate the intersection between in-classroom disciplinary and theoretical knowledge and vocational learning in the workplace, which focuses on applied knowledge. To do this effectively, their approach must emphasise the importance of equal access to both theoretical and specialised knowledge frameworks while also creating a work-informed space for broad occupational practices and professional standards. With on-the-job training largely structured around the activities of individual workplaces, it is important that educators create or support learning opportunities for apprentices to develop higher skills and transversal abilities of relevance to their industry. This facet of their role is linked to apprentices' career advancement and broader policy goals, such as social mobility. It involves a commitment to acknowledging and challenging educational inequalities arising from differences in the distribution of knowledge, resources, power and privilege in our society.

Education may not be able to compensate for society (Bernstein, 1970), but the path to social mobility through apprenticeships is unlikely to be achieved through the implementation of 'theoretical' educational and skills policies alone. Instead, it will also require educators identifying and sharing successful pedagogic practices and theorising how those successes were achieved. It is crucial, therefore, that educators fully recognise the significance of their role in leading higher and degree apprenticeships. Leadership in this chapter encompassed many levels of pedagogic activity, including planning, teaching, designing and enhancing individual modules, academic courses and whole programmes.

Through specific examples and case studies from practice we demonstrated how educators balance the curricular intention of providing 'powerful knowledge' with an understanding of re-contextualising principles and experiential workplace knowledge. Designing and teaching such an integrated curriculum allows learning to bridge knowledge acquisition boundaries, using different types of knowledge that create new insights through interaction with the curriculum (Mitchell & Nicholas, 2006). Current debates surrounding knowledge differentiation and organisation in the curriculum and the role of autonomy in the workplace provide valuable guidance for educators preparing and teaching a curriculum that integrates in-classroom theoretical and specialised knowledge frameworks, as well as approaches to learning in the workplace that support the development of professional expertise.

References

Addis, M., & Winch, C. (2017). Introduction. *Journal of Philosophy of Education*, 51(3), 557–573.

Arts Council England (2020). *Equality Analysis: Development of Arts Council England's 10-year Strategy, 2020–30*. [Research Report]. Accessed from: https://www.artscouncil.org.uk/sites/default/files/download-file/Equality%20Analysis_Arts%20Council%20England_Strategy%202020-2030.pdf

Ball, S. (2021). *The Education Debate*. (4th ed.). Policy Press.

Battiston A., Williams, R., Patrignani, P., & Conlon, G. (2020). *Apprenticeships and Social Mobility: Fulfilling Potential.* [Research report] Social Mobility Commission. Available from: https://assets.publishing.service.gov.uk/media/5ef1bb3dd3bf7f6c053a28a4/Apprenticeships_and_social_mobility_report.pdf

Bernstein, B. (1970). Education cannot compensate for society. In D. Rubinstein & C. Stoneman (Eds.), *Education for Democracy*. Penguin Education (pp. 104–116).

Bernstein, B. (1999). Vertical and horizontal discourse: An essay. *British Journal of Sociology of Education*, 20(2), 157–173.

Bernstein, B. (2000). *Pedagogy, Symbolic Control and Identity: Theory, Research,* critique (revised ed.). Rowman and Littlefield Publishers.

Bernstein, B. (2003). *Class, CODES and Control* (Vol. IV). The structuring of pedagogic discourse. Routledge.

Bibila, S., & Nottingham, P. (2020). Planning practitioner projects. In R. Helyer, T. Wall, A. Minton and A. Lund (Eds.), *The Work-Based Learning Student Handbook*. (3rd ed.) Palgrave Macmillan (pp. 183–203).

Brockmann, M., Clarke, L., & Winch, C. (2010). The Apprenticeship Framework in England: A new beginning or a continuing sham? *Journal of Education and Work,* 23(2), 111–127.

Cavaglia, C., McNally, S., & Ventura, G. (2022). *The Recent Evolution of Apprenticeships: Participation and Pathways*. [Research Discussion Paper] Centre for Vocational Education Research. Available from: cverdp039.pdf

Clarke, L., & Winch, C. (2013). Apprenticeship and applied theoretical knowledge. *Educational Philosophy and Theory*, 36(5), 509–521.

Cullinane, C., & Doherty, K. (2020). Making degree apprenticeships work for social mobility. [Research report] *The Sutton Trust*. Available from: https://www.suttontrust.com/our-research/levelling-up/

Dewey, J. (1938). *Experience and Education*. Macmillan.

Evans, K., Guile, D., Harris, J., & Allan, H. (2010). Putting knowledge to work: A new approach. *Nurse Education Today*, 30(3), 245–251.

Fuller, A., Unwin, L., Cavaglia, C., McNally, S. & Ventura, G. (2017). Apprenticeship quality and social mobility. [Research report] *The Sutton Trust*. Available from: https://www.suttontrust.com/our-research/better-apprenticeships-quality-access-social-mobility/

Goodwin, S.(2021a). *Leadership in the Arts and Cultural Sector*. Unpublished module specification. University of Wolverhampton.

Goodwin, S.(2021b). *Strategic Evaluation for Cultural Leadership*. Unpublished module specification. University of Wolverhampton.

Hordern, J. (2014). Workforce development, higher education and productive systems. *Journal of Education and Work*, 27(4), 409–431.

Hordern, J. (2017). Bernstein's sociology of knowledge and education(al) studies. In G. Whitty and J. Furlong (Eds.), *Knowledge and the Study of Education: An International Exploration*. Didcot: Symposium (pp. 191–210).

Institute for Apprenticeships and Technical Education (IfATE). (2023). *Chartered Manager Degree Apprenticeship Standard.* Available from: https://www.instituteforapprenticeships.org/apprenticeship-standards/st0272-v1-1

Institute for Apprenticeships and Technical Education (IfATE). (2025). *Creative Digital Design Professional (Integrated Degree) Apprenticeship Standard*. Available from: https://www.instituteforapprenticeships.org/apprenticeship-standards/st0625-v1-0

Linford, N. (2016). History of apprenticeships dating back to days of Elizabeth 1st. *FE Week* [Press Article]. Available from: https://feweek.co.uk/history-of-apprenticeships/

Maton K. (2007). Knowledge-knower structures in intellectual and educational fields. In F. Christie and J. Martin (Eds.), *Language, Knowledge and Pedagogy: Functional Linguistic and Sociological Perspectives*. Continuum (pp. 87– 108).

Middlesex University. (2024). *BA Digital Design Degree Apprenticeship Programme Specification Document*. [Unpublished course resource] Available from: Programme Specification BA Digital Design (degree apprenticeship) 2024–25

Middlesex University. (2025). *Level 6 BSc (Hons) in B2B Sales Degree Apprenticeship: Consalia Ltd Partnership*. Available from: https://www.mdx.ac.uk/business-partnerships/academic-partnerships/our-uk-and-channel-island-partners/consalia-limited/

Minton, A., & Lowe, J. (2019). How are universities supporting employers to facilitate effective 'on the job' learning for apprentices? *Higher Education, Skills and Work-Based Learning*, 9(2), 200–210.

Mirza-Davis, J. (2015). *A Short History of Apprenticeships in England: From Medieval Craft Guilds to the Twenty-First Century* [Insight paper] House of Commons Library. Available from: Short history of apprenticeships in England: from medieval craft guilds to the twenty-first century

Mitchell, R., & Nicholas, S. (2006). Knowledge creation through boundary-spanning. *Knowledge Management Research & Practice*, 4(4), 310–318.

Moore, R., & Muller, J. (1999). The discourse of 'voice' and the problem of knowledge and identity in the sociology of education. *British Journal of Sociology of Education*, 20(2), 189–206.

Morrow, W. (2009). *Bounds of Democracy: Epistemological Access in Higher Education*. HRSC Press.

Muller, J. (2014). Every picture tells a story: Epistemological access and knowledge. *Education as Change*, 18(2), 255–269.

Nottingham, P., & Bibila, S. (2020). Implementing practitioner research projects. In R. Helyer, T. Wall, A. Minton and A. Lund (Eds.), *The Work-Based Learning Student Handbook* (3rd ed.). Palgrave Macmillan (pp. 204–224).

Nottingham, P. M., & Mao, Y. (2023). Understanding the role of learning communities of practice within a degree apprenticeship to enhance inclusive engagement. *Higher Education, Skills and Work-Based Learning*, 13(5), 1009–1022.

O'Brien, D., & Ianni, L. (2023). New forms of distinction: How contemporary cultural elites understand 'good' taste. *The Sociological Review*, 71(1), 201–220.

Office for Standards in Education, Children's Services and Skills (Ofsted). (2019a). *The Education Inspection Framework*. Available from: https://www.gov.uk/government/consultations/education-inspection-framework-2019-inspecting-the-substance-of-education

Office for Standards in Education, Children's Services and Skills (Ofsted). (2019b). *Education Inspection Framework: Overview of Research*. Available from: https://www.gov.uk/government/publications/education-inspection-framework-overview-of-research

Onuoha, O.C. (2025a). *Earned Value Management (EVM), a Quantitative Tool to Monitor and Control the Progress of Project Activities*. Unpublished course materials. University of Exeter.

Onuoha, O.C. (2025b). *Applying Neuroscience in Leading Organisational Change*. Unpublished course materials. University of Exeter.

Pullen, C. (2024). *Apprenticeships – A System Built for Adults*. University Vocational Awards Council [Research report]. Available from: UVAC_25th-Anni_Report-2_For-screen_1251_180924_AW-1.pdf

Reay, D. (2017). *Miseducation: Inequality, Education, and the Working Classes*. Policy Press.

Richard, D. (2012). *The Richard Review of Apprenticeships*. London: Department for Business, Innovation and Skills (BIS). Available from: Richard Review of Apprenticeships – GOV.UK

Richmond, T., & Regan, E. (2022). *No Train, No Gain. An Investigation into the Quality of Apprenticeships in England*. [EDSK Report]. Available from: EDSK – NO TRAIN, NO GAIN.

Riley, T. (2021). The creative industries and degree apprenticeships: The benefits and challenges of adoption for small and micro businesses. *Higher Education, Skills and Work-Based Learning*, 11(1), 1–17.

Snow, P. (1961). *The Two Cultures and the Scientific Revolution. The Rede Lecture 1959*. Cambridge University Press. Accessed from: http://sciencepolicy.colorado.edu/students/envs_5110/snow_1959.pdf

University of Exeter. (2023). *Senior Leader Apprenticeship Programme Structure*. [Unpublished marketing resource] Available from: L7_Senior_Leader_Apprenticeship_Brochure_Sept_2023_(2).pdf

University of Exeter. (2024). *Project Management Framework, Unpublished Module guide and Materials*.

University of Wolverhampton. (2022). *Senior Leader Apprenticeship Programme Structure*. [Unpublished marketing resource] Available from: https://www.wlv.ac.uk/courses/apprenticeship-courses/senior-leader-degree-apprenticeship/ (Senior Leader Degree Apprenticeship - University of Wolverhampton)

Wattam, R. (2024). Cultural consumption/participation and prospective social mobility. [Unpublished PhD thesis]. The University of Manchester.

Wheelahan, L. (2007). How competency-based training locks the working class out of powerful knowledge: A modified Bernsteinian analysis. *British Journal of Sociology of Education*, 28(5), 637–651.

Wheelahan, L. (2012). Accessing knowledge in the university of the future: Lessons from Australia. In L. Wheelahan (Ed.), *The Future University*. Routledge (pp. 39–49).

Wheelahan, L. (2015). Not just skills: What a focus on knowledge means for vocational education. *Journal of Curriculum Studies*, 47(6), 750–762.

Winch, C. (2010a). Three different conceptions of know-how and their relevance to professional and vocational education. In B. Kotzee (Ed.), *Education and the Growth of Knowledge: Perspectives from Social and Virtue Epistemology*. Wiley Blackwell (pp. 145–163).

Winch, C. (2010b). *Dimensions of Expertise: A Conceptual Exploration of Vocational Knowledge*. Continuum.

Winch, C. (2013). Curriculum design and epistemic ascent. *Journal of Philosophy of Education*, 47(1), 128–146.

Winch, C., & Addis, M. (2022). Autonomy and expertise in the English workplace. *Journal of Vocational Education & Training*, 74(1),146–165.

Winch, C., Wolf, A., Gewirtz, S., Bayrakdar, S., Maguire, M., Laczik, A., Newton, O., Weavers, A., & Khazbak, R. (2024). Apprenticeship policy in England since 2010. Change and continuity. *Journal of Vocational Education & Training*, 77, 1–21. https://doi.org/10.1080/13636820.2024.2443914

Young, M. (2008). *Bringing Knowledge Back in: From Social Constructivism to Social Realism in the Sociology of Knowledge*. Routledge.

Young, M. (2014). Curriculum theory: What it is and why it is important. *Cadernos de Pesquisa*, 44(151), 190–202.

Young, M., & J. Muller. (2010). Three educational scenarios for the future: Lessons from the sociology of knowledge. *European Journal of Education*, 45(1), 11–27.

Young, M., & Muller, J. (2013). On the powers of powerful knowledge. *Review of Education*, 1(3), 229–250.

10

The Educator

Leading and delivering sustainable apprenticeship programmes in higher education

Sophie Cole, Susan Dawson, and Julie Derbyshire

Introduction

Through the lens of three experienced apprenticeship providers and programme leaders, this chapter reflects on the complexity of that role, demonstrating the pedagogical, strategic, and institutional challenges that apprenticeship educators must navigate.

Higher and Degree Apprenticeships (H&DAs) employ bespoke pedagogies (Shulman, 2005) to develop learners' theoretical knowledge, practical skills, and professional behaviours (Evans & Cloutier, 2023). However, literature on H&DAs remains limited, often focusing on learners and employers (Powell & Walsh, 2018) while overlooking the complexities faced by educators, who must balance academic and practical curriculum design, navigate high-stakes quality assurance, and cultivate employer relationships.

This chapter provides an exploration of the educator's role, examining their motivations, pedagogical strategies, and institutional challenges (Cahill & Bowyer, 2015). It highlights the administrative burdens of programme leadership, which often make it difficult to fully integrate academic practice. Many practitioners transitioning from industry to academia as 'pracademics' (Dickinson, Fowler & Griffiths, 2022) experience 'impostorism' (Parkman, 2016) and struggle to establish themselves within research-intensive institutions (Knights & Clarke, 2014). The lack of time for research further impedes

DOI: 10.4324/9781003567844-11

career progression, reinforcing calls for alternative promotion pathways that value practice-based contributions (Kitchener, 2023). However, as H&DAs continue to expand, more educators are engaging in the transformative process of co-delivering innovative programmes alongside exceptional apprentices and forward-thinking employer partners, offering a dynamic environment for professional growth and expertise development as an academic working in HE.

Section 1: Educator leadership in shaping Higher and Degree Apprenticeships

The implementation of H&DAs reflects a collective commitment among educators to expand learning opportunities that bridge academia and industry. Grounded in first-hand experiences as educators, leaders, and researchers, our engagement with H&DAs stems from witnessing the transformative potential of these programmes – for apprentices, their employers, and providers.

Through collaborative curriculum design and delivery, educators work closely with employer organisations to develop communities of practice that equip apprentices with relevant, future-focused capabilities (Wenger-Trayner & Wenger-Trayner, 2014). These partnerships support the development of applied knowledge, critical thinking, and industry-relevant behaviours, aligning higher education (HE) with professional trajectories.

Despite this potential, H&DAs introduce pedagogical and structural complexities that often sit uncomfortably within traditional HE frameworks. Regulatory demands, institutional systems, and varied employer capacities require ongoing negotiation, adaptability, and leadership from educators (Dawson & Osborne, 2020).

H&DAs necessitate the integration of academic theory with practical, work-based learning –a dynamic that challenges long-standing separations in HE pedagogy. Educators employ experiential learning techniques such as simulation, live projects, and collaborative problem solving to encourage apprentices to apply academic knowledge within their professional contexts (Forster et al., 2017).

While some academics embrace this integration, others remain tethered to more traditional models, potentially limiting the effectiveness of H&DA programmes. However, the mutual learning that occurs when teaching experienced apprentices enhances curriculum relevance and fosters pedagogical innovation (Chernikova et al., 2020).

These programmes demand the development of high-level academic and professional competencies. Apprentices are expected to synthesise knowledge and solve complex problems, demonstrating adaptability, leadership, and critical thinking at an accelerated pace compared to many traditional routes (Tilson, Sandretto & Pratt, 2017).

National and provider-level recognition of apprenticeship achievements further highlights the value and legitimacy of these programmes, with success stories contributing to sector-wide shifts in perception.

As universities adapt to shifting financial and social priorities, H&DAs offer a sustainable and inclusive route for widening participation and addressing workforce needs (Anderson, Bravenboer & Hemsworth, 2012). Their growing presence prompts higher education institutions (HEIs) to re-evaluate structures, policies, and approaches to employer engagement (Lester, 2020).

This evolution has led to the emergence of new institutional roles – such as apprenticeship coaches and compliance officers – that support apprentices in balancing academic and professional demands. These roles, and the systems they sustain, reinforce the need for institutional readiness to support this new model of higher education.

H&DAs also strengthen university–employer partnerships, ensuring curricula remain aligned with real-world practice. Economic outcomes for apprentices—such as increased earnings and career progression – further underscore the value of these programmes. As recognition of their impact grows, H&DAs are increasingly positioned as core components of the future HE landscape.

Section 2: Pedagogical practices and institutional strategies

The educators role extends beyond traditional teaching to encompass curriculum design, employer engagement, regulatory compliance, the continuous adaptation of provision to meet workforce needs, and quality assurance monitoring for multiple frameworks. This section explores the key strategies involved in delivering H&DAs, focusing on curriculum design, assessment, quality assurance, employer collaboration, and safeguarding.

A fundamental challenge in apprenticeship delivery is integrating academic theory with work-based learning to build apprentices' professional competencies. Traditional higher education models often separate theory from practice, yet apprenticeships demand a seamless interplay between the two (Powell & Walsh, 2018). A flexible curriculum structure enables the delivery of academic content in ways that are responsive to the realities of workplace practice (Lillis & Bravenboer, 2020; Horackova et al., 2024; Power-Mason et al., 2025).

Curriculum co-design with employers ensures programme relevance and promotes alignment with occupational requirements. Educators design the best mode of delivery of Knowledge, Skills, and Behaviours (KSBs) blending them to be meaningful to both academic and industry contexts (Quew-Jones, 2022; Chankseliani & James Relly, 2015). While Chapter 3 provides a valuable theoretical lens on the curriculum design process through social realism and knowledge recontextualisation, this chapter focuses on how educators operationalise these principles within institutional systems and live programme delivery. Tensions can arise around curriculum ownership and control (Powell & Walsh, 2018), and educators can find themselves balancing institutional standards with employer priorities, acting as negotiators who safeguard academic integrity while supporting contextual learning (Mulkeen et al., 2019) and preserving business and income generation.

Apprenticeship assessment must capture both academic achievement and occupational competence. Traditional academic assessment alone cannot fully reflect learning in the workplace. As a result, educators design mixed-method approaches that include reflective portfolios, competency evaluations, and professional discussions (Houldsworth, Kilmister & Brigue, 2024; Rowe, Perrin & Wall, 2016).

Authentic assessment strategies, such as problem-based learning, direct employer feedback, and work-based projects, do really help apprentices demonstrate how they apply theory to professional settings (Lester, 2020). The soft or employability skills that these experiences develop cannot be manufactured and apprentices appreciate these low-stakes environments to gain feedback on their burgeoning professional identities. These approaches also build confidence, independence, and critical thinking in the Educator, as they reflect on the effect on the apprentice and how it translates to the professional field.

The End-Point Assessment (EPA) is a step away from this integrated and continuous model of assessment and can often feel separate. As a formal, high-stakes component of the apprenticeship journey, its successful execution requires close collaboration between education providers, employers, and independent assessors to ensure alignment with occupational standards

(Houldsworth, Kilmister & Brigue, 2024) but also to make apprentices EPA-ready. It is in this arena, particularly in the non-integrated apprenticeship, that the Educator can feel very exposed, and their work highly judged, and often out of context.

Ensuring quality and consistency in H&DAs requires compliance with multiple regulatory frameworks, including apprenticeship standards, institutional accreditation, and employer expectations (Cahill & Bowyer, 2015; Power-Mason et al., 2025; Quew-Jones, 2023). The administrative demands on programme leaders are significant, requiring them to manage compliance while upholding academic and professional rigor (Mulkeen et al., 2019).

Programme leaders often serve as boundary-spanners, meaning that they act as intermediaries who operate across institutional, regulatory, and employer domains to align expectations and processes (Aitken & O'Carroll, 2020). Effective quality assurance mechanisms, such as employer reviews, apprentice progress monitoring, and external verification, are crucial but the Educator must show flexibility and adaptability with the multiple threads of QA to represent workplace learning variations (Quew-Jones, 2022).

Sustained collaboration with employers is essential to effective apprenticeship delivery. Educators facilitate partnerships that go beyond curriculum co-design to include co-delivery, mentoring, and joint assessment (Dickinson, Fowler & Griffiths, 2022; Fabian et al., 2022). Maintaining these relationships requires frequent communication, shared expectations, and clarity around roles and responsibilities.

One key challenge is reconciling differing priorities. Employers may focus on immediate workforce needs, while educators aim to embed critical thinking and reflective learning. Navigating these differences requires advocacy and diplomacy, with educators championing the long-term value of work-integrated education (Hugo et al., 2023; Powell & Walsh, 2018). The use of action learning approaches has proven effective in developing apprentice problem-solving capacity and promoting collaborative employer engagement (Quew-Jones, 2022).

Delivering H&DAs requires flexibility, collaboration, and innovation from educators. Effective curriculum design integrates theory with practice, balancing academic integrity and industry needs. Assessment strategies must measure both academic achievement and workplace competency, using authentic, competency-based, and reflective methods alongside formal EPAs.

Section 3: Transforming practice: the impact of H&DAs on educators and institutions

Establishing and managing H&DA programmes presents both opportunities and challenges. Over the past decade, these programmes have expanded, requiring institutions to navigate complex regulatory landscapes (Quew-Jones, 2023). Universities have rapidly developed administrative systems to balance academic integrity, employer expectations, and compliance requirements; this challenge is common across universities, requiring system-wide adaptations.

One of the sector's key challenges is the administrative burden that is placed on programme leaders, who must ensure apprentices meet all apprenticeship requirements, including off-the-job learning requirements, maintain progress records, and work towards EPA (Mulkeen et al., 2019). The introduction of an apprenticeship management system in our institution has streamlined these processes, providing a centralised platform for tracking the whole apprenticeship journey and this has been hugely successful.

While Chapter 3 explores the broader theoretical value of educator–stakeholder collaboration in workplace learning, this section focuses on the lived realities of supporting apprentices through institutional systems and employer relationships. At our institution, for instance, some apprentices initially struggle with digital tracking systems, but quickly adapt with guidance from apprenticeship coaches, who translate academic expectations into workplace applications (Lillis & Bravenboer, 2020). However, workplace mentor engagement remains inconsistent, impacting retention rates, highlighting the importance of strong tripartite collaboration between universities, employers, and apprentices (Evans & Cloutier, 2023).

Despite these challenges, H&DAs deliver tangible benefits. At our institution, healthcare apprenticeships have achieved over 90% satisfaction rates from the National Student Surveys (NSS), with high degree classifications and full employment post-graduation. This highlights apprenticeships as a viable alternative to traditional HE pathways. Furthermore, engagement with apprenticeship research (Derbyshire et al., 2024) and national recognition, such as a national award for Apprenticeship Provider of the Year (2024), demonstrates our institutional impact.

H&DAs have widened participation, offering alternative career pathways through apprenticeship routes to individuals who would otherwise not have considered HE (Horackova et al., 2024). The Office for Students (OfS, 2019) proposes that apprenticeships have the potential to increase social mobility and diversity in higher education, creating alternative entry to professions whilst maintaining similar prestige as more traditional routes. However, for apprentices it is just as important that this is translated into the workplace, which is reliant on close collaboration between educational institutions and employers (Universities UK, 2019; Welbourn et al., 2019). This requires ongoing effort from programme leaders and academic staff to sustain, working closely with employers to ensure they are exposed to authentic learning experiences and supported in the workplace (Quew-Jones, 2023). Many of our apprentices are career changers or professionals already within their chosen sectors, seeking formal qualifications to advance.

One compelling example is an apprentice who previously worked as a hospital cleaner, progressed to healthcare assistant, then nursing associate, and is soon to qualify as a registered nurse. With institutional and employer support, they advanced their theoretical knowledge, achieved all professional competencies and leadership skills and excelled in their role, culminating in a nomination for National Apprentice of the Year (2025). This aligns with research suggesting that apprentices can transform practice through effective leadership, problem solving, and adaptability skills faster than traditional university students often due to their previous roles in practice combined with life experience (Konstantinou & Miller, 2020).

Programme leaders have a pivotal role in supporting apprentices to succeed, whilst working within shifting regulatory frameworks and ensuring high-quality learning experiences (OfS, 2019). H&DAs demand balancing academic leadership, employer partnerships, and compliance oversight and programme leaders play a pivotal role in enabling apprentice success, working within evolving regulatory frameworks to maintain high-quality provision.

For educators, one of the challenges for some academics is their credibility with work-integrated learning pedagogies and contemporary workforce practice. However, through maintenance of professional registration, co-teaching with industry professionals, embedding experiential learning, and mentoring apprentices, they gain a deeper understanding of workforce needs, contributing to a shift toward valuing applied, practice-based teaching (Morley et al, 2021).

Institutions have introduced innovative practice educator roles to address challenges and provide formal recognition for academic staff supporting apprenticeship, offering formal career development recognition for apprenticeship academics. These 'pracademics' are emerging roles that can bridge academic and industry expertise and add value to work-based learning programmes; however, they remain undervalued in promotion structures, as universities prioritise research outputs over applied teaching (Evans & Cloutier, 2023). Further institutional integration of pracademic career pathways is needed to enhance industry collaboration and student outcomes (Dickinson, Fowler, & Griffiths, 2022). Formalising industry expertise within academia ensures HE remains responsive to workforce demands, strengthening the sustainability of apprenticeship programmes (Lu & Peng, 2024). Programme leaders play a critical role in ensuring quality and sustainability, requiring clear workload models and structured career progression. Recognising and valuing applied, work-integrated teaching within promotion frameworks can strengthen institutional commitment to apprenticeships (Lillis & Bravenboer, 2020).

Institutions are developing dedicated infrastructures to support apprenticeship provision, reflecting a strong and sustained commitment to H&DAs. However, this level of support is not yet universal across the sector. To fully integrate H&DAs, institutions must implement apprenticeship-friendly policies that effectively support providers, apprentices, and employers. Although apprenticeship provision has expanded in many universities, existing policy frameworks and workload models have not always kept pace. In some cases, administrative complexity and institutional bureaucracy risk stifling innovation and responsiveness (Welbourn, Devins & Reynolds, 2019). Unlike traditional degrees, apprenticeships require extensive regulatory oversight, adding significant pressure on all those involved in apprenticeship provision (Tulasi, 2013). All institutions must embed degree and higher apprenticeships into their workforce strategies, streamline their processes, and reduce unnecessary costs in the system and, in turn, this will all have a positive impact on apprenticeship provision for all stakeholders (Universities UK, 2019).

H&DAs offer transformative opportunities for learners, educators, and institutions, but their sustainability depends on institutional support and policy adaptation. H&DAs widen participation, offering career-changing opportunities for non-traditional learners while fostering critical workforce skills. However, educators face new pedagogical challenges and significant workload pressures, often without formal recognition. To ensure long-term sustainability, universities must develop career pathways for pracademics, strengthen workload models, and enhance employer–university partnerships. By embedding collaborative curriculum design and applied academic development, H&DAs can reshape HE and workforce development for the future.

Conclusion

As H&DAs continue to evolve within the UK higher education landscape, the role of the Educator remains both central and complex. These programmes demand more than subject expertise – they require academic staff to lead collaboratively across institutional and industry boundaries, co-design innovative curricula, manage extensive quality and regulatory oversight, and provide tailored pastoral and academic support.

This chapter has highlighted how educators are not only navigating these challenges but also shaping new models of practice that align higher education with workforce development and social inclusion goals. From curriculum design to assessment, and employer engagement to compliance, apprenticeship educators demonstrate agility, professionalism, and strategic leadership in a fast-changing environment.

However, this contribution is often under-recognised in institutional frameworks that continue to prioritise research over applied, practice-led teaching. Addressing this imbalance is critical to the long-term sustainability of apprenticeship provision. Recognising pracademic roles, clarifying progression pathways, and embedding supportive workload models are necessary steps towards valuing the distinct expertise educators bring to this space. Together with the theoretical perspectives explored in Chapter 3 , this chapter illustrates how those ideas manifest in real institutional practice, contributing to a comprehensive understanding of the educator's role.

Ultimately, the success of H&DAs depends not only on apprentices and employers, but also on the systems to enable educators to thrive. Fully integrating apprenticeship provision into university strategies will ensure that this dynamic and inclusive form of higher education continues to grow in reach, impact, and credibility.

References

Aitken, G., & O'Carroll, S. (2020). Academic identity and crossing boundaries: The role of the programme director in postgraduate taught programmes. *Higher Education Research & Development*. https://doi.org/10.1080/07294360.2020.1737658

Anderson, A., Bravenboer, D., & Hemsworth, D. (2012). The role of universities in higher apprenticeship development. *Higher Education, Skills and Work-Based Learning*, 2(3), 240–255. https://doi.org/10.1108/20423891211271773

Cahill, A., & Bowyer, B. (2015). An exploration of how programme leaders in higher education can be prepared and supported to discharge their roles and responsibilities effectively. *Educational Research*. https://doi.org/10.1080/00131881.2015.1056640

Chankseliani, M., & James Relly, S. (2015). From the provider-led to an employer-led system: Implications of apprenticeship reform on the private training market. *Journal of Vocational Education & Training*, 67(4), 515–528. https://doi.org/10.1080/13636820.2015.1076499

Chernikova, O., Heitzmann, N., Stadler, M., Holzberger, D., Seidel, T., & Fischer, F. (2020). Simulation-based learning in higher education: A meta-analysis. *Review of Educational Research*, 90(4), 499–541. https://doi.org/10.3102/0034654320933544

Dawson, S., & Osborne, A. (2020). Re-shaping built environment higher education: The impact of degree apprenticeships in England. *International Journal of Construction Education and Research*, 16(2), 102–116. https://doi.org/10.1080/15578771.2019.1668888

Derbyshire, J., Porteous, D., Corder, K., Foggo, B., & Steven, A. (2024). Investigating the processes and influences involved in the transformational journeys of registered nurse degree apprentices: A realist-informed qualitative study. *Nurse Education in Practice*, 74, 103834. https://doi.org/10.1016/j.nepr.2023.103834

Dickinson, J., Fowler, A., & Griffiths, T.-L. (2022). Pracademics? Exploring transitions and professional identities in higher education. *Studies in Higher Education*, 47(2), 290–304. https://doi.org/10.1080/03075079.2020.1744123

Evans, M., & Cloutier, M. (2023). Integrating higher degree education with practice: Exploring the value proposition of executive MBA apprenticeships. *Higher Education, Skills and Work-Based Learning*. https://doi.org/10.1108/HESWBL-10-2022-0207

Fabian, K., Taylor-Smith, E., Smith, S., Meharg, D., & Varey, A. (2022). An exploration of degree apprentice perspectives: A Q methodology study. *Studies in Higher Education*, 47(7), 1397–1409. https://doi.org/10.1080/03075079.2021.1897094

Forster, A. M., Pilcher, N., Tennant, S., Murray, M., Craig, N., & Copping, A. (2017). The fall and rise of experiential construction and engineering education: Decoupling and recoupling practice and theory. *Higher Education Pedagogies*, 2(1), 79–100. https://doi.org/10.1080/23752696.2017.1338530

Horackova, C., Bloomfield, S., Pereira, C. R., & Mutwarasibo, F. (2024). Delivering the chartered manager degree apprenticeship: What are the challenges and implications for good practice? *Higher Education, Skills and Work-Based Learning*, 14(3), 625–640. https://doi.org/10.1108/HESWBL-09-2023-0262

Houldsworth, E., Kilmister, M., & Brigue, R. (2024). Improving assessment for work-based learning and degree apprenticeships in business through a co-designed peer review process. *International Journal for Students as Partners*, 8(2), 199–209. https://doi.org/10.15173/ijsap.v8i2.5698

Hugo, R., Panagiota, C., Rita, P.-C., Daniela, D., Elena, M., Juho, M., & Dimitris, P. (2023). University-business collaboration for the design, development and delivery of critical thinking blended apprenticeships curricula: Lessons learned from a three-year project. *Education Sciences*. https://doi.org/10.3390/educsci13010001

Kitchener, M. (2023). 'Don't take your briefcase': Navigating a career change from professional practice to the academic role. In *Professional Development for Practitioners in Academia: Pracademia* (pp. 11–24). Springer.

Knights, D., & Clarke, C. A. (2014). It's a bittersweet symphony, this life: Fragile academic selves and insecure identities at work. *Organization Studies*, 35(3), 335–357. https://doi.org/10.1177/0170840613508396

Konstantinou, I., & Miller, E. (2020). Investigating work-integrated learning and its relevance to skills development in degree apprenticeships. *Higher Education, Skills and Work-Based Learning*, 10(5), 767–781. https://doi.org/10.1108/HESWBL-05-2020-0112

Lester, S. (2020). Creating conditions for sustainable degree apprenticeships in England. *Higher Education, Skills and Work-Based Learning*, 10(5), 701–714. https://doi.org/10.1108/HESWBL-04-2020-0062

Lillis, F., & Bravenboer, D. (2020). The best practice in work-integrated pedagogy for degree apprenticeships in a post-viral future. *Higher Education, Skills and Work-Based Learning*, 727–739. https://doi.org/10.1108/HESWBL-04-2020-0071

Lu, K., & Peng, S. (2024). Balancing early-career paths as pracademics: A collaborative autoethnography study in China. *Development in Practice*, 35(2), 1–11. https://doi.org/10.1080/09614524.2024.2416199

Morley, D. A., & Jamil, M. G. (Eds) (2021). *Applied pedagogies for higher education: Real world learning and innovation across the curriculum*. Palgrave Macmillan.

Mulkeen, J., Abdou, H. A., Leigh, J., & Ward, P. (2019). Degree and higher level apprenticeships: An empirical investigation of stakeholder perceptions of challenges and opportunities. *Studies in Higher Education*, 44(2), 333–346. https://doi.org/10.1080/03075079.2017.1365357

Office for Students. (2019). *Guide to Apprenticeships in Higher Education*. OfS.

Parkman, A. (2016). The imposter phenomenon in higher education: Incidence and impact. *Journal of Higher Education Theory and Practice*, 16(1), 51–60.

Powell, P., & Walsh, A. (2018). Whose curriculum is it anyway? Stakeholder salience in the context of degree apprenticeships. *Higher Education Quarterly*. https://doi.org/10.1111/hequ.12143

Power-Mason, P., Charlton, H., Walker-Martin, F., & Bloomfield, S. (2025). A sector in crisis? Insights from how English higher education apprenticeships are weathering the storm. *Higher Education, Skills and Work-Based Learning*. https://doi.org/10.1108/HESWBL-09-2024-0253

Quew-Jones, R. (2022). Enhancing apprenticeships within the higher education curriculum: An action learning and action research study. *Action Learning: Research and Practice*, 19(2), 146–164. https://doi.org/10.1080/14767333.2022.2056135

Quew-Jones, R. J. (2023). Degree apprenticeships in UK higher education institutions—are they viable? Integrative literature review. *Higher Education, Skills and Work-Based Learning*, 13(6), 1250–1268. https://doi.org/10.1108/HESWBL-02-2023-0026

Rowe, L., Perrin, D., & Wall, T. (2016). The chartered manager degree apprenticeship: Trials and tribulations. *Higher Education, Skills and Work-Based Learning*, 6(4), 357–369. https://doi.org/10.1108/HESWBL-05-2016-0034

Shulman, L. S. (2005). Signature pedagogies in the professions. *Daedalus*, 134(3), 52–59.

Tilson, J., Sandretto, S., & Pratt, K. (2017). Connecting theory to practice: Using preservice teachers' beliefs, theories and video-recorded teaching to prompt a cycle of praxis. *Teaching and Teacher Education*, 67, 454–463. https://doi.org/10.1016/j.tate.2017.06.003

Tulasi, B. (2013). Significance of big data and analytics in higher education. *International Journal of Computer Applications*, 68(14). https://doi.org/10.5120/11648-7142

Universities UK. (2019). *Degree Apprenticeships: Realising Opportunities*. London: UUK.

Welbourn, J., Devins, D., & Reynolds, M. (2019). Degree apprenticeships: Reflecting on university–employer partnership practice to improve workforce development in the United Kingdom. *Industry and Higher Education*, 33(6), 403–413. https://doi.org/10.1177/0950422219877594

Wenger-Trayner, E., & Wenger-Trayner, B. (2014). Learning in a landscape of practice: A framework. In *Learning in Landscapes of Practice* (pp. 13–30). Routledge.

11

Public and private providers

Experiences of Higher and Degree Apprenticeship provision: the good, the bad, and the ugly

Kieron Chadwick

Introduction

For nearly a decade, I have crafted a career in the higher- and degree-level apprenticeships (H&DA) space, initially working as a coach, and progressing through the layers of quality assurance, operations management, and head of department, before transitioning to my current role as a lecturer in academia, teaching H&DAs programmes. During this time, I have witnessed how the role of private independent training providers (ITPs) in delivering H&DAs has evolved, as the demand for flexible, industry-aligned education has grown, and employers seek innovative programmes. Similarly, I have seen higher education institutions (HEIs) emerge as key players in the apprenticeship landscape while navigating the intersection of academic rigour and employer-led skills development. In this chapter, I utilise Johnson et al.'s (2011) four lenses of strategy development to organise pertinent literature and my own anecdotal experiences, to highlight the approaches, contributions, challenges in delivery, regulatory compliance, and the impact on apprentices, employers, and the wider sector that HEIs and ITPs have respectively.

The four lenses model, first introduced by British academic Kevan Scholes, but later developed with other key contributors, is a model providing structure to the way in which organisations develop strategy. The four

DOI: 10.4324/9781003567844-12

lenses – experience, ideas, design, and discourse – allow for organisations to engage in strategic thinking (Mintzberg, 1994). I will use the lenses in a re-ordered manner to perform the act of reflection, allowing readership insight into the headspace of a HEI or ITP when considering the direction of H&DA provision. Firstly, I consider 'design', incorporating external (market) scanning and internal process analysis. Next, I explore 'discourse', investigating the human element – the people at the coalface of H&DA delivery and how HEIs and ITPs use organisational communication, culture, and power dynamics to influence their professional identity. As I move from literature to practice, I then draw on 'experience', allowing my lived experience and thoughts, paired with the aforementioned underpinning literature, to fuel creative solutions which I lay out in the final lens, 'ideas', covering the way in which HEIs and ITPs can use disruptive thinking to maximise their potential in H&DA management and delivery.

Design lens

Market conditions

Since their inception in 2015, H&DAs have grown significantly in popularity. There were just 19,800 H&DA starts in 2015, which represented 3.96% of apprenticeship starts at any level. By 2022, this had grown to 106,400, a vast 30.5% of any level (Powell, 2023; Cleaver, 2022). This coincided with a drop by a third in spending on Level 2 apprenticeships, while Level 7 spending grew from £11 million in 2017–2018, to a staggering £216 million in 2021–2022 (Camden, 2024). With demand comes supply, and H&DAs require the input of a wide range of provider types, predominantly HEIs and ITPs, but not discounting the other critical types, such as employer providers.

Analysis of the Apprenticeship Provider and Assessment Register, undertaken in February 2025 as part of the background research for this book chapter, explores the make-up of H&DA provision further, as shown in Figure 11.1. A total of 1505 providers are registered in England to deliver apprenticeships at any level (GOV.UK, 2025a). Of these, 120 are HEIs, as defined by the Higher Education Statistics Agency (HESA) (2024) as an institution with degree-awarding powers and university title granted by the Privy Council or relevant devolved administration, or other bodies offering recognised UK degrees. According to GOV.UK (2023), there were 288 HEIs

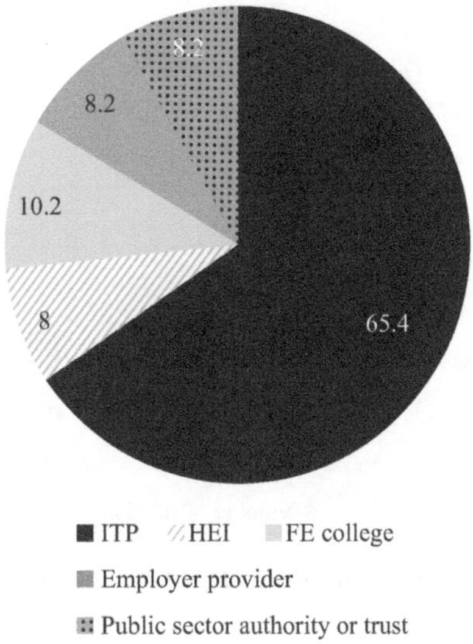

Figure 11.1 *Breakdown of H&DA providers by type*

operating generally in the UK as of the 2021–2022 academic year (the latest available data), and although the number fluctuates from one year to the next, with 295 noted in the previous year, less than half of HEIs (41.67%) are pursuing H&DAs, with the other half remaining firmly focused on their standard undergraduate and postgraduate portfolios. Of those that do offer H&DAs, Mackay (2022) points to 2019–2020 academic data which shows 64% are offering Level 6 H&DAs, while 66% offer Level 7 (many institutions offer both). A contributing factor to what HEIs offer in terms of apprenticeships is ultimately dictated by the range of apprenticeship standards (market instruments) available for selection. A breakdown of these by level is provided in Figure 11.2, and highlights that 294 of the 651 available apprenticeship standards are at Level 4 or above. Specifically, 105 are at Level 4, 38 at Level 5, 99 at Level 6, and 52 at Level 7 (GOV.UK, 2025b). For clarity, apprenticeship levels correlate with the skill level expected of an apprentice by the end of their programme. For example, many Level 6 H&DAs are three or four years in duration, with delivery commencing at Level 4 and moving through the levels as a typical undergraduate course would. This means some apprenticeships advertised at Level 4 or 5 culminate in the achievement of a Certificate or Diploma of Higher Education, abbreviated to 'CertHE' or 'DipHE', and topping up is not captured in apprenticeship funding, although may be a next step in an individual's progression.

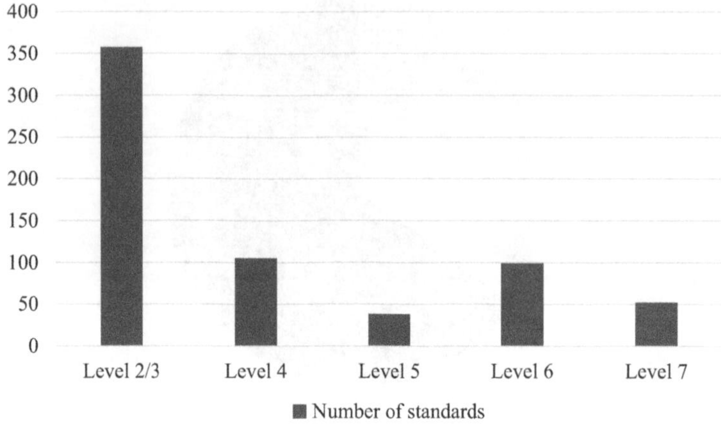

Figure 11.2 Available H&DA standards by level

A prominent H&DA standard, the Chartered Manager (Degree) Apprenticeship (CMDA), soon to be rebranded the Leadership and Management Professional (Integrated Degree) Apprenticeship (IfATE, 2025) is a useful case study to highlight the typical market conditions HEIs and ITPs are operating in. According to GOV.UK (2025c), there are 80 providers of this particular standard: 52 HEIs, 17 further education (FE) colleges, and 11 ITPs. Meanwhile, CMDA's 'sibling', the Level 7 Senior Leader Apprenticeship (SLA), features 157 providers, of which 71 are HEIs, 11 FE colleges, and 75 ITPs. This data demonstrates the significance of the role of ITPs in H&DA provision. It should, however, be acknowledged that while CMDA requires undergraduate degree completion as a mandated component, SLA does not require completion of a master's and may be delivered without an academic element, meaning it is more accessible for ITPs to deliver. The H&DA market is, however, in a period of transition. The government has set out plans for a new Skills Levy which may see some Level 7 apprenticeships axed, as part of a broadening of the current Levy arrangement aimed at giving employers greater flexibility, such as the provision of standalone qualifications, short courses, and even small modules; as opposed to only apprenticeships (Camden, 2024; Evans, 2024).

Quality

Recent literature highlights the complex nature of the governance of H&DAs, notably the impact of varied agencies responsible for oversight, including the Department for Education (DfE), the Institute for Apprenticeships and Technical Education (IfATE), the Office for Standards in Education, Children's Services and Skills (Ofsted), the Office of Qualifications and Examinations Regulation (OfQUAL), and the Office for Students (OfS) (Holland and Edifor, 2025). Although it may be assumed HEIs have more resource than ITPs to handle multi-governance of this manner effectively, Atherton et al. (2024) point out that the majority of HE providers in England are small and do not have the right to offer their own degrees. They are instead 'listed bodies' operating on behalf of a 'recognised body' with an extension of degree awarding power (DAP). It is therefore reasonable to argue that both HEIs and ITPs face resource constraints and find the degree of emphasis on quality overwhelming; with formal metrics paired with informal metrics, such as provider reviews, making compliance, consistency, and resource allocation a battle of conflicting priorities (Holland and Edifor, 2025). While HEIs and ITPs must remain adaptable to changes in governance requirements, the challenge lies in being pulled in various directions by different bodies. The OfS strategy 2022–2025 (OfS, 2022) acknowledges that they share 'regulatory interests' in apprenticeships with IfATE and Ofsted, expressing a willingness to collaborate and engage with them. However, there appears to be little follow-up in the literature regarding the effectiveness of collaboration between these governance bodies.

Literature argues the culture in the sector is one of Total Quality Management (TQM), with no slip ups allowed, no margin for error, and an emphasis on micro-management-style 'governance by numbers' instead of a focus on creativity and innovation (Hydén, 2016). Bringing HEIs into the arena at the time when H&DAs were introduced offered a chance for creativity and innovation regarding quality to occur. However, this has been a damp squib, with Lomas (2025) acknowledging HEIs' refusal or inability to adapt quality mechanisms to support the unique nature of H&DAs has ultimately led to HEIs H&DA quality strategies being typical academic processes with little focus beyond academic content. This is reflective of what Jackson (2010) refers to as 'institutionalised constraints'. Literature does, however, offer some positive steps forward; notably prompting further understanding on the part of HEIs and ITPs about how actors (staff on the frontline) help and hinder policy implementation (Considine, 2005), with a view to ensuring future quality direction is firmly embedded in organisational culture. Furthermore, Felce (2019) refers to working together to successfully manage the quality of apprenticeships in the HE arena; for example, by HEIs and ITPs collaborating to innovate and develop approaches and mechanisms together.

Discourse lens

Professional identity

H&DA provision features varied roles depending on ITP or HEI status. Circa 2017, delivery staff roles changed somewhat, and there was a transition from 'assessing' to 'mentoring' or 'coaching'. This coincided with the separation of assessment that came with the move away from apprenticeship frameworks to standards, and the subsequent implementation of End-Point Assessment (EPA). From a delivery perspective, a Level 3 Award in Education and Training (previously PTLLS) was previously deemed by many a sufficient qualification for delivery staff to hold, but suddenly expectations around teaching qualifications and experience increased and the need to have a high-level teaching qualification, as previously stressed by DIUS (2012), became paramount. This was not the first time the conceptualisation of professionalism among teachers in ITPs had shifted, with Evetts (2011) previous noting changes in what ITP delivery actually entailed. Aside from the recent drive for high-level teaching qualifications among ITP delivery staff, literature sets out a relatively simple professional identity for ITP staff, aligned with two forms of Continuing Professional Development (CPD) – organisational and occupational (Loy, 2024). For example, ITP delivery staff may engage in mandatory e-learning such as Safeguarding and Prevent annual training (deemed 'organisational CPD'), while undertaking further industry qualifications or spending time back in industry to retain occupational sharpness ('occupational CPD'). Bathmaker and Avis (2013) highlight the most significant barrier preventing achievement of this is giving staff the time and space to do it. They also find CPD time is not equitably allotted in the ITP setting, suggesting that while ITPs make time for organisational CPD, they often fail to facilitate occupational CPD.

Professional identity in HEIs is significantly more complex than in the ITP setting. Martin et al. (2018) notes there is pressure on H&DA-focused lecturers, who were purposely recruited to deliver solely on H&DA provision, to maintain the same levels of academic identity as their counterparts delivering on traditional undergraduate and postgraduate degree pathways or engaged in the research field. This source goes on to say that some of these individuals face negative perceptions from their peers, who view them as not being "proper academics". Many H&DA-focused academics made the transition from industry to teaching, and labels like "pracademics" (Hodgson and Garner, 2023) or "scholar practitioners" (Campbell, 2022) are assigned to them in literature. While such terms were likely coined with good intention, they may contribute to the narrative that those who teach H&DAs are not "proper academics", and that, somehow, they deal with only practice and not academia. The reality, in fact, is that work-based learning is the bridge between academia and practice (Konstantinou and Miller, 2021), fulfilling calls by society to recouple theory and practice through the vehicle of H&DAs (Forster et al., 2023). In addition, Bell and Bell (2020) explain H&DAs feature significant numbers of mature learners who, even before their apprenticeship, may have extensive work experience. They refer to this population needing less traditional lecturer-led passive learning (referred to as 'mode one'), instead needing more constructivist approaches ('mode two'). Given their practical, industry background, pracademics are well-suited to this. The professional identity of "pracademic", while acknowledging the limitations of the label, plays an important part in dictating the CPD engaged in by such educators. Similar to their ITP counterparts, this may be organisational and occupational as previously described, however; in the academic setting, this may be insufficient to develop, or even sustain, a long-term career. This is an issue explored somewhat by Gerhardt and Kelly (2024), who state defining oneself as a pracademic risks shutting the door on the potential to become a well-rounded "tri-professional", a term they use to describe an educator with pedagogical expertise, subject expertise, *and* research expertise.

Experience lens

Having experienced both HEIs and ITPs, I would like to commence my discussion by first challenging an assumption about the latter. Powell and Walsh (2018) describe the opening of HEI provision to private providers as a transfer of power to those with potentially no commitment to wider public values and subsequently threaten the international standing of HE in the UK. I challenge this notion – ITPs, in my experience, absolutely contribute to wider public values. While there are plenty of ITPs that run higher apprenticeships, not many run degree apprenticeships – yet. ITPs do, however, offer a threat to HEIs; not around the reputation of HE as alluded to, but in terms of their openness to change and subsequent dynamic reactions. March (1991) describes this as "organisational ambidexterity"; in other words, balancing the old certainties with an exploration of new possibilities. As more ITPs enter the DA arena (and more will); HEIs face challenges from a provider type who are simply more willing to be innovative. Applying March's theory to H&DAs as a broader concept, it can be argued that academic qualifications are the "old certainty", while society clambers for the new possibilities of sensory processing abilities, dexterity, endurance, precision, and global citizenship (WEF, 2023) which H&DAs offer. Skill needs are also changing: at a time when academia faces challenges around traditional assessment methods based on reading, writing, and mathematics not being fit for purpose due to the rise of Artificial Intelligence (AI), this is a prime example of the evolving dynamic of modern skills.

Having used the term 'ITP' throughout, I somewhat dislike the 'bundling' occurring with the term. The assumption about ITPs may be that they are profit-oriented, shareholder-driven setups, but this is far from reality in many cases. Many ITPs are small, local enterprises with niche offerings or a particular clientele. Others are sizable charities, and let us not forget the contribution of Colleges of Further Education (FE), who are the largest and most significant providers of vocational learning in England (ETF, 2022). I had the pleasure of working in a range of ITPs which were private limited companies, public limited companies, and not-for-profit setups; all making unique contributions and acting as forward-thinking hubs of innovation in their own ways. In my experience, ITPs are simply more dynamic and responsive than HEIs – confirming the findings of varied literature over a sustained period (Simmons, 2024; DES, 1991; Williams and Woodhall, 1979). Unfortunately, even ITP innovation is in decline, however. Smith and Rowe (2024) point out that government regulation is forcing firms to spend a disproportionate amount of their limited resources on meeting ever-increasing expectations associated with apprenticeship delivery (Smith and Rowe, 2024). This is set to change, and I generally take a positive stance to the 'loosening' of policy, including reducing the mandatory apprenticeship length from 12 months to eight, as this had previously been a barrier to innovations such as programme modularisation, which mirrors the fast-paced society we live in (Chadwick et al., 2024). Those quickest to react will be those that capitalise on this.

Reflecting on my time working in HEIs since transitioning from ITPs, I sense a great deal of unrest in the industry, not confined to a single HEI but felt in many. The HE market has been volatile for some time, which escalated somewhat in 2023 when the Conservative government indicated a crackdown on what they deemed 'rip off' university degrees to instead fund apprenticeships (GOV.UK, 2023). A good move in theory; however, multiple sources highlight that there is no evidence to suggest that 13% of subsequent missing undergraduate students would take up apprenticeships instead (Farquharson et al., 2024; Williams, 2024). This move only exacerbated existing worries triggered by real-term income attributed to UK students being 25% lower than it was in 2015–2016, according to a report highlighting HEI instability by the House of Commons (2024), resulting in financial pressures and resulting in course closures and staff redundancies (House of Lords, 2024). In response, HEIs had ramped up international student recruitment, which the Institute for Fiscal Studies (2024) noted is not a sustainable solution to address the challenges faced in the sector. In light of visa changes, HEIs have again shifted their focus: to H&DAs. And in yet another turn in an unpredictable market, Tweedie (2025) estimates HEIs could lose up to £177,660,000 in income due to the loss of the Apprenticeship Levy in its current state, if Level 7 provision is removed.

Based on this, I heed the warning to HEIs: do not put your eggs in one basket. Avoid cutting courses to pivot excessively to apprenticeships. Having worked in ITPs of varying success, I have seen them fail because they do not have a diverse portfolio. Meanwhile, I have seen them excel because they have spread their risk accordingly. ITPs must continue to do this, and HEIs the same. By having a portfolio made up of varied funding streams from different sources, HEIs and ITPs safeguard against politically-correlated knee-jerk reactions. Considering the field of business and management H&DAs specifically (my subject matter expertise), Quew-Jones (2024) called for further investigation and analysis of the value of investment of H&DAs, which Pius (2024) followed up, noting vocational degrees (interpreted as H&DAs) contribute positively in the management sector in terms of Knowledge, Skills, and Behaviours, making management a relevant field which should be captured in H&DA provision scope. Despite this, Richmond (2025) recommends that management training courses should be removed from the apprenticeship system and funded as non-apprenticeship training instead, within the Growth and Skills Levy. This highlights that aforementioned volatility around H&DAs is potentially worse in the field of business and management; and, considering this is a popular area for both HEIs and ITPs, this is alarming.

In summary, given the current struggles of HEIs, I believe H&DAs are an opportunity to get people who would not typically go into HE on the path.

If H&DA provision is grown sustainably by HEIs, and truly valued and embraced; H&DAs could be the saviour of our institutions. However, if relied upon too heavily or seen as a cash cow to prop up standard pathways by absorbing costs, H&DAs could be the nail in the coffin for HEIs. To truly value and embrace H&DAs, HEIs must accept times are changing and operations cannot be done the way they have for many years. It is time to de-institutionalise, and H&DAs may act as a reliable product to support our institutions while they transition to new ways of working.

Ideas lens

The shifting policy landscape of H&DAs presents both opportunities and risks. While the expansion of H&DAs could enhance access to higher education and offer a practical alternative to traditional degree routes, excessive reliance on apprenticeships as a financial lifeline for HEIs could further the existing pressures. Institutions must avoid reactionary pivots driven solely by financial imperatives and instead focus on a diverse wide range of sustainable, high-quality provision that genuinely serves a broad audience, including students, apprentices, employers, and the wider economy. Considering the resources required to deliver this, HEIs should accept that existing academic staff cannot simply pivot to delivering H&DAs. Instead, they should be given time and space to engage in appropriate CPD. Similarly, staff described as practitioners or scholarly practitioners should be encouraged to engage in research also, ensuring they become well-rounded "tri-professionals". The target of developing a workforce of tri-professionals should extend beyond the walls of HEIs and be embraced by ITPs. While ITPs generally do not seek funding to engage in research practice, doing so is pivotal in the professional identity of the workforce delivering H&DAs. There is an opportunity for ITPs to collaborate with HEIs, who are well-versed in research practice, to do so.

Another potential route for collaboration is mergers. Further education (FE) colleges did this effectively, reducing from 427 at incorporation, to 257 (Ainley and Bailey, 1997). It is possible HEIs could merge, as could ITPs; but it is also possible for cross-boundary public–private partnerships to be struck to allow the infrastructure of a HEI to be supported by the innovative working of an ITP. While mergers, acquisitions, and formal partnerships are somewhat at the top end of the continuum for ways forward, lighter solutions may involve collaboration in less formal manners. The Education and Training Foundation (ETF) made effort to set up Vocational Education and Training (VET) Centres of Excellence and Innovation (CoVEs), whereby groups of schools act as policy hub ecosystems to innovate technologically and digitally, thus boosting creativity (Galvin Arribas, 2020). A similar setup encouraging dialogue between HEIs and ITPs will not only stimulate creative thinking and lay foundations for future formal partnerships, but also act as a collective force which may somewhat influence policymaking by feeding good practice. This may be supportive during times of an evolving market, and with the concept of 'stackable qualifications' emerging, this may be critical. Stephenson (2024) notes the announcement of the Lifelong Learning Entitlement (LLE) loan, described as a "flexi-travelcard to jump on and off learning as opposed to being confined to a single advance ticket". The idea of this is for people to use several smaller LLE loans for stackable 30-credit modules rather than sign up and commit to a full qualification. While the source notes the full implementation of this has been delayed from 2025 to 2027, when it does emerge, education will reflect fast-moving society. HEI–ITP collaborations could yield some fantastic products in relation to this if bridges are forged soon.

In conclusion, this chapter has given insight into the market conditions of H&DAs, and the important roles played by both public higher education institutions (HEIs) and private independent training providers (ITPs). Through the application of Johnson et al.'s (2011) four lenses of strategy development, a structured analysis of the sector has been presented, highlighting key market dynamics, quality concerns, professional identity considerations, and the lived experiences of those operating within these frameworks. Findings indicate the growing, but unstable significance of H&DAs as a successful mechanism of UK vocational skills development which bridges the gap between academia and industry. HEIs, while bringing academic rigour and institutional credibility, often struggle with adaptability and the bureaucratic constraints that hinder responsiveness to market needs. In contrast, ITPs demonstrate agility and innovation but face substantial regulatory pressures that threaten their ability to make a reasonable profit, and subsequently their long-term sustainability depending on their setup: for example, profit driven, not-for-profit, or charity. The sector is, therefore, at a critical juncture, where HEIs and ITPs alone may struggle, and collaboration rather than competition may offer the most viable path forward.

References

Ainley, P. & Bailey, B. (1997). *The Business of Learning: Staff and Student Experiences of Further Education in the 1990s*. Cassell.

Atherton, G., Lewis, J. & Bolton, P. (2024). Higher education in the UK: systems, policy approaches, and challenges. https://commonslibrary.parliament.uk/

Bathmaker, A.-M. & Avis, J. (2013). Inbound, outbound or peripheral: The impact of discourses of 'organisational' professionalism on becoming a teacher in English further education, *Discourse: Studies in the Cultural Politics of Education*, 34(1), 731–748. https://doi.org/10.1080/01596306.2013.728367

Bell, R. & Bell, H. (2020). Applying educational theory to develop a framework to support the delivery of experiential entrepreneurship education, *Journal of Small Business and Enterprise Development*, 27(6), 987–1004. https://doi.org/10.1108/JSBED-01-2020-0012

Camden, B. (2024, September 23). Level 7 apprenticeships face the axe in levy reform, sources say, *FE Week*. https://feweek.co.uk/level-7-apprenticeships-face-the-axe-in-levy-reform-sources-say/

Campbell, C. (2022). Afterward? Moving onwards for developing pracademia and pracademics in education, *Journal of Professional Capital and Community*, 7(1), 98–108. https://doi.org/10.1108/JPCC-01-2022-104

Chadwick, K., Dimungu Hewage, D. & Hazzam, J. (2024). Barriers to effective higher and degree-level apprenticeships: A systematic literature review and future research agenda, *Higher Education, Skills and Work-Based Learning*, ahead-of-print. https://doi.org/10.1108/HESWBL-07-2024-0208

Cleaver, L. (2022, February 23). Academic governance and degree apprenticeships in England – getting it right. *Advance HE*. https://www.advance-he.ac.uk/news-and-views/academic-governance-and-degree-apprenticeships-england-getting-it-right

Considine, M. (2005). *Making Public Policy: Institutions, Actors, Strategies*. Polity.

Department for Education and Science (DES). (1991). *Education and Training for the 21st Century*. HMSO.

Department for Innovation, Universities and Skills (DIUS). (2012). *The Further Education Teachers' Continuing Professional Development and Registration (England) (Revocation) Regulations 2012*. The Stationery Office Ltd.

Education and Training Foundation (ETF). (2022). So What is the FE Sector? A Guide to the Further Education System in England. *ETF*. https://www.et-foundation.co.uk/wp-content/uploads/2020/08/200729-ETF-FE-Sector-Guide-RGB-v10.pdf

Evans, S. (2024). Flex and match: A new Skills Levy for growth and opportunity. https://learningandwork.org.uk/wp-content/uploads/2024/06/Flex-and-match-a-new-Skills-Levy-for-growth-and-opportunity.pdf

Evetts, J. (2011). A new professionalism? *Challenges and Opportunities, Current Sociology*, 59(4), 406–422. https://doi.org/10.1177/0011392111402585

Farquharson, C., Ogden, K., Tahir, I. & Waltmann, B. (2024, May 29). High-skilled apprenticeships have high returns – but funding via a 'crackdown' on higher education courses is challenging. *IFS*. https://ifs.org.uk/articles/high-skilled-apprenticeships-have-high-returns-funding-crackdown-higher-education-courses

Felce, A. (2019). Managing the quality of higher education in apprenticeships', *Higher Education, Skills and Work-Based Learning*, 9(2), 141–148. https://doi.org/10.1108/HESWBL-10-2018-0106

Forster, A. M., Pilcher, N., Murray, M., Tennant, S., Craig, N. & Galbrun, L. (2023). Construction and engineering Higher Education: the role of pracademics in recoupling classical experiential educational norms, in *Professional Development for Practitioners in Academia: Pracademia* (pp. 211–227). Springer International Publishing.

Galvin Arribas, J. (2020). Centers of Vocational Excellence and Innovation (CoVes): A new era for Vocational Education and Training (VET) institutions? *Academia (Greece)*, 18(1), 58–84.

Gerhardt, T. & Kelly, R. (2024). Reflection, pracademics and cognitive apprentices, *Work Based Learning e-Journal International*, 12(2), 106–122.

GOV.UK. (2023, July 17) Crackdown on rip-off university degrees. *GOV.UK*. Available from https://www.gov.uk/government/news/crackdown-on-rip-off-university-degrees

GOV.UK. (2025a). *Download the Apprenticeship Provider and Assessment Register (APAR)*. https://download.apprenticeships.education.gov.uk/apar [Accessed 28 February 2025].

GOV.UK. (2025b). *Apprenticeship Training Courses*. https://findapprenticeshiptraining.apprenticeships.education.gov.uk/courses?keyword=&levels=2 [Accessed 28 February 2025].

GOV.UK. (2025c). *Training Providers for Chartered Manager* (Degree) (Level 6). https://findapprenticeshiptraining.apprenticeships.education.gov.uk/courses/55/providers?location=-1 [Accessed 28 February 2025].

Higher Education Statistics Agency (HESA). (2024). *HE Provider Types*. [online] https://www.hesa.ac.uk/support/providers [Accessed 4 April 2025].

Hodgson, R. & Garner, I. (2023). Are staff with professional and industry expertise proper academics? *Wonkhe*. https://wonkhe.com/blogs/are-staff-with-professionaland-industry-expertise-proper-academics/ [Accessed 1 November 2023].

Holland, S. R. & Edifor, E. E. (2025). Quality metrics: Navigating the quality landscape of degree apprenticeships in higher education institutions, in Matthew Barr (Ed.), *Approaches to Work-Based Learning in Higher Education*, 159–178. Routledge.

House of Commons. (2024). *Higher Education Finances in England*. https://researchbriefings.files.parliament.uk/documents/CBP-10037/CBP-10037.pdf [Accessed 17 March 2025].

House of Lords. (2024). *Higher Education Funding*. https://lordslibrary.parliament.uk/higher-education-funding [Accessed 17 March 2025].

Hydén, G. (2016). The role and impact of funding agencies on higher education and research for development, in Halvorsen, T., & Nossum, J. (Eds.), *North-South Knowledge Networks: Towards Equitable Collaboration between Academics, Donors and Universities* (pp. 1–40). African Minds.

Institute for Apprenticeships and Technical Education (IfATE). (2025). *Revisions and Adjustments Status Report - March 2025.* https://www.instituteforapprenticeships.org/developing-new-apprenticeships/revisions-status-report/ [Accessed 4 April 2025].

Institute for Fiscal Studies (IFS). (2024). *Higher Education Finances: How Have They Fared and What Options Will the Incoming Government Have?* https://ifs.org.uk/publications/higher-education-finances-how-have-they-fared-and-what-options-will-incoming [Accessed 17 March 2025].

Jackson, G. (2010). Actors and Institutions, in *Oxford Handbook of Comparative Institutional Analysis*. Oxford University Press. https://ssrn.com/abstract=1408664

Johnson, G., Scholes, K. & Whittington, R. (2011). *Exploring Corporate Strategy: Text and Cases*. 9th edn. Pearson Education.

Konstantinou, I. & Miller, E. (2021). Self-managed and work-based learning: problematising the workplace–classroom skills gap, *Journal of Work-Applied Management*, 13(1), 6–18. https://doi.org/10.1108/JWAM-11-2020-0048

Lomas, J. (2025). Higher education apprenticeship pedagogies: A multilateral approach, in *Approaches to Work-Based Learning in Higher Education* (pp. 24–44). Routledge.

Loy, L. (2024). Redefining teachers' continuing professional development in further education providers in England, *Research in Post-Compulsory Education*, 29(3), 520–540.

Mackay, J. (2022). An assessment of degree apprenticeships as a vehicle for widening participation [Unpublished doctoral dissertation]. University of Bath.

March, J.G. (1991). Exploration and exploitation in organizational learning, *Organization Science*, 2(1), 71–87. https://doi.org/10.1287/orsc.2.1.71

Martin, L., Lord, G. & Warren-Smith, I. (2018). Juggling hats: Academic roles, identity work and new degree apprenticeships, *Studies in Higher Education*, 45(3), 524–537. https://doi.org/10.1080/03075079.2018.1550478

Mintzberg, H. (1994). *The Rise and Fall of Strategic Planning*. Free Press.

Office for Students. (2022). Office for Students Strategy 2022 to 2025. https://www.officeforstudents.org.uk/media/h13hk34t/ofs-strategy-2022-final-1452024.pdf

Pius, A. (2024). Exploring the experience of degree apprentices and academics in fostering managerial-level competencies: A case of vocational degrees within the UK, *International Journal of Sustainable Approach to Education Practice*, 3(1).

Powell, A. (2023). Apprenticeship statistics for England. *House of Commons Library*. https://commonslibrary.parliament.uk/research-briefings/sn06113/

Powell, P. & Walsh, A. (2018). Whose curriculum is it anyway? Stakeholder salience in the context of Degree Apprenticeships, *Higher Education Quarterly*, 72(2), 90–106.

Quew-Jones, R. (2024). Degree apprenticeships in higher education: Improving understanding and practice in work-integrated learning. [Unpublished doctoral dissertation]. University of Portsmouth.

Richmond, T. (2025). A level of uncertainty: How to resolve the debate over the future of Level 7 apprenticeships. https://www.tom-richmond.com/wp-content/uploads/2025/01/A-level-of-uncertainty-January-2025.pdf

Simmons, R. (2024). A private function: Independent providers of vocational education and training in post-war England, *British Journal of Educational Studies*, 72(6), 765–782.

Smith, N. & Rowe, L. (2024). The impact of neoliberalist government reform and regulatory oversight on private training providers in the UK technical education sector, *Journal of Work-Applied Management*, ahead-of-print. https://doi.org/10.1108/JWAM-06-2024-0083

Stephenson, R. (2024, June 10). Degree apprenticeships and the lifelong learning entitlement; The HE general election issues, Day 6, *HEPI*. https://www.hepi.ac.uk/2024/06/10/degree-apprenticeships-and-the-lifelong-learning-entitlement-the-he-general-election-issues-day-6/

Tweedie, L. (2025, January 13). Apprenticeships data highlights shift in focus for higher education in 2025, *RSM*. https://www.rsmuk.com/news/apprenticeships-data-highlights-shift-in-focus-for-higher-education-in-2025

Williams, G. & Woodhall, M. (1979). *Independent Further Education*. Policy Studies Institute.

Williams, T. (2024, May 29). More apprentices 'shouldn't come at higher education's expense. *Times Higher Education*. https://www.timeshighereducation.com/news/more-apprentices-shouldnt-come-higher-educations-expense

World Economic Forum (WEF). (2023). *Future of Jobs Report 2023*. https://www3.weforum.org/docs/WEF_Future_of_Jobs_2023.pdf

12 The Learner Coach

Surfacing tripartite practice

Helen Charlton and
Phil Power-Mason

Introduction

> Sadly, the coaching role is still not recognised...Academics do not see it as an important part and only focus on the degree and in most cases employers and apprentices do not know any difference regarding the huge additional support apprentices get from their...coach. They are often the glue which sticks everything together.
>
> (Construction)

The apprenticeship tripartite relationship comprises apprentice, employer representative (i.e. mentor or line manager), and higher education representative, and there is growing cross-sector evidence that the success of the tripartite relationship is critical to apprenticeship success (Minton and Lowe, 2019; Taylor-Smith et al., 2023). The apprenticeship tripartite model is a fundamental and distinct approach within UK higher education (HE), differing even from other work-aligned learning and experiential delivery models. In response, a community of practitioners representing HE providers in the tripartite relationship have emerged reactively as a novel workforce. Diverse models have been variously shaped by institutional norms and approaches. Even within institutions, differences in practice arise from disciplinary pedagogies and histories, rooted in vocational, industrial, and professional, statutory, and regulatory body alignments.

As academics deeply involved in HE apprenticeships, we have observed the emergence of the tripartite practitioner as a new, yet somewhat 'hidden' workforce. The titles of these roles in different institutions, and even within, is exceptionally diverse. Without consensus in the sector around professional

DOI: 10.4324/9781003567844-13

terminology, the identity and community work that would support these activities remains underdeveloped (Charlton and Power-Mason, 2025). In recognition of this, we refer to the role as higher education tripartite practice, and the role holders as higher education tripartite practitioners (HETPs). We argue that these roles are unique in HE, complex, multifaceted, and diverse. The impetus for this chapter arises from this divergence, the lack of clarity on how such activity is conceptualised or performed, and a recognition that few external benchmarks or forums to evaluate best practices exist in this area of apprenticeship delivery. We therefore explore the divergence across institutions and disciplines, surfacing key experiences and challenges that emerge across contexts (for a detailed discussion of one example, see Chapter 10).

This situation partly reflects the rapid expansion of apprenticeships in UK HE and historical perceptions that relegated work-based learning mainly to further education (FE), with consequent limited HE involvement in the establishment of Higher and Degree Apprenticeships (H&DAs) (Anderson, Bravenboer, and Hemsworth, 2012). Regulatory influences also shape tripartite practices: the Education and Skills Funding Agency (ESFA) rules have defined tasks within the tripartite relationship, but not roles to support this, while Ofsted oversight adds complexity with new requirements such as fundamental values and safeguarding. Such aspects are fundamental to compliance within apprenticeships and so shape the structures and approaches HE institutions have adopted. Consequently, growing institutional demands for granular apprenticeship data have driven additional processes and systems (Power-Mason et al., 2025). In response, staffing has evolved into multifaceted configurations to meet these external requirements and support students. In this, the limited homogeneity noted across international apprenticeship models at the macro level (Smith, 2023) extends to the meso and micro levels, with stark institutional, disciplinary, and practitioner plurality, resulting in diverse locally adapted configurations (Charlton and Power-Mason, 2025).

To explore this emerging practice, we begin by examining English HE tripartite practitioners through three lenses: dual professionalism, heuristic apprenticeship practice, and the continual management of inherent tensions. We ground our discussion in two key perspectives: theoretical understanding of these roles in vocational education and training internationally; and the lived experiences of tripartite practitioners in UK H&DAs across disciplines and institutions. Although we have long engaged with apprenticeships, we are not engaged in the day-to-day tripartite role ourselves, nor are we experts in every discipline. Therefore, we illustrate our views with those of tripartite practitioners themselves to add insight, candour, and diversity.

Tripartite practitioners as dual professionals

The tripartite practitioner role straddles the academic and practice communities, requiring expertise and fluency in both. This 'dual professionalism' is well recognised in other areas of HE; for example in the experiences of industry professionals moving into academic careers. Insights from the 'industry–academic transition' literature emphasise the complexity of this identity shift, and the tensions experienced moving from established industry practices to the pedagogical norms of academia (Myers et al., 2024).

Within apprenticeship delivery internationally such dual identity is both well recognised and understood (e.g. Köpsén and Andersson, 2017), but is perhaps new to UK HE given the rapidly changing regulatory landscape in which these roles have emerged. In the UK, vocational and educational training (VET) has often characterised the workplace as separate from the college (Esmond, 2020), and the significant personal cost of maintaining both professional and academic identities within degree and higher apprenticeship delivery (Martin, Lord, and Warren-Smith, 2018). We can therefore surmise that maintaining both identities is simultaneously valuable and problematic.

International evidence concurs, suggesting that, within VET, practitioners who can do so are better prepared for their roles (Fejes and Köpsén, 2014), but achieving pedagogical competence requires a shift between practice and academic thinking which can be difficult (Sarastuen, 2019). Such competence is further complicated by the emphasis on maintaining professional currency coming at a cost of pedagogical skills development (Schmidt, 2019), and even when continuing professional development (CPD) is both mandated and specifically designed, such as in Sweden, engagement may be limited (Andersson and Köpsén, 2015). This suggests that straddling the boundaries of this pedagogical and professional duality concurrency is key, despite the difficulties.

This is emphasised when we consider the stakeholder-facing role of coaches. In the more established setting of HE community engagement, the boundary spanning required to align diverse stakeholders is recognised as requiring significant identity work, not least in navigating the uncertainty around how these roles are both structurally located inside the institution, but also perceived externally (Lauvås and Vie, 2022). Given the emergent nature of tripartite practice roles, similar ambiguity is unsurprising.

Given this evidence of complexity within the dual roles of industry expert and educator present in apprenticeship delivery, it is predictable that the lived experience of the role reflects these challenges. The following reflections underlines the 'boundary-spanning' nature of the tripartite practitioner role and illuminates how real-world credibility, professional identity, and pedagogical responsibilities can simultaneously strengthen and complicate apprenticeship coaching and delivery.

Navigating duality as coach and practitioner

> The dual role can be difficult as the expectations and requirements for both are often contradictory and it can be very hard to balance both. Being able to give real-world examples due to having real-world industrial experience is a major advantage to being able to contact and gain respect from the employers and apprentices. Sadly, the large majority of HE providers are new to apprenticeships and are often career academics and have difficulty understanding the 'real' working world. I feel it would be beneficial to have more real-world experience in the support role as understanding the technical subject matter is one thing but being able to put it into real-world action is another. I have experience from FE before moving to HE and feel there is a lot HE can learn from the FE world in this area.
>
> (Construction)

> Dual professional identity provides both relevance and credibility within the coaching aspect of the learner and line manager. Whilst the learner is within an education process of understanding theoretical underpinnings, a key element to mapping in parallel or 'real time' the practice of applying the learning and creating both personal (learner development) and the current job role – value creation. A significant gap would emerge through the coaching process if practice experience was not applied.
>
> (Business)

> I feel a deep sense of fulfilment when I witness my learners' growth at each step of the process. This dual identity enables me to bring industry relevance into the learning environment while fostering a supportive and reflective academic

space. Overall, the impact is highly positive, dynamic, and rooted in continuous learning for both myself and my apprentices...Universities can better support practitioners by fostering efficiency and encouraging the optimal use of available resources and tools. Providing access to professional development opportunities, such as training in coaching techniques or updates on industry trends, can help practitioners maintain their industry relevance while improving their coaching capabilities. Additionally, streamlining administrative tasks and creating platforms for collaboration with industry partners can allow practitioners to focus more on meaningful engagement with apprentices.

(Business)

Insight

This discussion highlights how apprenticeship coaching requires concurrent expertise in disciplinarity (i.e. the professional area) and modality (i.e. apprenticeships as an educational format), with practitioners simultaneously acting as subject matter experts and negotiators of complex procedural requirements. Tripartite practitioners provide in-depth knowledge and technical insight to support apprentices' professional development, alongside administrative and compliance processes that underpin successful apprenticeship completion. Such duality, and the boundary straddling this requires, is complex. HE institutions should recognise this unique contribution of these dual professionals, valuing and fostering their vocational expertise, specific pedagogical insights, and their ability to connect academic and industry domains. By fostering this balance, tripartite practice becomes a robust model for enhancing student learning, aligning the necessity of integrating regulatory compliance, such as detailed documentation of progress reviews, with the development motivations of their coaching practices. It is to this we now turn.

Apprenticeship coaching as a heuristic practice

Work-based learning fosters rich educational experiences and professional identity (Brown, 2015), while reflective practice engages learners and facilitators in negotiating uncertainty, shared meanings, and understanding (Illeris, 2004; Khin and Fatt, 2010). This requires nuanced contexts of personal history, setting, and theoretical positions to avoid perfunctory models of support. Accordingly, apprenticeship coaching can be seen as a heuristic practice, with implications for identity formation (Helyer, 2015) and the development of resilience, problem solving, and praxis (Dalrymple, Kemp and Smith, 2014). Heuristic approaches account for individual differences, disciplinary norms, and career aspirations.

Across all disciplines, tripartite practitioners do this through co-developing structured plans, encouraging flexible action, and critically evaluating outcomes. This demands considerable adaptability, since personal histories and employment contexts continually introduce new challenges requiring a response from all three parties. Such personalised coaching and mentoring boosts emotional resilience, essential for navigating professional challenges (Eccles and Renaud, 2018), although inconsistent practices can create disengagement (Fabian et al., 2022).

As a result, heuristic approaches take various forms. In business apprenticeships, flexible curricula and stakeholder engagement are frequently cited (Evans and Cloutier, 2023). Specific examples of strategies used on one business programme can be found in the case study in Chapter 10. Meanwhile, engineering contexts emphasise indirect guidance, open questioning, feedback on technical design, and balancing autonomy with instruction (Puente Gómez, Doulougeri, and Bruns, 2022), and nursing literature highlights clinical performance, communication, and palliative care responsiveness (Richardson et al., 2023).

Effective tripartite practice therefore bridges academic learning and workplace application through tailored discovery-based approaches. Paradoxically, the journey is rigidly regulated yet adaptive, shaped by the interplay of context and people. Tripartite practitioners balance independent reflection with structured guidance, nurturing apprentices' capacity to integrate work, study, and life.

Approaching coaching in tripartite practice

> It can be difficult to support apprentices in their personal and academic challenges whilst holding them to the expectations of the apprenticeship; however, this can be done in a collaborative way by forming a good rapport with them from the start. This requires being consistent in meeting and making time for the apprentice.
>
> (Health and Science)

> Another important aspect is to bring reflection into the conversation...Asking open questions that while are not on the Performance Review Meeting forms...can help them to relate how empowering the learning experience can be when they are learning at university and being able to apply theoretical things at work.
>
> (Construction)

> My approach is continually evolving as apprenticeship standards and expectations change. As I grow as an academic and professional practitioner, I have transitioned from using a structured checklist-based approach to a more coaching-driven, personalised strategy...I now focus more on understanding individual learners' needs, tailoring my support to integrate their workplace responsibilities with university learning. This approach enables apprentices to develop both short-term solutions for immediate challenges and long-term strategies for career growth.
>
> (Business)

Insights

Taken together, these reflections underscore the 'heuristic' nature of apprenticeship coaching: a fluid, adaptive process shaped by ongoing reflection, co-produced strategies, and the need to align institutional requirements with an apprentice's individual development journey. They also underscore the adaptive skill of the tripartite practitioners, balancing mentoring and coaching roles. So, while mentoring offers emotional and motivational support, inspiring long-term aspirations and fostering career development, coaching, in contrast, emphasises task-oriented, goal-specific guidance aimed at achieving immediate objectives. Combining these ensures apprentices receive holistic support for both their current responsibilities and future potential. Another key balance lies between forward-looking and backward-looking coaching. Forward-looking practices set new growth goals and opportunities, while backward-looking approaches involve reviewing progress and reflecting on past experiences. These multiple positions create inherent tensions, and it is to this last aspect we now turn.

Tensions in higher education tripartite practice

It is clear, therefore, that tripartite practice inherently contains tensions, not least from the duality of professional identity, coupled with the developmental versus compliance focus of the role. The tripartite relationship itself compounds this, existing as a complex interplay of competing priorities among apprentices, employers, and educational providers, against a background of regulatory demands. Time multiplies these pressures – progress reviews, End Point Assessment checkpoints and institution-wide record-keeping compress the hours available for deep formative conversation. These tensions are conceptualised by Fuller and Unwin's (2003) 'expansive–restrictive' continuum, where expansive models, which promote integrated learning and skill application, are often constrained by restrictive practices prioritising regulatory compliance over meaningful professional development.

The tripartite setting creates multiple environments where these competing priorities are in constant focus. Apprentices negotiate complex demands between professional and personal responsibilities, constant granular levels of bureaucratic record-keeping, and the aim of long-term competency through academic achievement. As result of these tensions, Fabian et al. (2022) identifies three distinct apprentice perspectives: aligned student-workers who balanced academic and professional goals; busy professionals focused on immediate workplace demands; and the cast adrift, who felt unsupported or disconnected. They relate this to Fuller and Unwin's model, noting that alignment between workplace and academia is key to the development of 'expansive' apprenticeships, and emphasising the role of workplace mentors in this. Yet mentors also face tensions, between long-term workforce development and day-to-day contributions.

What remains unexposed is the role of the tripartite practitioner in negotiating and holding space for these tensions in the tripartite. The reflections below illuminate how tripartite practitioners are adopting tailored interventions to align employer, apprentice, and institutional expectations, whilst fostering apprentices' professional growth. These strategies, while resource-intensive, are critical for ensuring the efficacy and sustainability of the tripartite model.

Experiencing tensions in tripartite settings

> [One] difficulty in navigating priorities is navigating study leave for apprentices. They all received their allocated 20% off the job but different employers have different approaches to study leave. Some provide additional work time to study and some do not. It can be very difficult to negotiate this between individual apprentices and employers and also across different employers.
>
> (Health)

> I try to help [apprentices] see the...programme as a unique opportunity that not many have. I ask [them] to imagine they have a scholarship from the government and other institutions. These institutions will have expectations [which]...are reflected on the training plan, attendance at university and work, and having PRMs regularly. I make them understand that as money is involved, for these institutions the only way to know if they are doing the work they supposed to be doing, is by recording their activities.
>
> (Construction)

> I have countless times when I have had to navigate the competing priorities and at times work with the employer and apprentice 'against' the university for assorted reasons [and] I have obviously worked with the university and apprentice if the employer is not holding up their side of the bargain or even with the employer and university if there is an issue with the apprentice. This is all in the aim of what is best for the apprentice in the long term even if this might seem counterproductive.
>
> (Construction)

Insights

It is clear, therefore, that tensions in tripartite practice stem from balancing competing priorities across multiple boundaries and stakeholders, alongside reconciling holistic (expansive) and fragmented (restrictive) approaches. While a holistic focus fosters overall growth and reflection, immediate, task-specific demands risk fragmenting the experience. The challenge facing individual tripartite practitioners, institutions, and the sector more broadly, is how to meet compliance goals without losing sight of broader developmental aims.

Concluding remarks, reflections, and ways forward

Tripartite practitioners stand at the heart of H&DAs, with significant transformative potential for apprentices, industry, and academia. Occupying a pivotal, tripartite role, these coaches embody a dual professional identity, merging technical expertise with educational insight. By bridging academia and industry, they ensure apprentices not only meet mandated requirements but also grow into reflective, capable professionals. These roles rely on a nuanced, heuristic approach that balances rapid compliance demands with deeper developmental goals that remain personalised and responsive to individual apprentices' learning journeys within distinct employer contexts. As such, they adapt practices and strategies to cultivate mastery and personal growth, acknowledging the educational significance of their role. Inevitably, tensions arise between short-term compliance objectives and broader developmental visions, between aligning immediate targets with the holistic formation of practitioner identity, and carefully avoiding narrow proceduralism.

For universities, practitioners, and policymakers, embracing and supporting this role is vital to advancing apprenticeships. Their position across academic and professional boundaries offers opportunities to foster stronger employer partnerships, aligning skill development with industry needs. Recognising these roles as central to apprenticeship delivery requires adequate workload provision, institutional support, and professional communities where tripartite practitioners can refine methods and share insights.

Further resources

Universities Vocational Awards Council Higher Education Tripartite Professionals Knowledge Network – https://uvac.ac.uk/higher-and-degree-apprenticeships-knowledge-networks-webinars-and-workshops/

ASET, The Work Based Learning and Placement Learning Association – https://www.asetonline.org/

References

Anderson, A., Bravenboer, D. and Hemsworth, D. (2012) 'The role of universities in higher apprenticeship development', *Higher Education, Skills and Work-Based Learning*, 2(3), pp. 240–255. https://doi.org/10.1108/20423891211271773

Andersson, P. and Köpsén, S. (2015) 'Continuing professional development of vocational teachers: Participation in a Swedish national initiative', *Empirical Research in Vocational Education and Training*, 7(7), pp. 1–20. https://doi.org/10.1186/s40461-015-0019-3

Brown, P. (2015) 'Communities of practice: A heuristic for workplace reflection in higher education', *Rapport: The International Journal for Recording Achievement, Planning and Portfolios*, 1. Available at: https://viewer.joomag.com/rapport/0727239001439797282

Charlton, H. and Power-Mason, P. (2025) 'Higher education tripartite practitioners as an emerging role in UK higher education', *Vocation, Technology and Education*, 2(forthcoming).

Dalrymple, R., Kemp, C. and Smith, P. (2014) 'Characterising work-based learning as a triadic learning endeavour', *Journal of Further and Higher Education*, 38(1), pp. 75–89. https://doi.org/10.1080/0309877X.2012.699516

Eccles, S. and Renaud, V. (2018) 'Building students' emotional resilience through placement coaching and mentoring', in Morley, D. (ed.) *Enhancing Employability in Higher Education through Work Based Learning*. Palgrave Macmillan, pp. 153,172.

Esmond, B. (2020) 'Emerging apprenticeship practitioner roles in England: Conceptualising the subaltern educator', *Vocations and Learning*, 13(2), pp. 179–196. https://doi.org/10.1007/s12186-019-09233-0

Evans, M. and Cloutier, L.M. (2023) 'Integrating higher degree education with practice: Exploring the value proposition of executive MBA apprenticeships', *Higher Education, Skills and Work-Based Learning*, 13(2), pp. 283–298. https://doi.org/10.1108/HESWBL-10-2022-0207

Fabian, K., Taylor-Smith, E., Smith, S., Meharg, D. and Varey, A. (2022) 'An exploration of degree apprentice perspectives: A Q methodology study', *Studies in Higher Education*, 47(7), pp. 1397–1409. https://doi.org/10.1080/03075079.2021.1897094

Fejes, A. and Köpsén, S. (2014) 'Vocational teachers' identity formation through boundary crossing', *Journal of Education and Work*, 27(3), pp. 265–283. https://doi.org/10.1080/13639080.2012.742181

Fuller, A. and Unwin, L. (2003) 'Learning as apprentices in the contemporary UK workplace: creating and managing expansive and restrictive participation', *Journal of Education and Work*, 16(4), pp. 407–426. https://doi.org/10.1080/1363908032000093012

Helyer, R. (2015) 'Learning through reflection; The critical role of reflection in work-based learning', *Journal of Work-Applied Management*, 7(1), pp. 15–27. https://doi.org/10.1108/JWAM-10-2015-003

Illeris, K. (2004) 'A Model for Learning in Working Life', *Journal of Workplace Learning*, 16(8), pp. 431–441. https://doi.org/10.1108/13665620410566405

Khin, E.W.S. and Fatt, C.K. (2010) 'The role of reflective practitioner heuristic inquiry in institutional learning and research', *International Journal of Education*, 2(1). https://doi.org/10.5296/ije.v2i1.236

Köpsén, S. and Andersson, P. (2017) 'Reformation of VET and demands on teachers' subject knowledge: Swedish vocational teachers' recurrent participation in a national CPD initiative', *Journal of Education and Work*, 30(1), pp. 69–83. https://doi.org/10.1080/13639080.2015.1119259

Lauvås, T. and Vie, O.E. (2022) 'Boundary spanners enabling knowledge integration for sustainable innovations in university–industry research centres', in Fernandes, C., Ramírez-Pasillas, M. and Ferreira, J.J. (eds.) *Universities, Entrepreneurial Ecosystems, and Sustainability*. Berlin/Boston: De Gruyter, pp. 243–264. https://doi.org/10.1515/9783110670219-013

Martin, L., Lord, G. and Warren-Smith, I. (2018). 'Juggling hats: Academic roles, identity work and new degree apprenticeships', *Studies in Higher Education*, 45(3), 524–537. https://doi.org/10.1080/03075079.2018.1550478

Minton, A. and Lowe, J. (2019) 'How are universities supporting employers to facilitate effective "on the job" learning for apprentices?', *Higher Education, Skills and Work-Based Learning*, 9(2), pp. 200–210. https://doi.org/10.1108/HESWBL-10-2018-0099

Myers, F., Baxter, J., Selby-Fell, H. and Pachón, A.M. (2024) 'Navigating from industry to higher education: Practitioner transitions to academic life', *British Educational Research Journal*, 00, pp. 1–19. https://doi.org/10.1002/berj.4109

Power-Mason, P., Charlton, H., Walker-Martin, F. and Bloomfield, S. (2025) 'A sector in crisis? Insights from how English higher education apprenticeships are weathering the storm', *Higher Education, Skills and Work-Based Learning*, 548–561. https://doi.org/10.1108/HESWBL-09-2024-0253

Puente Gómez, S.M., Doulougeri, K. and Bruns, M. (2022) 'Coaching practices in challenge-based learning: Characteristics in students' projects', in Gudjonsdottir, M.S., et al. (eds.) *18th CDIO International Conference, CDIO 2022 – Proceedings*. Chalmers University of Technology, pp. 991–1002. Available at: http://w.cdio.org/knowledge-library/documents/coaching-practices-challenge-based-learning-characteristics-students%E2%80%99

Richardson, C., Wicking, K., Biedermann, N. and Langtree, T. (2023) 'Coaching in nursing: An integrative literature review', *Nursing Open*, 10(10), pp. 6635–6649. https://doi.org/10.1002/nop2.1925

Sarastuen, N.K. (2019) 'From vocational worker to vocational teacher: a study of identity transition and loss', *Journal of Vocational Education and Training*, 72(3), pp. 333–349. https://doi.org/10.1080/13636820.2019.1607533

Schmidt, T. (2019) Industry currency and vocational teachers in Australia: what is the impact of contemporary policy and practice on their professional development? *Research in Post-Compulsory Education*, 24(1), pp. 1–19. https://doi.org/10.1080/13596748.2019.1584431

Smith, E. (2023) 'Apprenticeships: The problem of attractiveness and the hindrance of heterogeneity', *International Journal of Training and Development*, 27, pp. 18–38. https://doi.org/10.1111/ijtd.12281

Taylor-Smith, E., Smith, S., Fabian, K. and Bratton, A. (2023) 'Apprentices' perspectives of the tripartite collaboration at the heart of degree apprenticeships: a longitudinal study', *Journal of Workplace Learning*, 35(8), pp. 779–795. https://doi.org/10.1108/JWL-01-2023-0007

13

The Learner Coach

Supporting the Learner's apprenticeship journey through coaching and mentoring interventions

Hilary Duckett, Stavroula Bibila, Michelle Civile, Fernando Correia, Peter Goodwin, Michael Matthews, Julie Pepper, and Peter Stephenson

Degree apprenticeships and experiential learning

A brief background

From the publication of the Wolf Report (2011) and the Richard Review (2012) in the early 2010s, to the introduction of the Apprenticeship Levy in 2017 and the recent announcement of the UK government's plans (DfE, 2024) to rebalance apprenticeship provision in favour of younger people, the apprenticeship system in England has been undergoing extensive changes.

During this time, pedagogic staff across further and higher education have experienced the development of over 400 apprenticeship standards at Levels 4–7 mapped onto occupational standards across apprenticeship curricula, the introduction of new methods of assessment (e.g. synoptic

DOI: 10.4324/9781003567844-14

End-Point Assessments – EPAs), and the rise of Higher and Degree Apprenticeships (H&DAs) as an entry route to many professions.

As part of reforming apprenticeships, employers (as trailblazer groups[1]) were given the important role of designing learning opportunities and pathways for the workforce, through the creation of apprenticeship standards that focus on building Knowledge, Skills and Behaviours. Pedagogic staff also found themselves with a new, and equally important, role; that of mediating the learning relationship between the apprenticeship provider, individual employers, and their apprentices, the latter being required to spend time learning 'off the job' and to complete an independent End-Point Assessment (EPA). It is this role, often coming with the job title of a skills coach, a learning facilitator, or an academic mentor, that the chapter brings to the fore, through a discussion based on empirical data, our professional observations and insights, and key aspects of the evolving apprenticeship landscape.

Theorising the Learner Coach

It has long been argued that the development of tomorrow's leaders will not be achieved through the teaching of theoretical concepts alone (e.g. Day, 2000; Schon, 1983). The leaders of tomorrow cannot rely on the theory of today and educators are tasked with developing the necessary skills and behaviours to allow today's students the abilities required for a lifelong journey of becoming tomorrow's leaders (Schedlitzki, 2019).

Our starting point is the belief that a successful understanding of work-based learning pedagogies focuses first on the learning processes themselves, and secondly on the teaching or coaching methods used. These learning processes are underpinned by Bandura's (1977) social cognitive theory, allowing us to explicitly go beyond individual factors in behaviour to account for environmental and social factors, and recognising that learning from experience includes learning from others. The deeper philosophical roots of our theorisation lie in the conviction that knowledge is created by doing and through an active transformation of experience (Dewey, 1916; Reynolds, 2011). The challenges that H&DA programmes face is a pedagogical shift from teaching traditional academic knowledge to teaching threshold concepts set up to support the ongoing refinement of skills and behaviours.

The mutuality of the experiential learning process

To understand the importance of experiential learning to the apprenticeship journey it is important to explore its tripartite nature (employer, apprentice, academic tutor). Nearly a decade after their inception, there is compelling evidence that H&DAs have had a positive impact for apprentices and employers. A Department for Education report (2024) found that businesses cited multiple benefits from apprenticeships with the most common being the development of specific skills relevant to their organisation (85%) and increased productivity (78%). Apprenticeships act as a pipeline for talent development across various sectors (Nawaz et al., 2023).

The Employer perspective

Employers have attested to value of H&DAs as a talent management tool to attract, engage, and retain talent (Quality Assurance Agency [QAA], 2024). Furthermore, they have been reported to positively influence organisational performance, contributed to strategic goals and support diversity (QAA, 2024). Much of the success of the apprenticeship model is attributed to the inclusion of coaching and mentoring processes which enable effective tripartite communication (learner, employer, and provider) and provide signposting and support and increased likelihood of higher levels of engagement and completion (Nawaz and Edifor, 2024). Research has shown that employers unanimously emphasised the importance of workplace mentors (QAA, 2024). Mentors provide coaching and pastoral support to apprentices while also helping them identify opportunities to integrate theoretical knowledge with practical application (France et al, as cited in Laczik et al., 2024).

The apprentice perspective

Nearly three-quarters of apprentices in the QAA report (QAA, 2024) felt that H&DAs were meeting their expectations and over 80% reported that they facilitated career progression. According to Smith et al. (2023), mentors and coaches contribute to apprentice development in four key ways: (1) increasing confidence; (2) enhancing personal and professional growth, particularly in decision-making, leadership and emotional intelligence; (3) fostering a sense of achievement, often associated with career progression; and (4) providing support in balancing challenges. At the University of Exeter

(UoE) experience of reapproving job changes, to ensure that new roles meet the standards, demonstrates that large numbers of apprentices achieve job promotion whilst on programme.

A qualitative study by Pepper and Ashbullby (cited in Laczik et al., 2024) reinforces the importance of personal growth which mentoring and coaching processes support. It finds that degree apprentices see themselves as lifelong learners with distinct qualities, including industry experience, connections and resilience. Feedback received at UoE from students following the EPA period validates the strength of support provided to apprentices:

> My Academic Supervisor (Y) did a fantastic job at keeping me on top of my evidence collection, to what otherwise could appear as a daunting and process heavy activity. She gave me ample in-advance notice as to what is coming, simplifying the tasks as much as possible, and always happy to listen to any concerns and frustrations I'm facing along the way.
>
> (EPA Student 4)

The academic perspective

There has been less focus on those teaching and academic mentoring on degree apprenticeships. An interview study with 30 academics teaching H&DAs found that while positive for students the picture for staff was nuanced (Martin et al., 2018). Participants felt that additional demands arose from managing partnerships and workplace learning and that teaching apprenticeships did not always fit with what it meant to be an academic.

However, initial case data from the UoE suggests that tutors and mentors felt their engagement with apprenticeships and involvement in coaching and mentoring was valuable, providing them with business knowledge and reusable case examples:

> you're also learning from students yourself in the sense of, you know, they will tell you how, for example (their company) might apply a process of coaching in order to assimilate new staff into the workforce fairly quickly, so, you know, you learn quite a lot about different approaches yourself and that in turn becomes part of your practise, you know, when you're describing examples to other cohorts.
>
> (Academic 1)

To assess how apprentice teams at UoE manage the expectations of work-based learning we will begin by exploring the importance of the coaching relationship and illustrate how the concept of the Learner Coach might be characterised.

Defining coaching in the context of apprenticeships

Coaching is defined by Whitmore (1992) as "unlocking a person's potential to maximise their own performance. It is helping them to learn rather than teaching them – a facilitation approach" (p. 8). Coaching interventions, *normally* take the form of one-to-one conversations and place the Learner at the centre of the relationship with the purpose of facilitating transformative outcomes (Freire, 2000; Gray, 2007; Jones, 2020). Central to coaching practice is cultivating a sense of learner agency and self-efficacy, thereby developing confidence (Bandura, 1977). Encouraging the Learner to reflect and set goals are central coaching practice, which, over time, enable the Learner to become a self-coach (embodying the *Learner Coach).*

Coaching outcomes

Work-based coaching has been linked to a wide range of positive outcomes. Research has demonstrated that personal and organisational outcomes from coaching include: relevant practice-based learning, unlocking potential, improvement through reflective practice, evidence-based and solutions-focussed behaviours, action-centred and goal-setting development, increased confidence and reduced stress (Hughes & Saieva, 2019; Milad, 2017; Passmore, 2020; Sammet & Wolf, 2022; Whitmore, 1992; Yates & Yates, 2022). At UoE, coaching is integrated into apprenticeship learning as the survey data suggests:

> The coaching that they receive from the mentors regarding where to find information, how to approach assessments, and the coaching they receive from tutors during the modules when tutors put on sessions to support the assessments and webinars, are key aspects of learning.
>
> (Academic 7)

Coaching approaches and skills

The fundamental principles of coaching are rooted in constructs such as learning from others and self-efficacy, the belief that one can influence outcomes and make sense, and the ability to critically reflect and understand one's situation (Bandura, 1977; Weick, 1995). The same constructs are also intrinsic to the coaching process. Accordingly, the approach requires the coach to utilise a broad range of skills. At different times and in varying degrees a coach needs an ability: to observe and make sense of situations and behaviours; to demonstrate active and empathetic listening; and to pose thought-provoking powerful questions. It also requires the willingness to help reframe situations and explore solutions, and to be able to offer feedback and positive affirmations, and also a capacity to provide warmth and understanding (Antiss, 2020; Hughes & Saieva, 2019; Milad, 2017; Passmore, 2020).

As an example, the EPA process evaluates apprentices' knowledge, skills, and behaviours through methods such as a strategic business proposal or work-based project, a presentation with questions and answers, and a professional discussion based on a portfolio of evidence, ensuring they meet the required standards for certification. A structured approach to coaching can support all aspects of this process.

Feedback received from a UoE student at EPA illustrates the value of coaching support:

> X has been an excellent academic mentor. He was able to take his experience from both his previous roles and this role to guide me through the process. He applied the right amount of pressure at the right time to ensure I hit deadlines and guided me through the creation of the portfolio with real calmness, which was a huge support, given that the process can be stressful, especially when balancing work, academic and apprenticeship commitments.
>
> (EPA Student 1)

Challenges in the apprenticeship journey

The challenges that H&DA programmes face is a pedagogical shift from teaching traditional academic knowledge to a focus on supporting the ongoing refinement of skills and behaviours.

The role of the Educator

A coaching-oriented and reflexive pedagogical approach requires the Educator to balance their role as 'expert' on the theory with facilitating the student's application of their practical experience. In this process the issue of balancing power relationships can become a significant obstacle (Iszatt-White et al., 2017). As Vince (1998) highlighted, the experience students (and educators) draw on in the context of tertiary education is "constructed, shaped, and contained by social power relations" (p. 309). In addition, the educator's role as 'expert' in regard to the relevant theory establishes a power imbalance rarely acknowledged in the consideration of pedagogical practice (Collinson & Tourish, 2015).

To address this imbalance some have advocated for a complete shift in the identity of the Educator from instructor to facilitator (e.g. Hibbert & Cunliffe, 2015). This, however, has been shown to have the potential to detrimentally affect both the Educator and the student (Iszatt-White et al., 2017). The loss of identity for the Educator was, in Iszatt-White et al.'s (2017) findings, equally problematic for the students who felt the lack of an 'expert' opinion (Nicholson & Carroll, 2013). The solution proposed by Iszatt-White and her colleagues was "for educators and students to collectively experiment with a greater identity and pedagogical repertoire around the value and use of theory" (Iszatt-White et al., 2017, p. 594).

An example of how UoE has adapted to this was the creation of the 'Academic Mentor' role. The academic mentor is not a subject matter expert but acts as a coach to facilitate student learning. The role is not to have answers for the students but to pose questions that help in spotting opportunities to apply content and connect the workplace to the classroom. This specific role was created to act as a personal coach for every student.

Developing skills and behaviours

Achieving the learning outcomes for H&DA students requires a nuanced understanding of how skills and behaviours are developed. Unlike knowledge acquisition which can focus on conceptualisation and understanding, developing skills and behaviours involves application of learning to workplace experiences and continued cycles of reflection (Kolb, 2014; Rynes et al., 2003. Behaviours are learnt through continued reinforcement (e.g., Pavlov 1897; Skinner, 1938; Watson, 1930) and through the social environments around us (Bandura et al., 1961). This presents challenges around ensuring students have the job scope and relational support to apply content; and, secondly, the time and metacognitive skills for continued development. At UoE, these are two areas that have been a centre of our Degree Apprenticeship curriculum.

The H&DA curriculum is unique in that it allows for learning outcomes to be met in the workplace rather in traditional written assessment formats. Students must understand threshold concepts and apply them to their workplace and evaluate their success (Bloom et al., 1994; Meyer, 2003). The academic curriculum sets clear structures for the student and their organisations on what criteria needs to be met.

Consequently, experiential learning is not simply learning through doing; importantly, it is also the cycle of evaluation, connection to theory, and refining plans for continued development that make it effective (Kolb, 1984). At UoE, we have implemented reflective learning and career development modules within each programme's curriculum. In many instances, these modules span a longer duration of the programme to provide the time and space for metacognition, and recognising the value this brings to overall learning. The following survey data vignette illustrates the multiple uses of reflective practice within apprenticeship modules at UoE:

> Reflective practise as a skill is incorporated into the modules that I teach. We begin at induction by explaining what reflective practice is. And then, in the first module, we give them lots of examples of reflective practices, talk them through various models, give them hints and links to library resources which exist. We give them examples of reflective practice that have been done previously, so they can see how they might apply it as a technique themselves.
>
> (Academic 8)

For tutor, coaches, and mentors to be effective, structures around additional staff resourcing, work integrated assessments, and time are required. These tools are important for coaching effectiveness, and to equip students to navigate the complexities of modern leadership. The process for managing the challenges of portfolio-based experiential learning will now be explored through the practices used at UoE.

Experiential learning in practice at UoE

UK Apprenticeship Standards[2] determine what is required from an apprentice for them to succeed at a specific job role. Underpinning these requirements is a set of core attributes, known as Knowledge, Skills and Behaviours (or KSBs), that an apprentice must demonstrate in their EPA.

At the start of UoE's Senior Leader Apprenticeship (SLA), each student is assigned to an Academic Mentor, who will not only provide guidance and support for academic and administrative matters but also agree with the student the content of work-based learning/reflective projects, and regularly discuss progress through a coaching approach. Academic Mentors act as 'de facto' coaches guiding individuals to discover their own solutions, develop their skills, and achieve their goals, by a process of asking open-ended questions, actively listening, and providing constructive feedback.

To reinforce social learning, at the start of the first module, students are allocated to Action Learning Sets (ALS) with their peers (approximately 6 per set), which they will use throughout as peer-coaching platforms to support them with workplace challenges, that they can use also as the focus of their assignments. Feedback from academics and students suggest that the ALSs are valuable:

> Groups continue to work as a formal action learning set..., a support group or co-coaching group...using the social support.
>
> (Academic 2)

> I have been very lucky that I have been part of a really engaged action learning set, and we have met up outside of the course and helped and motivated each other.
>
> (Student 3)

A reflective and experiential learning approach was embedded across the more 'formal' teaching components of the programme. The programme is comprised of three 'content-focused' modules, aiming to cover the knowledge elements of the KSBs. For each module, students will produce two assignments, with one being a more personal reflective and developmental piece, and the other a workplace development piece, which they are encouraged to discuss and agree with their workplace mentors. A coaching approach and the embedding of reflective practice across teaching was frequently cited as valuable by staff in the UoE survey data and the following data vignette illustrates the technique:

> The working in practise module is a really powerful module, and I asked some powerful probing questions. Things like what's your purpose, your individual purpose, your bigger purpose here, why are you on this earth? What, what are you wanting to contribute? And what are your values?...and it feels like people are really thinking about those questions and you know, thinking about values. Are they the values that I really want to live by, or are they actually the ones that I am living by.
>
> (Academic 1)

The 'Applied Leadership Skills and Behaviours' module runs in parallel to the content focussed modules. It has a strong 'applied' focus, where students work to complete a portfolio of evidence that showcases the application of their learning at work through a series of practical case studies. Again, academic and workplace mentors will have a key role in supporting the identification and development of appropriate evidencing case studies. At UoE, Academic Mentors and their apprentices meet for Progress Review meetings every 12 weeks. During these meetings open dialogue occurs and portfolios and any supporting evidence are reviewed with agreement reached on next steps.

Preparation for End-Point Assessment (EPA)

A key part of the EPA is a process of open reflection and discussion by the student with an independent assessor, focused on the student's portfolio and strategic proposal or work-based project. To prepare apprentices, UoE's SLA programme offers a 'Strategic Business Proposal' module and a coaching approach underpins this process by facilitating critical reflective practice and asking powerful questions to clarify ideas. Fisher (2003) identifies the aim of critical reflection as challenging one's perception of how an organisational problem or opportunity is interpreted. Gray (2007) considers critical reflection a "route to collective action and a component of organizational learning".

In examining broader influences on reflective practice in the professions, Holdo (2023) advocated diverse ways of thinking and viewing things. UoE has applied this premise to move the students beyond the casual acceptance of their own perceptions of the root cause of organisational problems towards the examination of the problem through the application of primary and secondary research. The academic tutors and mentors engage apprentices in one-to-one discussions about their proposals and, through the coaching technique of asking powerful questions, apprentices are encouraged to refine their ideas and develop responses. This coaching technique results in a more critical interrogation of the problems, challenges, or opportunities identified and a more reasoned examination of a range of appropriate solutions. At the end of this process, UoE's aim is that students can produce a more critically informed 'Strategic Business Proposal' for their EPA.

Completing the programme and accreditation

The EPA process itself is completed by an independent third party (the Chartered Management Institute [CMI], in the case of SLA) and comprises a 20-minute presentation followed by a professional discussion to assess the apprentice against the standard. Apprentices are given extensive support and guidance throughout this process, using a range of coaching and mentoring interventions. Academic Mentors use practice discussion questions and mock presentation sessions to help preparation. They employ powerful questions to ensure clarity of thought and provide guidance, and feedback and advice on the quality of case studies written and evidence provided by apprentices. At UoE, the Senior Leader Apprenticeship achieves a 97.5% distinction achievement at EPA which illustrates the effectiveness of the coaching and mentoring systems. The following apprentice extract is indicative of apprentice feedback following EPA:

> I would like to extend my heartfelt thanks to you and everyone involved in supporting me throughout this journey. In particular, I want to express my deepest gratitude to Z, who has been an outstanding academic mentor. His guidance, expertise, and encouragement have been invaluable in helping me navigate this programme and achieve this result.
>
> (EPA Student 3)

> This accomplishment is a reflection of the incredible support system I have had along the way, and I am truly grateful for the opportunities and learning experiences this apprenticeship has provided. Thank you once again for being a part of this meaningful journey.
>
> (EPA Student 4)

Conclusions and future solutions

It's clear that in response to the delivery of apprenticeships higher education institutions are undergoing a rapid transformation in their approach to learning. Social and experiential learning theory and the application of critical reflective practice provide a clear foundation for the design and delivery of the curriculum. This case study has demonstrated how a well-planned and supported curriculum which develops KSBs can ensure that learning is workplace-relevant and has life through value. By structuring work-based learning and providing coaching and mentoring support apprentices can achieve high-level learning outcomes. This case has illustrated how the role of a university academic has been widened to encompass coaching, mentoring, and facilitation. Academic Mentors provide ongoing support and guidance throughout the apprenticeship journey and through coaching interventions (regular feedback, use of powerful questions, feedback and assurance etc.) ensure that portfolios are compliant with the standards and that evidence is robust and sufficient to ensure success at EPA. The tripartite relationship between apprentices, their employers and the university's expert team of tutors and mentors has created a supportive community of practitioners. The *Learner Coach* is realised as the apprentices, work-based mentors and university academic and mentoring teams learn new knowledge, skills and behaviours.

Notes

1 Trailblazer groups / Institute for Apprenticeships and Technical Education.
2 Specification of apprenticeship standards for England (SASE) - GOV.UK.

References

Andrea Laczik, A., Emms, K., and Patel, J. (2024). Investigating the experiences of the many stakeholders of degree apprenticeships. *SHRE News Blog*, September 11, 2024.

Antiss, T. (2020). 'Affirmations, reflections and summaries in coaching.' Chapter 11 in Passmore, J. (Ed.). *The Coaches' Handbook: The Complete Practitioner Guide for Professional Coaches*. Abingdon: Taylor & Francis Group.

Bandura, A. (1977). Self-efficacy: Toward a Unifying Theory of Behavioral Change. *Psychological Review*, 84(2), 191–215.

Bandura, A., Ross, D., & Ross, S. A. (1961). Transmission of aggression through imitation of aggressive models. *The Journal of Abnormal and Social Psychology*, 63(3), 575.

Bloom, B., Anderson, L. W., Sosniak, L. A., & National Society for the Study of Education. (1994). *Bloom's 'Taxonomy': A Forty-Year Retrospective: Ninety-Third Yearbook of the National Society for the Study of Education*. Chicago, IL: University of Chicago Press.

Collinson, D. L. & Tourish, D. (2015). Teaching leadership critically: New directions for leadership pedagogy. *Academy of Management Learning and Education*, 14(4), 576–594.

Day, D.V. (2000). Leadership development: A review in context. *Leadership Quarterly*, 11(4).

Department for Education (DfE). (2024, 24 September). Prime Minister overhauls apprenticeships to support opportunity. [Press Release] *GOV.UK*.

Dewey, J. (1916). *Democracy and Education*. New York: Macmillan.

Fisher, K. (2003). Demystifying Critical Reflection: Defining criteria for assessment. *Higher Education Research & Development*, 22(3), 313–325. https://doi.org/10.1080/0729436032000145167

Freire, P. (2000). *Pedagogy of Freedom: Ethics, Democracy, and Civic Courage*. New York: Rowman & Littlefield.

Gray, D. E. (2007). Facilitating management learning: Developing critical reflection through reflective tools. *Management Learning*, 38(5), 495–517

Hibbert, P. and Cunliffe, A. (2015). Responsible management: Engaging moral reflexive practice through threshold concepts. *Journal of Business Ethics*, 127(1), 177–188.

Holdo, M. (2023). Critical reflection: John Dewey's relational view of transformative learning. *Journal of Transformative Education*, 21(1), 9–25. https://doi.org/10.1177/15413446221086727

Hughes, C. J., & Saieva, G. (2019). Degree apprenticeships – An opportunity for all? *Higher Education, Skills and Work-Based Learning*, 9(2), 225–236. https://doi.org/10.1108/HESWBL-10-2018-0113

Iszatt-White, M., Kempster, S., & Carroll, B. (2017). An educator's perspective on reflexive pedagogy: Identity undoing and issues of power. *Management Learning*, 48(5), 582–596.

Jones, R. J. (2020). The business case for coaching. Chapter 2 in Passmore, J. (Ed.). *The Coaches' Handbook: The Complete Practitioner Guide for Professional Coaches*. London: Taylor & Francis Group, pp. 13–23.

Kolb, D. (1984). *Experiential Learning*. Englewood Cliffs: Prentice Hall.

Kolb, D. A. (2014). *Experiential Learning: Experience as the Source of Learning and Development* (2nd ed.). Harlow: Pearson Education.

Martin, L., Lord, G., & Warren-Smith, I. (2018). Juggling hats: Academic roles, identity work and new degree apprenticeships. *Studies in Higher Education*, 45(3), 524–537. https://doi.org/10.1080/03075079.2018.1550478

Meyer, J. P. (2003). Four territories of experience: A developmental action inquiry approach to outdoor-adventure experiential learning. *Academy of Management Learning & Education*, 2(4), 352–363.

Milad, M. (2017) Applying the CREAM strategy for coaching teaching practices. *AFOR Journal of Education*, 5(1), 65–82.

Nawaz, R. and Edifor, E. (2024). Degree apprenticeships: Voices from the frontline – Impact, policy and good practice guide. *The Quality Assurance Agency*. https://www.qaa.ac.uk/docs/qaa/members/degree-apprenticeships-voice-from-the-frontline-impact-policy-and-good-practice-guide-2024.pdf

Nawaz, R., Edifor, E.E., Holland, S.R., Cao, Q. and Liu, L.S. (2023). The impact of degree apprenticeships: analysis, insights and policy recommendations. *Transforming Government: People, Process and Policy*, 17(3), 372–386. https://doi.org/10.1108/TG-07-2022-0105

Nicholson, H. and Carroll, B. (2013) Identity undoing and power relations in leadership development. *Human Relations*, 66(9), 1225–1248.

Passmore, J. (2020). Coaching Defined and Explored. Chapter 1 in Passmore, J. (Ed.). *The Coaches' Handbook: The Complete Practitioner Guide for Professional Coaches*. Taylor & Francis Group, pp. 1–10.

Pavlov, I. P. (1897). *The Work of the Digestive Glands*. London: Griffin.

QAA. (2024). *Degree Apprenticeship: VOICES From The Frontline* www.qaa.ac.uk/docs/qaa/members/degree-apprenticeships-voice-from-the-frontline-impact-policy-and-good-practice-guide-2024.pdf

Reynolds, M. (2011). Reflective practice: Origins and interpretations. *Action Learning: Research and Practice*, 8(1), March, 5–13.

Richard, D. (2012). *The Richard Review of Apprenticeships*. London: Department for Business, Innovation and Skills (BIS).

Rynes, S. L., Trank, C. Q., Lawson, A. M., & Ilies, R. (2003). Behavioral coursework in business education: Growing evidence of a legitimacy crisis. *Academy of Management Learning & Education*, 2, 269–283.

Sammet, J., & Wolf, J. (2022). *From Trainer to Agile Learning Facilitator: How Teaching and Learning Works in Digital Times* (1st ed.). Berlin/Heidelberg: Springer. https://doi.org/10.1007/978-3-662-65909-0

Schedlitzki, D. (2019). Developing apprentice leaders through critical reflection. *Higher Education, Skills and Work-Based Learning* , 9(2), 237–247.

Schon, D.A. (1983). *The Reflective Practitioner: How Professionals Think in Action*. London: Maurice Temple Smith.

Skinner, B. F. (1938). *The Behavior of Organisms: An Experimental Analysis*. New York: Appleton-Century.

Smith, K. et al. (2023). Success measures within Degree Apprenticeships. *Three Rivers Conference* July. Available at: https://www.researchgate.net/publication/372267807_Success_Measures_within_Degree_A pprenticeships?channel=-doi&linkId=64ad5158c41fb852dd69f15b&showFulltext=true (Accessed: 29 August 2024).

Vince, R. (1998). Behind and beyond Kolb's learning cycle. *Journal of Management Education* , 22(3), 304–319.

Watson, J. B. (1930). *Behaviorism* (revised ed.). Chicago, IL: University of Chicago Press.

Weick, K.E. (1995). *Sensemaking in Organizations*. Thousand Oaks, CA: Sage Publications.

Whitmore, J. (1992). *Coaching for Performance*. London: Nicholas Brealey

Wolf, A. (2011). *Review of Vocational Education: The Wolf Report*. London: Department of Education (DfE) and Department for Business, Innovation and Skills (BIS).

Yates, J., & Yates, J. (2022). The GROW model: A framework for interventions. In Julia Yates (Ed.), *The Career Coaching Handbook* (2nd ed., pp. 118–127). Abingdon Oxfordshire: Routledge. https://doi.org/10.4324/9781003104827-12

14

Trailblazers

Demand-led apprenticeships! Yes, but by whom? The representativeness of apprenticeship trailblazers

Peter Dickinson and Emily Erickson

Introduction

Apprenticeships, in their publicly funded format, have been through a number of reforms since their introduction in 1994. In general, the reforms have been designed to improve the quality of skills provision, extend the range of people who might become apprentices, and expand delivery to higher levels. An important core aspect of the reforms has been to make apprenticeships more 'demand-led', at least from an employer perspective. For example, from 2013 apprenticeship Frameworks were replaced by apprenticeship Standards the contents of which are determined by employer-led groups called 'Trailblazers'. This gave employers some degree of monopsony power as there was scope to tailor apprenticeships to particular organisational needs (at least at the margin). This, in part, helps to address the 'free-rider' problem which is seen as a major barrier to employers investing in apprenticeships. Unlike Germany (the apprenticeship system most lauded in the UK), there is nothing to prevent free riders recruiting the training firm's apprentices upon completion of their training. This reduces the benefit of apprenticeship training to the Employer as they will fail to recoup its costs.

DOI: 10.4324/9781003567844-15

The changing face of apprenticeships

If the intention was to increase the number and level (as a proxy for quality) of apprenticeships, the reforms begun in the 2000s mostly worked. As Figure 14.1 shows, the number of apprentice starts increased significantly throughout the 2000s. Between 2002/2003 and 2011/2012, the number of starts increased by 210%. This was initially driven by an expansion in 19–24-year-old apprentices, and then by those aged 25+. In 2002/2003 (when the age cap was 24), the proportion of apprentices aged under 19 was 58% and those aged 19–24 42%. Whilst the numbers in both age groups increased, by 2011/2012, the respective percentages were 25% and 31%, with 25+ apprentices constituting 44%.

A parallel trend was the gradual decline in Intermediate apprenticeships. Whilst the numbers grew between 2002/2003 and 2011/2012, the percentage fell from 71% to 63%, reflecting employer demand for higher-level skills. Both trends continued into the 2010s with a flattening of the decline in younger apprentices, and an acceleration in the fall of the proportion of Intermediate apprentices.

The gradual switch from apprenticeship Frameworks to Standards in 2013 did not affect employer uptake of apprenticeships. The most significant changes post-2011/2012 were, firstly, the replacement in 2013/2014 of

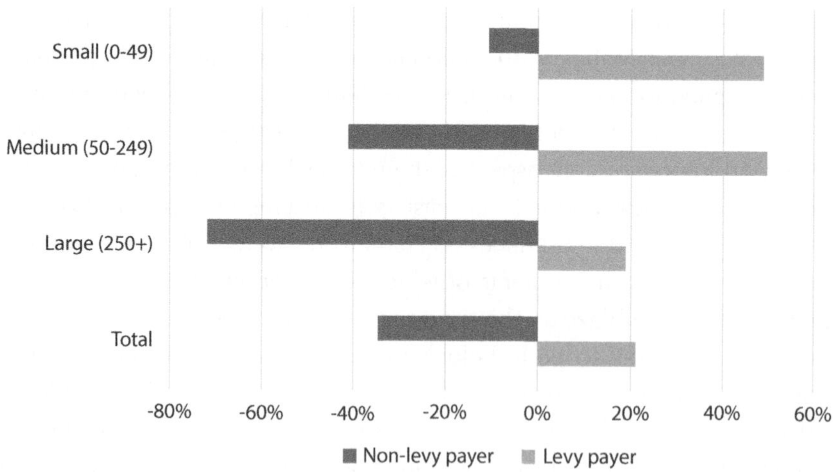

Figure 14.1 Change in apprenticeship starts 2017/18 to 2021/22 – levy and non-levy payers

Source: Authors' own analysis based on Department for Education apprenticeship data

Adult Skills Budget (ASB) grant funding with Advanced Learner loans for 24+ apprentices which reduced starts in the short term. And, secondly, a suite of reforms introduced in Spring 2017, the most impactful of which was the introduction of the apprenticeship levy (Dickinson and Hogarth, 2021). These reforms reduced the number of apprentice starts to levels not seen since 2009/2010.

Whilst the levy did not affect the longer-term trends of older (who tended to be existing employees rather than new entrants) and higher-level apprentices, the 2017 reforms (primarily the AL) introduced a new dimension which was the reduction in the proportion of non-levy-paying employers starting apprentices. As a result, the proportion of non-levy-paying employers fell by 43% (as well as numerically) between 2017/2018 and 2022/2023. In contrast, the proportion of levy-paying employers increased by 23% (as well as numerically) over the same period (Dickinson and Hogarth, 2021).

As levy payers tended to be larger organisations, the number of apprentice starts by smaller employers declined. As Figure 14.1 shows, the key factor was whether or not the organisations paid the levy. Across all employment sizes of employers, levy payers increased the number of apprentice starts whilst non-levy payers reduced theirs (Dickinson and Hogarth, 2021). The 2017 reforms have not been favourable to non-levy payers (who are predominantly smaller employers[1]). For levy payers, their levy pot has served as a ring-fenced budget for apprenticeships, whereas in the case of non-levy payers they had to contribute more funding to their apprenticeships because in the past they would have got it mostly for free (Dickinson and Hogarth, 2021).

Apprenticeships standards and trailblazers

Whilst the impact of the levy on smaller firms is clear from an analysis of apprenticeship data, no analysis has been undertaken of other apprenticeship reforms on employer size. This chapter fills that gap by developing a methodology for profiling the representativeness of employers involved in apprenticeship Trailblazers and analyses the extent to which they include smaller employers and sectors representing relevant occupations.

Apprenticeship Standards were introduced in 2014 as an eventual replacement of Frameworks, and the 2017 reforms committed to phasing them out altogether by 2020. Having employer designed Standards was a recommendation of the Richard Review in order to make apprenticeships: "...more relevant and therefore more attractive to existing and new employers" (Richard, 2012).

Standards differed from Frameworks in both their content and their development. The Standard is to contain the Knowledge, Skills and Behaviour (KSBs) that is sufficient to: "...ensure full competence in the relevant occupation is acquired" (HM Government, 2012). And to include a method of assessing those competencies at the end of the apprenticeship (the End-Point Assessment [EPA]). Standards are produced by a development group of employers, although other organisations can also be represented such as professional/membership bodies, sector organisations, providers and employer organisations (Dickinson and Erickson, 2022).

The requirements of Trailblazer groups were set out by the Institute for Apprenticeships and Technical Education (IfATE), to be: "...a group of employers recognised by the Institute and reflective of those who employ people in the occupation, including small employers".[2]

Trailblazer groups develop the occupational standards, which are a central component of the Standards, as well as the EPA, on which achievement of the apprenticeship is based. As Standards can take several years to develop, sitting on a Trailblazer is a significant commitment for which organisations are not paid. They consist of a group of employers but can involve other important stakeholders such as: employer and sector representative bodies; professional bodies; former sector skills bodies; and training providers. An average of nine organisations sit on each Trailblazer group, with the majority being employers. Some organisations sit on more than one Trailblazer. For example, BAE Systems, BAM Construction, BT, Rolls Royce, Ministry of Defence and Siemens sit on more than 30 each.

IfATE sought to ensure that Trailblazer members were representative of employers who employed people in the Standards' occupations by analysing the size and sector of Trailblazer organisations. IfATE may withdraw support for a Trailblazer group if it: "...considers that the Trailblazer group no longer has the support of a representative cross-section of employers in the occupational area, or refuses to work with other individual employers or groups of employers when requested to do so by us".[3] It is unclear whether or by what means IfATE measures representativeness, and whether they have ever withdrawn support for this reason.

By the end of 2022, 647 apprenticeship Standards had been approved for delivery.

Methodology

In 2022, the Gatsby Foundation commissioned the Warwick Institute for Employment Research (IER) to undertake an analysis of the size and sector of employers on the Trailblazer employer groups.

The analysis is based on a cross-section of Standards across the three levels of apprenticeships (Intermediate, Advanced and Higher [including Degree Apprenticeships]), based on the number of starts in 2018/2019, the last full year before the pandemic.

Within the top ten Standards by level and number of starts, nine Standards were selected (three per level), as shown in Table 14.1. Within each level there is a range of Standards covering different occupations and sectors, including sector-specific (e.g. hair professional) and generic (such as management) occupations.

Table 14.1 Apprenticeship standards sample

Level	Title	No. of starts 2018/2019	No. of Trailblazer organisations 2018/2019
Intermediate	Adult care worker	14,820	11
	Hair professional	6,700	17
	Commis Chef	2,200	19
Advanced	Team leader/ Supervisor	22,840	28
	Business administrator	10,790	45
	Installation electrician/ maintenance electrician	5,960	8
Higher	Accountancy/ taxation professional (Level 7)	6,810	27
	Nursing associate (Level 5)	4,310	17
	Associate Project Manager (Level 4)	3,350	25

Source: Warwick IER

The type of organisation on the nine Trailblazers was identified and (for employers) their size and sector were identified through web searches (including LinkedIn) and information from Companies House:

- The employment size of the organisation used the following bands: small (<50); medium (50–249); and large (250+); and,
- The sector was identified to 3-digit SIC (2007).

The occupations most closely related to the Standard were identified[4] and data collected about the number of workers, and the sectors and sizes of organisations they worked in. Data on the occupation and the sectoral profile of employment came from the Annual Population Survey (APS). Relevant occupations were converted into their 4-digit Standard Occupation Classification (SOC) designation(s). Then each 4-digit SOC was analysed against the Standard Industrial Classification (SIC) sector (3-digit SIC) of employment, and by employment size (small, medium and large).

Using the Accountancy/Taxation Professional – Level 7 Standard as an example, Table 14.2 shows the sectors and size bands of people working in the relevant occupations.[5] As a generic occupation, accountants and

Table 14.2 Largest employment sectors by size for Accountancy/Taxation Professional – Level 7 occupations – top five sectors of employment[a]

Sector (3-digit SIC)	Employment size			
	Small	Medium	Large	Total
69.2 Accounting and auditing activities	25,621	14,560	23,144	63,325
70.2 Management consultancy activities	23,361	5,597	18,605	47,562
84.1 State Admin & social/ econ. policy	2,740	3,868	23,675	30,282
62.0 Computer programming and consultancy	3,564	6,017	7,641	17,222
66.1 Activities auxiliary to financial services, except insurance and pension funding	2,830	3,139	7,046	13,014
Other sectors	37,932	42,246	71,757	151,935
All sectors	96,046	7,5427	151,868	323,340

[a] Numbers may not add up due to rounding.
Source: Warwick IER analysis of APS data 2019

taxation professionals work in a large number of sectors (140 3-digit SIC sectors). Because of this the top five only are shown; together these account for 53% of the total employment of accountants and taxation professionals.

The distribution of employment by sector was compared to the distribution of the employers represented on the Trailblazers. Table 14.3 shows that in 2022 there were 18 Trailblazer employers involved in setting the Accountancy/Taxation Professional – Level 7 apprenticeship Standard. Most of these employers (72% of Trailblazer employers) were in the SIC '69.2 Accounting and auditing activities sector'. The remaining five employers came from one sector each – only two of these appear in Table 14.2 (84.1 and 62.0). Ten other organisations were involved in this Trailblazer (see below).

The employment (APS) column shows the proportion of people in relevant occupations employed in these sectors. For example, the '69.2 Accounting and auditing activities sector' accounted for 20% of employment of occupations related to this Standard, but Trailblazer employers from this sector accounted for 72% of employers the Standards group.

Table 14.3 Comparison of the sector of Trailblazer employers for Accountancy/Taxation Professional – Level 7 occupations

Sector	Employment (APS) (%)	Trailblazer employers	
		No.	%
69.2 Accounting and auditing activities	20	13	72
84.1 Administration of the State and the economic and social policy of the community	9	1	6
62.0 Computer programming and consultancy	5	1	6
86.1 Hospital activities	2	1	6
56.3 Beverage serving activities	–	1	6
42.1 Construction of roads and railways	<1	1	6
Total	51	18	100
Main employment sector(s) not included above (ASP)			
70.2 Management consultancy activities	15	–	–
66.1 Activities auxiliary to financial services, except insurance and pension funding	4	–	–

Source: Warwick IER analysis

Other sectors were more aligned. For example, the '62.0 Computer programming and consultancy' accounts for 5% of employment and 6% of Trailblazer employers. However, three sectors had employer representation which was greater than accounted for by their share of occupational employment. Two main sectors which employed a significant proportion of this Standard's related occupations were not represented on the Trailblazer group. These were: '70.2 Management consultancy activities' (employing 15% of relevant occupations); and '66.1 Activities auxiliary to financial services, except insurance and pension funding' (employing 4%).

Therefore, accounting and auditing activities employers can be said to be overrepresented on the Trailblazer group. Whilst management consultancies, and activities auxiliary to financial services employers are underrepresented.

In a similar way, the employment size (small, medium and large) of employers was compared to those on the Trailblazer group (Table 14.4). Almost half (47%) of the related occupations for this Standard worked for large employers, around one quarter (23%) for medium-sized employers, and almost one-third (30%) for small employers. However, just under three-quarters (72%) of employers on the Trailblazer group were large employers, one in ten (11%) were medium sized employers and less than one in five (17%) were small employers. Therefore, large employers can be said to be overrepresented on the Trailblazer group, and small and medium-sized employers underrepresented.

Involvement in Trailblazer groups can be time-consuming as Standards can take several years to be developed (Dickinson, 2020). This might be off-putting to medium and smaller employers. It might be the case that non-large employers are represented by sector groups or other employer representative organisations. For each Standard, an analysis was undertaken of non-employer organisations sitting on the Trailblazer group. For the Accountancy/Taxation Professional – Level 7 Trailblazer, ten other organisations were represented:

Table 14.4 Comparison of the employment size of Trailblazer employers for Accountancy/Taxation Professional – Level 7 occupations

	APS employment (%)	Trailblazer employers	
		No.	%
Small (<50 employees)	30	3	17
Medium (50–249 employees)	23	2	11
Large (250+ employees)	47	13	72
Total	100	18	100

Source: Warwick IER analysis

- Eight were professional or membership body organisations, such as, Chartered Institute of Taxation (CIOT) and the Institute of Chartered Accountants in England and Wales (ICAEW);
- One was an employer organisation i.e. NHS Employers; and
- One was a training provider: Health Education East of England.

Therefore, as far as non-large employers were concerned there were no sector or employer organisations representing them.

Analysis

Sector representativeness of sample Trailblazers

All nine selected apprenticeship Standards were analysed in a similar way. Table 14.5 shows the sectoral representativeness of the Trailblazer groups compared to the employment distribution of the related occupations. The

Table 14.5 Sector representation of Trailblazer groups (3-digit SIC)

	No. of sectors represented in Trailblazer	% employment in Trailblazer sectors (%)
Accountancy/Taxation Professional - Level 7	6	36
Adult Care Worker – Intermediate	5	49
Associate Project Manager – Level 4	17	34
Business Administrator – Advanced	21	29
Commis Chef – Intermediate	7	70
Hair Professional – Intermediate	1	97
Installation Electrician/ Maintenance Electrician – Advanced	4	37
Nursing Associate – Level 5	4	69
Team Leader/Supervisor – Advanced	17	26

Source: Warwick IER analysis

analysis shows that three of the Standards – Commis Chef Intermediate, Hair Professional Intermediate and Nursing Associate Level 5 – have high levels of sectoral employment accounted for by the sector of its Trailblazer employers (all greater than 69%). However, Team Leader/Supervisor and Business Administrator (both of which are generic occupations) represent less than 30% of the sectoral employment coverage of the related occupations. This suggests that key sectors of employment are not represented on the Trailblazer. For example, three sectors together employ 14% of Team Leader related occupations but are not represented on the Trailblazer.[6]

It therefore appears that the Trailblazers of the more generic Standards are unrepresentative of the sectors where many of the related occupations are employed.

Employment size representativeness of sample Trailblazers

Table 14.6 undertakes similar analysis for the employment size representativeness of the selected Trailblazers. It shows the proportion of small (<50 employees), medium (50–249) and large (250+) employers employing the Standard related occupations and compares them to the employment size of employers on the Trailblazer group. A negative figure shows that

Table 14.6 Employment size representation of Trailblazer groups

	Small (%)	Medium (%)	Large (%)
Accountancy/Taxation Professional – Level 7	−13	−12	25
Adult Care Worker – Intermediate	−40	−12	52
Associate Project Manager – Level 4	−23	−13	36
Business Administrator – Advanced	−27	−16	44
Commis Chef – Intermediate	−74	−18	92
Hair Professional – Intermediate	−39	13	26
Installation Electrician/Maintenance Electrician – Advanced	−23	8	15
Nursing Associate – Level 5	−52	−15	67
Team Leader/Supervisor – Advanced	−41	−10	51

Source: Warwick IER analysis

the size group is underrepresented, and a positive figure means that it is overrepresented. For example, 35% of organisations employing Associate Project Manager relevant occupations are small employers whereas 12% of employers on the Trailblazer group are small employers. This gives a figure of −23% indicating that small employers are underrepresented.

Table 14.6 shows that small employers are underrepresented on all the Trailblazer groups whilst large employers are overrepresented. Medium-sized employers are underrepresented on seven Standard groups and over-represented on two.

The overrepresentation of large employers is greatest for: Commis Chef (+92%); Nursing Associate (+67%); Adult Care Workers (+52%); and Team Leaders (+51%). These are also the Trailblazer groups where the underrepresentation of small employers is greatest.

The level of underrepresentation of medium-sized employers is similar across the seven Standards. Medium-sized employers are overrepresented in the Hair Professional and Installation Electrician Trailblazer groups.

Conclusions

This chapter has analysed the impact of apprenticeship reforms on the take-up of apprenticeships by smaller employers. It has looked at the impact of the AL on the number of starts by levy and non-levy payers and, by extension, larger and smaller employers. Non-levy payers have seen a significant fall in the number of starts. Conversely, it is levy payers (i.e. larger employers) where the number of apprentice starts has increased.

Other aspects of the reforms have not been researched, including the move to Standards. One element of the 2017 reforms was to phase out apprenticeship Frameworks completely by 2020 and replace them with Standards (a process started in 2014). The Trailblazer groups tasked with producing the Standards were expected to be representative of organisations who employ people in the occupation, including small employers. However, the analysis has shown that the nine Trailblazer groups selected for analysis in this study are mostly dominated by large employers. In addition, the spread of sectors Trailblazer employers cover is often narrower than where people in Standard-related occupations work. This is a greater issue for generic occupations such as accountants and project managers. It is not the case that smaller organisations are represented through other organisations. Very few of these 'other' organisations are sector or employer representative organisations. Most are training providers or professional/membership bodies.

Standards take a long time to develop and representation on Trailblazer groups requires a significant organisational commitment; this is likely to be the reason that larger organisations tend to dominate. However, being able to represent an organisation's interest has the capacity to influence the content of Standards and thereby contribute to the cost–benefit calculation for the returns on investments in training.

Similarly, Trailblazers tend not to include a number of sectors where Standard-related occupations work. Only three Trailblazers included employers in sectors that accounted for more than half of employment in Standard-related occupations. Unrepresentativeness is greatest in those Standards relating to more generic occupations such as project managers.

Undertaking the analysis for this study has been challenging because the data on Trailblazer representation is not organised. There is no information on the sector and employment size of Trailblazer employers. Given that representativeness is a key part of the remit for Trailblazers, such information should be collected as the norm. There should be agreement on a basic set of standardised information to be collected so their representativeness can be assessed.

Notes

1 Based on the median earnings of all employees in the UK, a wage bill of £3 million equates to 128 employees in 2017 and 108 in 2022. The levy threshold has not risen in line with average earnings.

2 https://www.instituteforapprenticeships.org/developing-new-apprenticeships/trailblazer-group/.

3 https://www.instituteforapprenticeships.org/developing-new-apprenticeships/trailblazer-group/.

4 Examples of the occupations the Standard covers is included in the occupational standard see https://www.instituteforapprenticeships.org/apprenticeship-standards/.

5 The most relevant 4-digit SOCs for this Standard were: 2421 Chartered and certified accountants; 2423 Management consultants and business analysts; and 3535 Taxation experts. https://www.instituteforapprenticeships.org/apprenticeship-standards/accountancy-or-taxation-professional-v1-0.

6 The three sectors are: '47.7 Retail sale of other goods in specialised stores' (6% of employment in related occupations); '81.2 Cleaning activities' (4%); and '55.1 Hotels and similar accommodation' (3%).

References

Dickinson, P. (2020). *Future-proofing apprenticeships*. Co-op Group.

Dickinson, P., & Erickson, E. (2022). *Profiling employers involved in Apprenticeship Trailblazer groups*. Gatsby Foundation.

Dickinson, P., & Hogarth, T. (2021). *The Benefits of Hindsight: Assessing the impact of apprenticeship reforms on employer behaviour*. Edge Foundation and Gatsby Foundation.

HM Government. (2012). *The future of apprenticeships in England: Guidance for trailblazers – from standards to starts*. Department for Business, Innovation and Skills.

Richard, D. (2012). *The Richard review of apprenticeships*. BIS.

References

PART II

Industry context

15 Health and social care

Transformative learning through apprenticeships

Rhidian Lewis, Naowarat Lewis, and Adrienne Sharples

Introduction

The University of Bedfordshire, whilst not unique in respect of its support for diverse learner groups, is an organisation that has achieved a significant degree of positive impact upon its apprenticeship population, with a significant number of apprentice learners achieving full-time employment or career progression after completion of their apprenticeship studies. The Faculty of Health and Social Sciences hosts the largest number of apprentice learners within the university and supports both clinical health and social work apprenticeship study. The delivery of such programmes is based upon a longstanding tradition of engagement between the faculty and local employers who themselves are challenged to meet the needs of a diverse and complex client base.

Apprenticeship programmes not only differ in their subject focus, but also in the demographic characteristics of their learners and the duration of service within the workplace environment. At the University of Bedfordshire, many of our apprentices come from a widening participation background, often with limited prior education experiences or financial constraints that prevent them from pursuing a traditional degree programme and accumulating student debt. As a result, these individuals may not have reached their full academic or occupational potential. Apprenticeships in nursing associate and social work roles have been an attractive and successful choice into registered practitioner roles for such individuals, and a way for organisations to develop their staff into workforce vacancies. Through this pipeline,

DOI: 10.4324/9781003567844-17

organisations can grow a labour force that meets a nationally agreed competency framework set by employers (Stone & Worsley, 2021; Church, 2024; Institute for Apprenticeships, 2022a, b), thus meeting learner aspiration and creating immediate and longer-term social impact.

The transformative nature of apprenticeships within the Higher Education section is multifaceted, reflecting not only the needs of the Learners, but also the organisations where the Learners are based. To explore this situation, we have elected to examine the Level 5 Nursing Associate and the Level 6 Social Worker Degree Apprenticeship, which represent the clinical and social care aspects of the faculty as well as representing both Higher and Degree Apprenticeship (H&DA) Study. Our case study approach will be based upon the learner experience, and their perceptions of their apprenticeship learning journey to explore the value and impact of undertaking an apprenticeship to their service users and wider employing organisations.

Case studies

Social work

The interviewee had, at the time of beginning the Social Worker Degree apprenticeship, worked for over a decade as a Community Care Officer and as such took the decision to undertake the degree apprenticeship. This undertaking was one made to not only support career development but also satisfy a personal interest in the broader aspects of social care.

The interviewee received full employer support and undertook the degree apprenticeship through a "day release" approach. The interviewee identified that the opportunity to achieve the Social Worker degree was only possible as self-funding a degree programme would not have been possible. The apprenticeship approach offered not only opportunities for new learning but also a mechanism by which learning could take place alongside relevant placement experience whilst maintaining employment within their current employer environment.

The interviewee identified that the degree apprenticeship gave an opportunity to not only build upon existing understanding but also explore a range of scenarios that would be encountered as a qualified Social Worker. Throughout the apprenticeship the opportunities to learn new theories, reflect upon exiting understanding and apply to practice scenarios were highlighted as of significant benefit. It was acknowledged that initially the depth and range of theoretical material was "challenging", but through reflective actions coupled with practice placements in a variety of scenarios it was possible to apply, refine and reinforce knowledge and skills. The interviewee recognised that personal development had been ongoing throughout the apprenticeship. These were identified as the ability to link theory to practice, to demonstrate increased capacity for critical thinking, to expand autonomous working, and to develop self-confidence within the professional setting.

The interviewee recognised that the apprenticeship is designed to increase in complexity and that this, in turn, supports the practice environments experienced both within the apprenticeship and in the workplace setting. In recognition of this, the interviewee articulated that as a learner the process of professional development is one that evolves from a conscious effort to align theory with practice to a state in which application of knowledge becomes "fluid" to the professional scenarios and takes place "almost subconsciously". The development throughout the apprenticeship was one limited to not only academic development but also a significant development in confidence to engage in different scenarios that would not have been possible without the apprenticeship. The interviewee recognised that, as a consequence of the apprenticeship, employment as a full-time Social Worker had been made available. Whilst at the initial stages of this new role senior managers continue to demonstrate significant confidence through inclusion in new and challenging opportunities.

Nursing associate

Zoe, the nursing associate interviewee, had always held ambitions to be a nurse from an early age. Life took over and Zoe took a series of non-healthcare roles. Nonetheless, her motivation to nurse was reignited when she needed treatment in a large city hospital. While Zoe had already achieved the necessary qualifications to enter nurse education, the cost of training was prohibitive. Therefore, she took a job as a healthcare assistant to gain care experience and when the apprenticeship route for nursing associates was first available in her organisation, Zoe was suitable to be selected given her extensive experience and qualifications.

The first thing Zoe noticed when she started her apprenticeship was the large gaps in her knowledge. While she had training and experience of undertaking certain procedures as a healthcare assistant, the underpinning theory was often missing.

> I knew for example, I would be taking a set of observations to check for signs of people being ill – but the underpinning anatomy, physiology – the "whys" and depth were missing – my apprenticeship gave me that knowledge from the start.

The apprenticeship also included placements, which gave Zoe exposure to other clinical environments outside her substantive community role – hospitals and doctors' surgeries and mental health services for example. Zoe noted these opportunities gave her a holistic understanding of the patient journey, and helped her to see the integration of health and social care services. It also offered a chance to practise and apply her skills gained on the job as an apprentice within other contexts. Zoe explains that an apprentice brings existing knowledge; during the apprenticeship, this is built upon so new knowledge slots into existing like a "jigsaw puzzle" with university modules linking together over time. There were opportunities during the apprenticeship to reflect, and reflective learning was a big part of her journey to uncover areas for development and further practise, and to develop her confidence and autonomy.

The apprenticeship also covered wider areas, including safeguarding and understanding national legislation, and policies and nursing ethics. The theory covered in the university sessions is then applied in practice placement and in her substantive job, supported by her academic tutors and work colleagues. These experiences helped her understand the care provided to longstanding patients in depth. Zoe explained that the nursing associate was a new registered role, regulated by the Nursing and Midwifery Council in 2018, and it could be difficult for longstanding colleagues to understand what her scope of practice was and to give her the autonomy the new role demanded. Nonetheless, her managers championed the role and trusted Zoe as they knew her well. This support was vital for colleagues and gave them the confidence to help her develop.

Modelling case study outcomes

The case studies presented here aim to demonstrate how adopting an apprenticeship approach can lead to positive outcomes for the apprentice, employer and wider stakeholders. Additionally, they examine the mechanisms by which new knowledge and skills are introduced, the opportunities for learners to refine and adapt their learning to new settings, and the development of professional competencies including:

- Criticality
- Self-determination
- Accountability
- Confidence

Whilst the apprentices interviewed as part of this study are following different career paths and, therefore, are studying for different apprenticeship standards (Nursing Associate – Higher Apprenticeship and Social Worker Degree Apprenticeship), both programmes of study possess defined periods of "practice placement". Here the Employer provides appropriate scenarios into which the apprentices will have the opportunity to apply and build upon newly acquired knowledge and skills within a range of workplace contexts. This approach, therefore, contributes towards developing a practitioner who can meet the challenges of ever-changing service user needs and service provision.

In reviewing the interviews undertaken with both apprentices we identified a number of commonalities revealed through personal testimony. The apprentices both recognised that the apprenticeship itself comprises formal settings in which learning activities were constructed as a means of introducing new knowledge and skills within their respective professional care environments. In addition to this, both were able to articulate the influence of lecturers and practice educators in supporting their professional development. Both interviewees highlighted the impact of those with primary responsibility for the delivery of training within the academic environment and that of the practice educator whose primary role is to support the apprentice during periods of practical engagement within the workplace setting.

As a means of collating the experiences of the individual apprentices, the authors believe it is important to review the learning opportunities and the ways in which apprentices develop throughout the duration of their apprenticeship. The modelling of learning is not a new concept, with the existence of a number of well-established models, including Dunn and Dunn (1979), Kolb (1984), Curry (1983, 1987) and Grasha (1994, 1996). The model initially proposed by Lewis (2019), as presented in Figure 15.1, is built upon

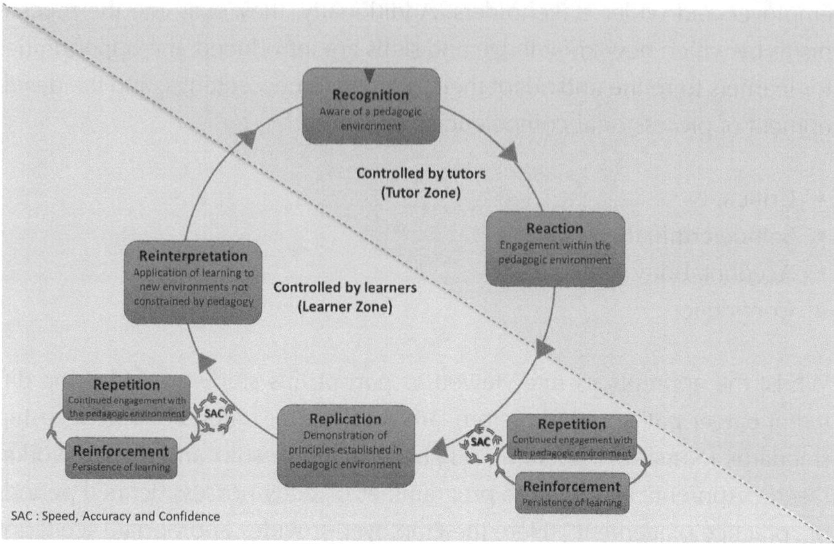

Figure 15.1 The iterative learning model (Lewis, 2019)

the initial work of Kolb (1984). However, the Lewis (2019) model introduces several additional features to that proposed by Kolb (1984). These include: the span of control afforded the tutor and learner; the phases through which a typical learner will pass when new knowledge or skills are presented; and the opportunities through which repetition and reinforcement are most often necessitated to support learner development.

The iterative learning model (Lewis, 2019)

The environment in which apprenticeships take place adds an additional layer of complexity to this model. Apprenticeships require learning to occur within a practice environment determined by the Employer in consultation with the training provider. This creates a duality of learning for the apprentice, where new knowledge and skills, initially encountered in the classroom, are expected to be applied and assessed within a health and social care setting. To account for this, a minor adaptation is made to the initial model (see Figure 15.2). While small, this adjustment is crucial and reflects statements made by the apprentices regarding their practice environment. In this setting, work experience is coupled with clear opportunities to reflect upon practice experience, review previously learned theory and adapt to

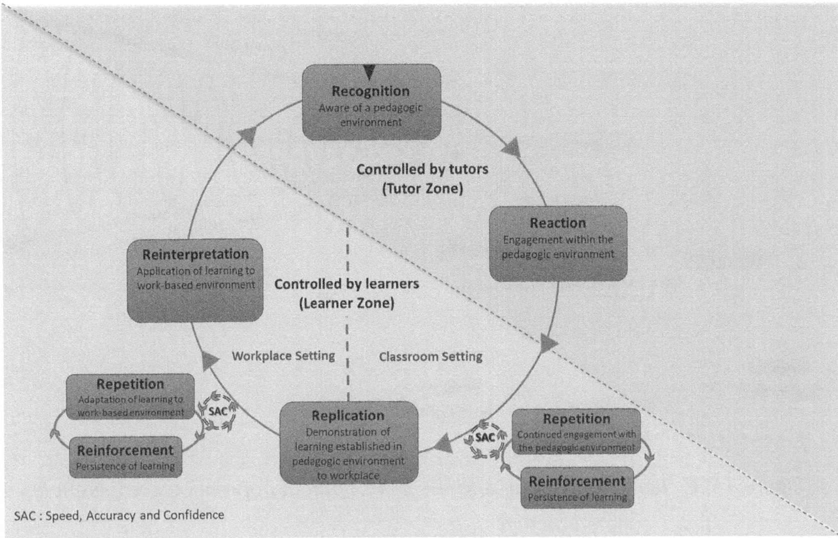

Figure 15.2 Adapting the iterative learning model to the apprenticeship setting

increasingly complex scenarios within their professional roles as the apprenticeship programme progresses.

In applying and adapting a modelling approach to the outcomes from the case study interviews it was noted that the apprentices referenced the ongoing development nature of the learning associated with the apprenticeship within the health and social care environments. As such, both apprentices recognised that whilst the formal structure of an apprenticeship was based upon acquisition of Knowledge, Skills and Behaviours these elements were not themselves isolated and form part of a continuum of development through each unit/module of learning. Both apprentices were keen to identify that encountering new theories and skills with the ongoing opportunity for their application to the work setting or defined "practice placements" supported a number of additional benefits, including the "confidence to challenge", "willingness to make decisions", "eagerness to add value to the end user" and "professional recognition by one's peers". In the apprentice's view, these outcomes were directly related to the structure of the apprenticeship, which builds upon knowledge and skills introduced at earlier points in the programme or within an individual unit/module and, as such, is highly relevant to the health and social care practice environment. To account for this, the model introduced in Figure 15.2 cannot be taken in isolation and is, as such, a single element in the overall learning process

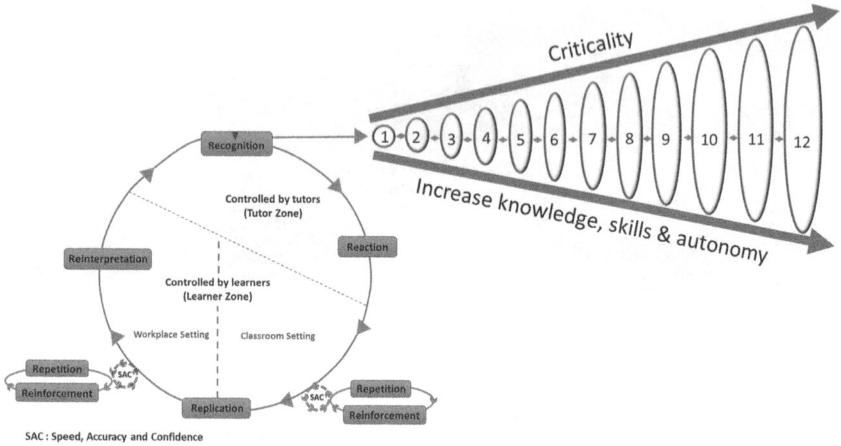

Figure 15.3 Iterative learning and the development apprentice competencies

which is experienced by the apprentice as they encounter new aspects of subject knowledge or are introduced to new skills and techniques. Expanding this model is therefore presented within Figure 15.3, which serves to highlight that the stages of recognition, reaction, replication and reinterpretation are themselves repeated throughout the delivery of each unit/module through the influence of the tutor/practice educator and the application demonstrated by the apprentice in the context of health and social care settings. This model therefore seeks to visualise the transformative nature of the learning process as experienced by the interviewees and as the apprentice becomes increasingly familiar with the content and application of each unit/module they ultimately gain subject area knowledge and the ability to apply knowledge through the familiarity of a skills approach, as well as intrinsic benefits such as enhanced autonomy, criticality and self-determination.

Exploration of the apprenticeship learning journey using the iterative learning model (Lewis, 2019)

In our experience, the apprenticeship route provides a learning journey that fosters the development of health and social work practitioners who are fit for contemporary practice through several different methods. As illustrated in the case studies, apprentices begin their first year of training with some practical skills competence, but a limited theoretical understanding of the work they regularly perform. During their first year of their apprenticeship, they are guided by their academic tutors and colleagues in practice to become a practitioner who can apply a theoretical base to their pre-existing knowledge and current practise through a critical lens. This development allows individuals to progressively identify their skills and knowledge gaps in their new role as the apprenticeship progresses. By the end of their apprenticeship, it provides a strong foundation for building proficiency and supports the growth of the apprentice into an evolving, lifelong autonomous learner in practice.

Furthermore, the apprenticeship framework promotes a highly supportive partnership between academics and practitioners within the apprentice's own workplace. This approach strengthens the apprentice's personal psychological resources, enabling them to meet the demands of contemporary practice and reducing attrition within the sector. The curriculum introduces learners to reflective practice, a tool that is key in developing personal resilience (Grant & Kinman, 2019). Benefits to the Learner gained from embedded opportunities to practise and develop skills are best achieved through the implementation of a supportive environment in which workplace colleagues and lecturers play key roles. This learning approach promotes mastery of the subject matter, thereby informing and promoting practice-focused self-efficacy (Guerrero et al., 2024). Innovative assessment tasks that are strongly reflective of the skills needed in professional practice promoted within the University of Bedfordshire in the taught curriculum support individual learning differences, thereby promoting academic and professional self-confidence. The creation of an environment for learning in which the apprentice acquires new knowledge and skills both within the traditional teaching and in employer environments is one which offers opportunities for not only personal development but also an increase in intellectual capital within the Employer setting and, ultimately, creating wider societal benefits as the apprentice achieves professional competence.

The desire to achieve mutually beneficial outcomes through the development or employment of an apprentice is well-established in policy. As such, this ambition expands the scope of learning beyond the traditional learner–tutor relationship, emphasising the increased importance of the Employer and workplace environment in the learning process. The development of the apprentice throughout the duration of the apprenticeship, whilst following a linear approach typical of higher education programmes, includes many opportunities for self-reflection and conscious reengagement with both knowledge and skills as a means of assuring adaptation to different practice-based scenarios. Whilst the design of assessments and the scenarios presented within the practice setting afford apprentices opportunities to demonstrate understanding and advancement, the development of professional characteristics such as self-awareness, autonomy and confidence are themselves developed through the process of reinforcement gained by repeated engagement with knowledge and skills introduced within the apprenticeship programme. A conscious approach which encourages reflection, repetition and reinforcement will, in turn, add value not only to the Learner (who becomes increasingly proficient and confident) but also to those who use their services and the Employer who benefits from an increase in staff potential. Maintenance and enhancement of the individual and wider workforce can, once the practices of self-reflection, repetition and reinforcement become familiar, be promoted through engagement with formalised training engagements or through the process of self-determined learning.

To achieve the wider ambition for apprenticeship programmes, where the Learner, employer and wider society all benefit, stakeholders must recognise the differences between an apprenticeship-based approach to learning and the traditional path of direct-entry students in the 'helping' professions. For our purposes, this distinction is based upon the premise that all apprentices by their nature are employees, and, as such, are continuously exposed to the work environment which for direct entry students, may be a component of their programme, but is (as is the case for practice placements) designed to provide valuable albeit limited experience.

For both students and apprentices, the primary goal remains that the Learner undergoes a process of "transformation", with the outcome marked by the achievement of an academic award. However, for apprentices, the key difference lies in the immediate application of newly acquired knowledge and skills within the workplace. This results in apprentices not only earning an academic award but also receiving recognition for their professional competence. To enable this outcome, it is necessary for apprentices to be provided with an environment of support that not only acknowledges the rigorous academic and professional practice nature of the programme but also values the development of the individual through self-examination, reflection, personal growth and continued learning.

References

Church, E. (2024, September 2). The role of apprenticeships in growing the nursing workforce. *Nursing Times*. https://www.nursingtimes.net/education-and-training/the-role-of-apprenticeships-in-growing-the-nursing-workforce-02-09-2024/

Curry, L. (1983, April 11–15). *An Organization of Learning Styles Theory and Constructs* [Conference Session]. The Annual Meeting of the American Educational Research Association, Montreal, Quebec. http://files.eric.ed.gov/fulltext/ED235185.pdf

Curry, L. (1987). *Integrating Concepts of Cognitive or Learning Style: A Review with Attention to Psychometric Standards*. Canadian College of Health Service Executives.

Dunn, R. & Dunn, K. (1979). Learning styles/teaching styles: Should they ... can they ... be matched? *Educational Leadership*, 36(4), 238–244. https://files.ascd.org/staticfiles.ascd/pdf/journals/ed_lead/el_197901_dunn.pdf

Grant, L. & Kinman, G. (2019). Developing emotional resilience and wellbeing: A practical guide for social workers. *Inform*. https://adults.ccinform.co.uk/practice-guidance/guide-developing-social-workers-emotional-resilience/

Grasha, A. F. (1994). A matter of style: The teacher as expert, formal authority, personal model, facilitator, and delegator. *College Teaching*, 42(4), 142–149. https://doi.org/10.1080/87567555.1994.9926845

Grasha, A.F. (1996). Teaching with style: The integration of teaching and learning styles in the classroom. *The Professional & Organizational Development Network in Higher Education*, 7(5) 1995–1996. https://podnetwork.org/content/uploads/V7-N5-Grasha.pdf

Guerrero, J. G., Attallah, D. M., Gomma, N. H., & Ali, S. A. (2024). Improvements in practising nurses' knowledge, skills, self-efficacy, confidence, and satisfaction after a simulated clinical experience of caring for a patient undergoing chemotherapy: A quasi-experimental study. *BMC Nursing*, 23(1), 66. https://doi.org/10.1186/s12912-024-01727-0

Institute for Apprenticeships and Technical Education. (2022a, February 21). Registered nurse degree (NMC 2018). *Apprenticeships*. https://www.instituteforapprenticeships.org/apprenticeship-standards/st0781-v1-1

Institute for Apprenticeships and Technical Education. (2022b, October 31). Social worker (integrated degree). *Apprenticeships*. https://www.instituteforapprenticeships.org/apprenticeship-standards/st0510-v1-1

Kolb, D. A. (1984). *Experiential Learning: Experience as the Source of Learning and Development*. London: Prentice-Hall. https://www.fullerton.edu/cice/_resources/pdfs/sl_documents/Experiential%20Learning%20-%20Experience%20As%20The%20Source%20Of%20Learning%20and%20Development.pdf

Lewis, N. (2019). *Pedagogy through Technology: Investigating Different Technology Approaches to the Pedagogic Environment of Undergraduate Education*. https://aru.figshare.com/articles/thesis/Pedagogy_through_technology_investigating_different_technology_approaches_to_the_pedagogic_environment_of_undergraduate_education/23764671 [arror.anglia.ac.uk]

Stone, C. & Worsley, A. (2021). 'It's my time now': The experiences of social work degree apprentices. *Social Work Education*, 41(4), 675–690. https://doi.org/10.1080/02615479.2021.1873936

16

Education

The academic professional apprenticeship: runway or roadblock to professional development in higher education?

Debbie Reel

The APA model: Entry to expertise

The design of the Academic Professional Apprenticeship (APA) is full of promising and exciting intentions as a programme led by a set of professional competencies designed specifically for those new to developing learning and teaching in higher education (HE). Whilst promising and exciting intentions for professional development are an important foundation for the APA, it must be acknowledged that the model brings a financial gain via the apprenticeship levy which helps the higher education institution (HEI) pay for the delivery of the APA. O'Leary et al. (2019), as well as Brindley et al. (2024), posit this as a significant driver across the HE sector for implementing the APA. However, any initial financial gain arguably does not out measure the long-lasting professional development experiences the APA has the potential to create.

Before its introduction, universities offered Postgraduate Certifications in Higher Education linked to Professional Practice. These carry numerous names including: PGCAP, PCAP, PGCertHE. Whatever the title given, however, the programmes are designed to provide staff new to teaching in HE theoretical and practical guidance and grounding in effective learning and

DOI: 10.4324/9781003567844-18

teaching practices. Many of these programmes are also accredited by Advance HE's Professional Standard Framework (PSF) (Advance HE, 2023), leading to the international recognition of Fellowship. The introduction of the APA has not replaced the postgraduate qualification; instead, the two work in conjunction, with the APA providing the umbrella under which the postgraduate qualification sits along with the other components of the APA. So, why the change? Why add to a postgraduate programme that already offers theoretical and practical opportunities to enhance learning and teaching? With these questions, the introduction of the APA has not been without complication and some level of frustration (Figure 16.1).

It is important to understand that the APA and its key components as an education-based apprenticeship reach beyond that of a traditional PG Cert. With two specialist routes to choose from, either teaching or research, not only does it dovetail with any institution's accredited PG Cert, but it also offers dedicated time for:

Regular tripartite meetings attended by employers and providers of the apprenticeship who support, monitor and set targets for further professional development towards the meeting of the APA standards.

'Off the Job' activities where the apprentice can maximise opportunities for engagement in professional development specifically related to their needs.

Completion of the Knowledge award (PG Cert), usually accredited by Advance HE, leading to the additional award of Fellowship.

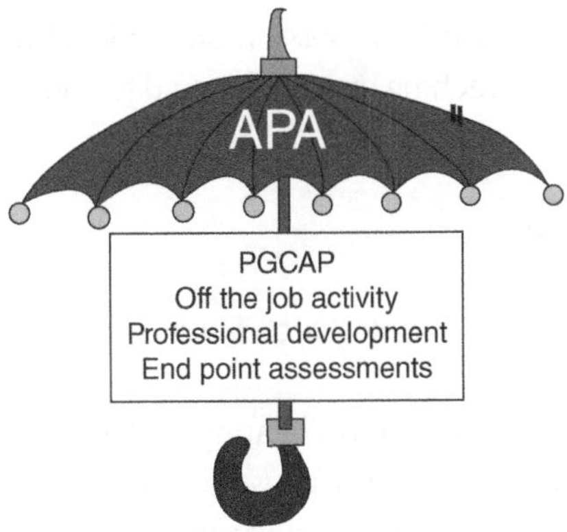

Figure 16.1 Umbrella diagram showing the relationship between the APA and PGCAP

This culminates in multiple awards including:

- PGCert HE, which carries M level credits
- L7 Academic Professional Apprenticeship
- Advance HE Fellowship.

The depth to which these are achieved is framed by the 39 APA components that must be evidenced across the programme, regularly reviewed and finally assessed through three submission points that have been described by Brindley et al. (2024) as more complex than the traditional PGCert HE. There is the danger of the components being met as part of a tick box exercise as the requirements are distinct and definite in nature. With this, it can be assumed that the APA focusses more on the logistics of the programme, as purported by Brindley et al. (2024), rather than on the needs to the apprentices themselves as they navigate a new career trajectory. It is here, however, that opportunities arise. With strategic planning and support and the real time afforded to the completion of the programme, this education apprenticeship model, designed to stretch and challenge, to apply skills, to create collegiate experiences and transform practice, can encourage the novice lecturer to engage with, lead on and develop strategies that they may not otherwise consider.

Case Study

This case study demonstrates the powerful impact of the PGCAP and the APA on enhancing teaching practices and transforming practices. The lecturer's journey, which began with a PGCAP session on Student Voice, led to significant improvements in their teaching approach and development, professionally.

Key outcomes

1) Engagement in an Action Research Study

In response to a PGCAP session on hearing and acting upon student voices, the lecturer conducted a small-scale study interviewing international students before and after implementing changes, gathering honest feedback about the curriculum, teaching methods, and a sense of belonging.

2) Meaningful Changes – Based on the feedback, the lecturer made several module improvements:

    - Diversified the guest speaker programme.
    - Incorporated global examples into teaching.
    - Developed activities to better prepare students for the global economy.

3) Professional Growth – The APA provided additional time and resources, enabling the lecturer to:

    - Present findings at conferences.
    - Assume an Academic Course Lead role and now an Associate Head role.
    - Lecture annually to new APA cohorts about their experience.

4) Impact on International Students

The study addressed the often-marginalised voices of international students, aligning with research showing that international students may be reluctant to speak up or seek help due to cultural differences. By actively seeking and responding to their feedback, the lecturer created a more inclusive learning environment. This case exemplified the value of listening to student voices, particularly those from diverse backgrounds, and demonstrated how incorporating student feedback can lead to more effective, culturally responsive teaching practices. The approach taken by the lecturer aligned with recommendations for providing tailored support to international students during their transition to a different academic culture.

5) Professional Development through PGCAP and APA

The combination of PGCAP and APA proved instrumental in the lecturer's growth, with the PGCAP initiating the focus on student voice and the APA providing the time and resources to extend the research and implement change. This highlights how these programmes supported the lecturer to become more reflective and impact transformative approaches to education.

> The additional time and resources facilitated by the APA gave me the tools and understanding to go on to develop my career in higher education in a variety of ways. I was able to play a significant part

in the rewriting and revalidation of our course and the course work I completed during the APA has also led to my PhD, which seeks to understand the transformational potential of higher education for health and social care higher and degree apprentices.

(APA Learner)

The APA model: Pragmatic perspectives

Managing identities: What does being an APA apprentice look like?

Whilst the intentions of the APA in moving the new lecturer from novice level to expertise are indeed admirable and often tangible, the realities of this always being the case creates debate. This begins in its simplest form as the term 'Apprentice', as part of Level 7 Degree Apprenticeship, has created uncertainty and ambiguity amongst extremely professional staff who are new to HE. There is inevitable complexity in dual identity and agency as highly trained professionals are asked to identify as an apprentice and/or a student (Brindley et al., 2024; Fabian et al., 2022). This begins at the onboarding stage, where these staff are asked to complete an application process to secure a student identity, and complete Basic Key Skill Builder tests in maths and English as well as complete mandatory training that duplicates that already completed as a member of staff new to an HEI. Until February 2025, they have had to present GCSE certificates. Many of these tasks are synonymous with that expected of a traditional student, with whom, arguably, staff do not recognise themselves as being. Smith et al. (2021) attribute this matriculation into student life as a problematic part of an apprenticeship. This relates to the suitability and challenges across career stages. Smith et al. (2021) continue by acknowledging the tensions within apprenticeship programmes as they can create a 'One-Size-Fits-All Dilemma' and it is crucial to recognise the potential pitfall of applying uniform work and study restrictions across diverse apprentice populations as this approach fails to differentiate between:

- Recent school leavers entering the workforce.
- Experienced professionals transitioning into HE roles.
- Dual role challenges for HE professionals.

This situation often leads to frustration amongst lecturers who find themselves in the role of both educator and student. They must navigate their professional responsibilities while adhering to an apprenticeship framework that can feel overly restrictive and time-constraining, especially for those with significant prior career experience in industry.

The challenge, therefore, lies with the inflexibility of an education apprenticeship model that struggles to accommodate the varied needs and personal experiences of apprentices at different career stages, particularly within the HE sector alongside the time to reflect on and transform practices.

Who advocates for the apprentices' time?

Although the APA incorporates dedicated "Off the Job" hours that should be protected to foster professional growth, the time for these crucial development opportunities is frequently underappreciated and underutilised. This disconnect stems from:

- Competing priorities in the workplace.
- Lack of understanding about the importance of structured learning time.
- Pressure to focus on immediate job tasks over long-term skill development.

The result, then, is a tension between the ideals of work-based learning and the realities of implementing it effectively within busy professional environments. Whilst the concept of learning through practical experience is inherently valuable, the execution can be problematic.

This dichotomy is further perpetuated by the provider/employer relationship. As part of the APA, the institution acts as both. Poole et al. (2023) refer to the significant levels of negotiation that must take place between provider and employer to ascertain when and how sufficient time will be afforded to the Learner to ensure all apprentice tasks can be completed in a timely manner. The fact that these two are often found in the same organisation compounds the issue as it is often the provider (those delivering the programme) having to negotiate with the Employer (often Line Managers) for the time allocation to be honoured.

The impact of both the complexities and the intricacies of this programme can significantly affect the fundamental principles of apprenticeship delivery. Whilst employers recognise the necessity of time allocation, their focus often remains on the broader perspective of managing their teaching team and overall programme delivery. This includes the challenge of effectively operating with one team member on study leave for a day each week.

Meanwhile, providers find themselves in a challenging position, balancing their own programme management needs while also advocating for learners. As Poole et al. (2023) highlight, providers invest considerable time negotiating on behalf of apprentices, who may find themselves at odds with their employers (Jackson, 2019).

To address these challenges, Vasant (2023) proposes a holistic approach that is referred to as a 'whole employer approach'. This strategy aims to minimise conflict and promote a more cohesive and integrated approach to off-the-job training hours. The recommendation for a full day per week dedicated to training, rather than fragmented hours here and there, appears to be a more sustainable and practical method for supporting effective long-term professional development. This approach not only addresses immediate training needs but also fosters a more harmonious relationship between employers, providers, and apprentices, potentially leading to more successful outcomes for all parties involved.

Who advocates for the apprentices' voice?

Apprenticeship success is significantly influenced by the apprentice's perspective, attitude, and ability to fully engage with the programme. The dual identity of being both an employee and a student, coupled with time constraints, can impact the overall apprenticeship's effectiveness. However, the concept of "Apprenticeship Awareness" introduces an additional layer of complexity that can either support or hinder the success of educational apprenticeships.

Unlike traditional degree pathways, where students use their own voices and make their own choices, apprenticeships, particularly in cases like the APA, are often driven by financial considerations and staff development linked to probationary periods (James Relly & Laczik, 2021). Mclaughlin (2024) refers, within a Bourdieu framework, that it is a sense of belonging and feeling of fitting in that influences decision-making in where and what to study. However, with the case of an educational apprenticeship, as in the case of the APA, this situation creates a scenario where apprentices may have limited or no voice or choice in their participation, potentially affecting their engagement and motivation. The lack of agency and Apprenticeship

Awareness in deciding to pursue an apprenticeship programme can have significant implications:

Motivation: Apprentices who feel they had no choice in their educational path may struggle with motivation and engagement.

Understanding: Without proper awareness, apprentices might not fully grasp the benefits and expectations of their programme.

Identity conflict: The imposed nature of the apprenticeship may exacerbate the tension between professional and academic identities as previously discussed.

Success factors: Key elements for apprenticeship success, such as employer support and the quality of mentorship, may be undermined if the apprentice is not fully invested in the process.

To mitigate these issues, supportive strategies can be implemented, for example:

Proactive engagement: It is crucial to identify and connect with prospective apprentices at the earliest opportunity. A comprehensive induction process should be developed, showcasing the programme's key features, benefits, and expectations. This early intervention serves to demystify the apprenticeship journey, alleviating potential anxieties and misconceptions. By providing clear, accessible information from the outset, apprentices can shift their focus from initial uncertainties to the positive aspects of their role and the long-term advantages the programme has to offer. This approach prepares apprentices for a more engaged and motivated participation in the programme, cultivating a sense of ownership and engagement.

Bridging theory and practice: The education apprenticeship model, while standardised, often encounters challenges due to the diverse nature of disciplines and varying individual capacities to meet set standards. Dismore (2014, p. 589) refers to the challenges in the shift from a 'transfer of educational knowledge' to people moving between different contexts as they engage in an apprenticeship. To address this, it is crucial to implement a more nuanced approach. By identifying and engaging well-trained mentors and tutors early in the process, a more personalised alignment between job roles and both on-the-job and off-the-job learning can be achieved. These experienced professionals can play a pivotal role in bridging the gap between theoretical knowledge and practical application, effectively helping apprentices navigate and reconcile their dual identities as both employees and students. This tailored support system can significantly enhance the relevance and effectiveness of the apprenticeship experience. Establishing this level of comprehensive support can guide apprentices through the complexities of balancing work and study commitments.

By adopting these approaches, organisations can create a more conducive environment for apprenticeship success, even when initial participation may not have been entirely voluntary.

The APA model: Enhancing the educational workforce

The chapter so far has highlighted that although faced with challenges, the primary objective of an educational apprenticeship should encompass a shared commitment from both the Employer and the training provider to:

- Upskill the education workforce.
- Create pathways for career development and progression within the educational field.

In the context of the apprenticeship programme a distinctive feature has already emerged that supports this, in that the Employer and the provider are often part of the same institution, albeit representatives from different departments. This shared institutional background fosters a common understanding of the apprentice's needs.

The alignment between employer and provider within the same institution can offer significant advantages:

- Enhanced programme delivery: The shared understanding of the apprentice's needs facilitates a more tailored and effective learning experience.
- Improved continuity: With both parties operating within the same organisational framework, there is potential for smoother transitions between theoretical learning and practical application.
- Holistic development: The institution can leverage its comprehensive resources and expertise to support the apprentice's growth more effectively.

This innovative approach to educational apprenticeships fosters a symbiotic environment that can potentially yield enhanced outcomes for both apprentices and the institution. One of the primary benefits of this model is its ability to address skills gaps. Educational apprenticeships serve as a catalyst for bridging the divide between 'knowing in practice' and the 'acquisition of abstract knowledge' (Horden, 2015, p. 187). Whilst 'knowing in practice' typically refers to profession-specific skills acquired on the job, apprenticeships offer a unique opportunity to close the 'acquisition of knowledge' gap.

These programmes provide apprentices with diverse experiences across the organisation, enabling them to forge relationships with colleagues from various disciplines. This cross-functional exposure creates a framework for the professionalisation of practice, revealing previously unrecognised talents and potential. As apprentices develop professional competencies and gain discipline-specific skills, their career aspirations and progression opportunities are positively impacted. Moreover, research by Hughes and Saieva (2021) has highlighted an unexpected benefit – the cultivation of leadership qualities, which further enhances career advancement prospects. By integrating practical experience with theoretical knowledge, educational apprenticeships create a comprehensive learning environment that prepares individuals for success in their chosen fields while simultaneously benefiting the institutions that host them.

This case study examines the journey of a novice educator in a HEI, illustrating how the apprenticeship programme was strategically leveraged to facilitate professional advancement through self-directed off-the-job activities. The apprentice, armed with extensive industry experience, embarked on the APA with a clear vision: to craft a trajectory towards a Senior Lecturer position while simultaneously bolstering their candidacy for an Academic Course Lead role.

Recognising the potential of the apprenticeship as a catalyst for career progression, the individual approached the programme with a deliberate focus on aligning their chosen off-the-job activities with their professional aspirations. Intentional learning opportunities were created which aligned current practice with potential future career opportunities. This strategic approach demonstrates how apprenticeships can be tailored to support specific career goals within the HE sector, bridging the gap between industry expertise and academic proficiency.

The apprentice worked with mentor, tutor and professional colleagues, university-wide to integrate their own role with off-the-job activity which included:

- Programme creation
- Module leadership
- Academic Conduct Officer role
- Attendance at conferences
- Assessment development

By showcasing this apprentice's proactive stance, the case study underscores the flexibility and potential of apprenticeship programmes in HE to foster targeted professional development and career advancement. Consequently, the transformative potential of educational apprenticeships in shaping professional trajectories can have a significant positive impact on employee retention. By creating bespoke professional development opportunities, these apprenticeships can create a sense of institutional loyalty as apprentices gain institution-specific experiences and competencies, which may encourage them to remain with their current employer rather than transferring their newly acquired skills elsewhere.

> I have since become an Academic Course Lead and deliver workshops and teaching each year to later PGCAP cohorts on the importance of academics understanding the links between research, relational pedagogy and student experience and outcomes.
>
> (APA Learner)

Hunt et al. (2025) conducted a study on the impact of apprenticeships and found a recurring theme among participants in that they recognised that the apprenticeship could support their transition into managerial roles and felt a sense of professional progression in their work. These findings position educational apprenticeships as having medium- to long-term value, rather than being limited to immediate, short-term benefits apparent during the apprenticeship period (Quew-Jones, 2022). The long-term rewards of educational apprenticeships, which extend beyond the duration of the programme itself, offer continued value as apprentices progress in their careers. However, it is crucial that all stakeholders. including the institution, mentors, and apprentices themselves, recognise and nurture this long-term potential. This ensures that apprentices can fully reap the benefits of their investment in the programme, creating a win–win situation for all parties. By fostering a culture of continuous learning and professional growth, educational apprenticeships can not only enhance the skills and capabilities of individuals but also contribute to the overall strength and stability of the institution's workforce.

However, despite the evident advantages of the APA and its positive influence on the professional workforce, its long-term sustainability has recently come under threat. In May 2025, the government's 'Plan for Change' introduced a sweeping overhaul of the apprenticeship system, posing a significant risk to the future of the APA. The government's strategy aims to prioritise funding for young people embarking on apprenticeships at the start of their careers. While this focus is important, it will inevitably lead to reduced funding for new entrants to Level 7 apprenticeships, including the APA.

The government seems optimistic that employers will continue to invest in professional development and support staff in gaining new Knowledge, Skills, and Behaviours while in employment. However, the financial pressures currently facing English higher education institutions, evidenced by a growing number of course closures as universities attempt to stabilise their finances, suggests that there will be little, if any, budget available to support programmes that were previously funded creating a significant risk to the future of the APA (OfS, 2024).

Concluding remarks, reflections and ways forward

The APA serves as a launchpad for newcomers to academia, offering a structured pathway to create, develop, and refine experiences along a trajectory from novice to expert. This journey can lead to innovative opportunities and enhanced professional development experiences that are often not readily accessible to those new to academia so early in their careers. The limited availability of such opportunities due to one's newcomer status, challenges in developing a sense of belonging, and lack of awareness about available resources underscores the invaluable nature of the APA.

However, this runway to academic expertise is not without its challenges. Throughout this chapter, we have explored several potential roadblocks, including:

- Identity crises.
- Time constraints.
- Misunderstandings about the nature and purpose of apprenticeships.

- Questions about stakeholder interests.
- The perceived value of the apprentice's voice throughout their journey.
- Challenges to funding.

These issues can pose significant challenges to the smooth execution and success of the programme. Nevertheless, given that the fundamental aim of this programme is to enhance the educational workforce, it should serve as a catalyst for educational institutions to:

- Adapt their practices.
- Allocate sufficient time.
- Allocate sufficient funding
- Engage collaboratively with apprentices.

By doing so, institutions can ensure that continuous learning, professional growth, and the cultivation of well-developed staff remain at the forefront of their priorities. This approach not only benefits the individual apprentices but also contributes to the overall strength and quality of the institution's academic workforce.

In essence, whilst the APA presents challenges, its potential to transform academic careers and institutional capabilities makes it a valuable investment for all parties involved. The key lies in recognising these challenges and proactively working to overcome them, thereby maximising the benefits of this innovative approach to academic professional development.

Suggested further reading

Blog. https://www.santanuvasant.com/2023/12/06/the-academic-professional-apprenticeship-adjusting-to-change-and-how-to-make-it-work/

References

Advance HE (2023) Professional Standards Framework for teaching and supporting learning in higher education (PSF 2023) [PDF]. Available at: https://www.advance-he.ac.uk/sites/default/files/2022-06/The_Draft_Revised_Professional_Standards_Framework_0.pdf (Accessed: 24 November 2025).

Brindley, J., Poole, R., Cook, F., & Sims, S. (2024) Identity formation and conflicting priorities of early career academics studying the academic professional apprenticeship in England, *Journal of Vocational Education & Training*, 1–28. Available at: https://doi.org/10.1080/13636820.2024.2443919

Dismore, H. (2014) Experiencing the transition from an apprenticeship to higher education, *Journal of Education and Work*, 27:6, 585–607. Available at: https://doi.org/10.1080/13639080.2013.802831

Fabian, M., Alexandrova, A., Coyle, D., Agarwala, M. & Felici, M. (2022) Respecting the subject in wellbeing public policy: beyond the social planner perspective. *Journal of European Public Policy*. Available at: https://doi.org/10.1080/13501763.2022.2093947

Horden, J. (2015) Higher apprenticeships in England: professional and vocational formation, *International Journal of Training Research*, 13:3, 174–193. Available at: https://doi.org/10.1080/14480220.2015.1051350

Hughes, C., & Saieva, G. (2021) The journey of higher degree apprenticeships, in: D.A. Morley and M.G. Jamil, eds. *Applied Pedagogies for Higher Education: Real World Learning and Innovation across the Curriculum*. Cham: Palgrave Macmillan, Chapter 11.

Hunt, I., O'Connor, S., Young, K., Ryan, A., Butler, E., Power, J., & Hennessy, M. (2025) Generation apprenticeships – a perspective through the lens of industry learners, *International Journal of Logistics Research and Applications*, 1–19. Available at: https://doi.org/10.1080/13675567.2025.2458691

Jackson, J. (2019) Physiotherapy apprenticeships - Building on the experiences of in-service physiotherapy students, *Physiotherapy*, 105, e118–e119.

James Relly, S., & Laczik, A. (2021) Apprenticeship, employer engagement and vocational formation: a process of collaboration. *Journal of Education and Work*, 35(1), 1–15. https://doi.org/10.1080/13639080.2021.1983524

McLaughlin, S. (2024) Using Bourdieu's concept of habitus to explore higher education decision-making for working class women on an access to higher education course, *Studies in the Education of Adults*. Available at: https://doi.org/10.1080/02660830.2024.2374617

O'Leary, R., Mudd, S., & King, H. (2019) Reflecting on the academic professional apprenticeship: Lessons learnt at a large higher education institution, *Educational Developments*, 20(4), 19–22.

OfS. (2024) Navigating financial challenges in higher education. *OfS Insight*, 21. Available at: https://www.officeforstudents.org.uk/media/kegazm0o/insight-brief-21-financial-challeges.pdf

Poole, R., Cook, F., Sims, S., & Brindley, J. (2023) Challenges, barriers and strategies for engaging in level 7 apprenticeship studies, *Journal of Education and Work*, 36:2, 153–168. Available at: https://doi.org/10.1080/13639080.2023.2167953

Quew-Jones, R. (2022) Enhancing apprenticeships within the Higher Education curriculum – an action learning and action research study, *Action Learning: Research and Practice*, 19:2, 146–164. Available at: https://doi.org/10.1080/14767333.2022.2056135

Smith, S., Caddell, M., Taylor-Smith, E., Smith, C., & Varey, A. (2021) Degree apprenticeships - a win-win model? A comparison of policy aims with the expectations and experiences of apprentices, *Journal of Vocational Education & Training*, 73:4, 505–525. Available at: https://doi.org/10.1080/13636820.2020.1744690

17 Business and management

What is the price of progress amidst apprenticeship funding reform?

Clare Taylor and Stephanie Reynolds

The evolving landscape of business and management apprenticeships

Business and Management Higher and Degree Apprenticeships (H&DAs) are some of the most popular apprenticeships in the UK.

In the academic year 2023/2024, 339,580 new apprenticeships commenced. Of those, 94,880 apprentices (28%) chose apprenticeship programmes in Business, Administration, or Law (known as Tier 1 subject group), making them the most in-demand subject group that year. These Tier 1 apprenticeship standards include a wide range of disciplines, such as:

- Accounting and Finance
- Business Management
- Administration
- Marketing and Sales
- Legal and Law Services

Within this Tier 1 subject group, 35,510 apprentices (37%) started a Level 4, 5 or 6 Business Management apprenticeship and 18,960 apprentices (20%)

DOI: 10.4324/9781003567844-19

commenced a Level 7 Business Management apprenticeship, showing the continued growth and popularity of these programmes (Department for Education, n.d.).

Against this landscape, in May 2025, the UK government announced that Level 7 DAs would no longer be eligible for apprenticeship levy funding (Jeffreys, 2025). However, in a rapid U-turn in August 2025, the government announced a Level 7 apprenticeship funding extension for five healthcare professions until 2028–2029, to allow delivery of the government's ten-year healthcare plan (Mellor, 2025). From January 2026, popular Business and Management Level 7 standards will be directly impacted by the revised funding regulations, signaling a major shift in the H&DA landscape with potentially significant and wide-reaching impacts (Moss, 2025). Ministers said this will "rebalance" funding towards lower levels (2, 3 and 4). Education Secretary Bridget Phillipson went on to say that Labour will invest in a "shared, stronger economic future through Britain's young people" and that "we're backing the next generation by giving young people more opportunities to learn a trade, earn a wage and achieve and thrive" (GOV.UK, 2025).

However, there is growing concern among employers, training providers and professional bodies – such as the Chartered Management Institute (CMI), The Law Society, and the Institute of Chartered Accountants in England and Wales (ICAEW) – regarding the potential consequences of withdrawing Level 7 funding. Specifically, there is a risk that this policy change could reduce the appeal of lower-level DAs as a viable alternative to traditional university degrees. This could potentially undermine social mobility by restricting access to higher education for individuals from disadvantaged backgrounds (Prospects, 2025). FE Week (2025, July 26) goes on to support this, stating that data shows 60% of Senior Leader apprentices come from some of the UK's most deprived areas. The collapse of this standard will have a significant impact on targets for social inclusion and mobility, but will also, importantly, remove the opportunity for continuing professional leadership development for aspiring leaders and managers in a wide range of sectors across England.

With the change in funding policy, undoubtedly more attention will now be paid to Level 6 DAs as they too have been successful in bolstering the economy, fueling social mobility and tackling skills shortages (Nawaz et al., 2022). Level 6 DAs remain a cost-effective and impactful route for the upskilling of employees of any age by employers and continue to be eligible for levy funding (Mayne, 2025).

Anne Dibley, head of post-experience and apprenticeship programmes at Henley Business School (Mayne, 2025) agrees:

> Strong offerings at Level 6 and below that meet crucial skills gaps should secure the attractiveness and reputation of apprenticeships into the future. The target audiences may change, but younger learners will benefit, which is very positive.

But Petra Wilton, Director of Policy & External Affairs at the CMI, an organisation that has been a trailblazer (see Chapter 14) in the design and implementation of leadership and management apprenticeships, plus an awarding body for the Senior Leader standard, said:

> *The decision to significantly cut funding for Level 7 apprenticeships remains a disappointment.*
>
> (Moss, 2025)

In response to the consultation with employers and professional bodies ahead of the final announcement on funding in May 2025, the government granted two exceptions: learners who are under 21 at the start of their programme will continue to have access to Level 7 apprenticeship funding, as well as those who are care leavers or have an Education, Health and Care Plan (EHCP), with eligibility up to 25 years of age (Chowen, 2025a).

Even with such exceptions, Wilton is very pessimistic about the future of Business and Management H&DAs and goes on to add:

> *The government's decision to restrict level 7 funding to those under 21 does not address the UK's ongoing skills gap in management capability. This decision to withdraw eligibility for those over 21 years wipes out virtually all funding for senior leader apprenticeships, and that early-career learners are not at the stage in their working lives to undertake senior leadership training.*

The Chartered Institute of Personnel and Development (Mayne, 2025) concurs:

> *The decision to restrict government funding for all level 7 apprenticeships to those aged 16 to 21 is unlikely to meaningfully boost youth*

participation given that fewer than one in 10 apprentices who train at this level fall within this age bracket.

While the most recent data on Level 7 apprenticeships does not provide a breakdown by individual standards, earlier analysis by FE Week (Chowen, 2025b) indicates that the Accountancy and Taxation Professional and Solicitor apprenticeships have been the most popular among younger learners. As a result, these standards may be marginally less impacted by the January 2026 funding changes compared to others that primarily attract older apprentices.

With this narrowing of eligibility, a critical question for training providers now emerges: will delivering courses to these smaller cohorts remain a viable proposition? With the announcement of these restrictions, the reality for Business and Management standards such as the Senior Leader means the applicant pipelines will be unsustainable resulting in the removal of these standards from provider portfolios altogether (FE Week, 2025).

Wilton goes on to share her organisation's regrets on the policy change for Level 7 DAs:

Independent research found that level 7 Senior Leader apprenticeships are a key driver of multi-million-pound economic growth and social mobility across the UK. They are overrepresented by people who were on free school meals and who were the first in their families to go to university. These raise aspirations and offer tangible gains for hard-working families across the country.

(Moss, 2025)

Government policy continues to provide strategic support for Level 6 DAs and evidence suggests that they are well-positioned to drive skills development, contributing to long-term growth and sectoral impact (Nawaz et al., 2022). Against this backdrop, this chapter examines two Level 6 DAs: Chartered Manager Degree Apprenticeship and Accounting and Finance Manager Degree Apprenticeship. Presented as short case studies, these DAs illustrate the breadth of the Tier 1 subject group curriculum, and the diverse Knowledge, Skills and Behaviours the apprentices develop throughout their programmes of study.

Each case study includes a brief overview of the standard and different stakeholder perspectives on the successes and challenges of each DA.

Case Study 1 Chartered Manager Degree Apprenticeship (CMDA)

Overview of the standard

The CMDA serves as a strategic asset for organisations by addressing the demand for work-ready business graduates and professionals capable of making an immediate impact (UVAC, 2024). Purposely designed to develop targeted competencies aligned with current leadership and management industry standards, the CMDA ensures that aspiring and early-career managers acquire essential business management capabilities relevant to today's workplace. Organisational trailblazers involved in its design include NHS England, NSPCC, Easy Jet, Amazon, Corndell & Morrisons (see Chapter 14 for more information).

The CMDA is an all-age apprenticeship for future managers and attracts a wide range of apprentices from all sectors – private, public, and third – and organisations of various sizes. Unlike those in traditional academic programmes, CMDA apprentices vary in age, academic backgrounds, and management experience, with some not having undertaken any kind of formal study for some time (Horackova et al., 2023). As a result, it is common for a CMDA cohort to include a mix of apprentices with varying levels of academic and workplace experience. This diversity can be highly beneficial, fostering collaboration and cross-boundary knowledge sharing, but it also presents challenges, as apprentices may be at varying career stages and face differing workplace demands. This topic is explored further in Chapter 4.

The CMDA remains the longest on-programme apprenticeship with a period of three to five years (Skills England, n.d.-a). Progression from the CMDA often leads to the Level 7 Senior Leader Apprenticeship, forming a continuing professional development pathway for many apprentices. However, with changes to funding rules, upward mobility will likely become restricted for those over the age of 21, potentially making the Level 6 CMDA the highest publicly funded standard available to them. As a result, greater attention will no doubt shift to this qualification, presenting a unique opportunity for trailblazers, training providers and employers to further develop and refine the standard to meet the evolving leadership and management needs of contemporary organisations – both large and small.

The CMDA programme is built around three core pillars that guide the development of apprentices' Knowledge, Skills and Behaviours:

1. **Organisational Performance**
   Delivering a long-term purpose – operational strategy, project management, business finance, sales and marketing and digital business & new technologies
2. **Interpersonal Excellence**
   Leading people, developing collaborative relationships and communication
3. **Personal Effectiveness**

Awareness of self and others, management of self and decision-making
Over the course of the three or four years, apprentices immerse themselves in a comprehensive programme designed to deepen their understanding of contemporary business, leadership and management practices, strengthen their workplace skills, and enhance their organisational behaviour – ultimately benefiting their teams, improving service delivery, and contributing to stronger organisational outcomes.

The flexible nature of the CMDA standard means that for open programmes, where apprentices from different organisations come together, the nature of the learning, teaching and assessment is often determined by the training provider and shaped by evolving workplace realities, with considerable flexibility in the timing, delivery, and format in alignment with CMDA standards. By contrast, for closed programmes, uniquely designed for a single organisation, the learning, teaching and assessments may be more closely co-created to reflect the specific organisational context, priorities, and strategic goals.

Achievements and success on the CMDA are monitored through regular assessments such as written reports, collaborative projects, live presentations and reflective portfolios, putting the apprentice and their workplace at the heart of the learning.

A CMDA apprentice from the charity sector reflected on their experience of a particular aspect of the learning and teaching process:

> *The module on Leadership...has been transformative for my role as Technology Innovation Manager. Understanding the nuanced differences between leadership and management through relevant theories, such as Transformational Leadership, has allowed me to reframe*

how I approach driving innovation. Comparing these theories to real-world practices within my organisation highlighted the importance of adaptive leadership to inspire and influence diverse teams.

The CMDA culminates in a two-stage End-Point Assessment (EPA) comprising:

1. A work-based project and presentation demonstrating how apprentices apply the required Knowledge, Skills and Behaviours through a business-related initiative.
2. A portfolio with Q&A elements, featuring work-based evidence and testimonials that showcase the apprentice's application of leadership and management in practice.

Our charity sector apprentice goes on to add:

Reflecting on my own coaching practice enhanced my ability to mentor and support team members effectively, creating a high-performance culture. This has enabled me to better articulate organisational values, ensuring inclusivity, accessibility and collaboration remain at the forefront. By providing me with practical tools for coaching, this has enhanced my ability to drive change and promote innovation.

Upon completing the CMDA, apprentices are awarded an undergraduate degree and Chartered Manager status from the CMI – a prestigious recognition of their leadership and management excellence. This designation signals a strong commitment to their ongoing professional development and demonstrates the apprentice's expertise to their employer and peers.

Reflections on this standard

Opportunities for diversification

Business and Management DAs offer flexible frameworks that can be adapted to meet sector-specific needs, thereby expanding opportunities for employers across diverse industries. At the University of Gloucestershire, the CMDA has been adapted to include a specialised hospitality pathway. This CMDA-Hospitality features bespoke modules such as *The Experience Economy* and *International Hotel and Tourism Management*, customised specifically to meet the demands of this unique sector.

Innovatively, it is delivered through a remote campus model based in central London hotels, bringing sector-specific learning and strategic insights directly to apprentices in their professional environments. This tailored approach is highly valued by employers, enabling vital professional development without prolonged absences from demanding work environments. It has also proven to be an effective tool for attracting high-calibre early-career talent into the UK's hospitality industry – an especially strategic advantage amid record vacancy levels in the sector (People Management, 2024). Looking ahead, the future for such programmes appears strong, with a likely renewed emphasis on Level 6 standards that continue to support and promote organisational resilience and leadership capability.

Changes in the standard

In 2026, the CMDA will be replaced by the Leadership and Management Professional Apprenticeship (LaMP). Developed in collaboration with the Trailblazer group, LaMP introduces a stronger emphasis on strategic 'golden threads' embedded throughout the curriculum. These threads reflect shifting priorities in contemporary leadership practice, including sustainability, ethics, equality, diversity and inclusion, as well as digital skills and artificial intelligence.

The revised standard moves away from a focus on individual business functions – such as law, marketing, and budgeting – and instead centres on the development of professional behaviours in the workplace, encouraging a more holistic approach to leadership and management beyond technical skill acquisition (Trailblazers, 2025).

The revised LaMP standard is anticipated to become the principal development pathway for aspiring managers.

Case Study 2 – Accounting Finance Degree Apprenticeship (AFDA)

Overview of the standard

On the AFDA, an apprentice develops the expertise to manage financial systems and processes and support strategic decision-making through budgeting, forecasting, and data analysis. They learn to lead teams, ensure compliance, and use technology to deliver accurate financial insights, bridging operational and strategic functions within finance.

Organisational trailblazers involved in the design of this standard included Ernst and Young, Coventry University, Thomson Reuters Professional (UK) Ltd, the University of Portsmouth, the Institute of Financial Accountants, Sage UK Ltd and Jaguar Land Rover (see Chapter 8 for more information).

An apprentice typically spends 36 months on programme and the standard emphasises the following domains of knowledge and skill acquisition (Skills England, n.d.-c):

1. Financial Management & Reporting
   Manage financial systems, internal controls, and reporting processes, conduct reconciliations, ensure compliance with tax regulations, legislation, governance, and ethical standards.
2. Strategic Analysis & Decision Support
   Analyse financial and non-financial data, market trends, and competitor activity, contribute to business planning, performance analysis, forecasting, financial insights to stakeholders.
3. Budgeting, Cash Flow & Risk Control
   Manage budgeting processes, analyse variances, monitor and forecast cash flows, manage credit control, identify sources of finance, develop internal controls to manage financial risk and safeguard assets.
4. Systems, Security & Compliance
   Oversee accounting systems for cyber security and data integrity, ensure compliance standards, support strategic implementation and decision-making.
5. Leadership, Communication & Team Management
   Lead and manage finance teams, maintain professional relationships with clients, suppliers, auditors, and regulatory bodies. Demonstrate strong communication, ethical conduct, and a commitment to continuous improvement.

For Ascentant Accountancy (2024), a specialist firm based in Derby providing outsourced legal cashiering services to law firms, employing apprentices has proven to be a strategic and highly effective approach to workforce development. The company's director, Kevin Drew, believes apprenticeships offer a sustainable pipeline for talent acquisition and team growth. Their firm integrates apprentices into the business every six months, so they can shape and develop individuals from the outset, aligning their training with the organisation's specific operational needs and culture. Drew highlights that apprentices bring enthusiasm, adaptability, and strong digital literacy – qualities that are increasingly essential in a tech-driven accounting environment. Their ability to quickly grasp new technologies often surpasses that of more experienced hires, making them particularly valuable in such a niche practice.

Like the CMDA, this DA is concluded with a project report with presentation, plus a further professional discussion underpinned by a portfolio of evidence of their Knowledge, Skills and Behaviour development whilst on programme.

Progression routes from this DA would normally be into a role as an Accountancy or Taxation Professional and on to Chartered Status via a Level 7 apprenticeship. Depending on the age of the apprentice at the end of this award, there is now only a slim chance they may still be eligible to continue onto the Level 7 Accounting or Taxation Professional Apprenticeship, but very low numbers of apprentices are under 21 years of age on finishing their DA (Chowen, 2025b).

Reflections on this standard

The accountancy sector has been an early adopter of apprenticeship pathways, driven by the need to expand the talent pool entering the profession, with the DA being a central pillar of this targeted workplace skills development. Accountancy remains one of the few sectors in the economy to offer a comprehensive progression route from Level 2 to Level 7, providing young people with opportunities to advance significantly within the field (Johnson, 2025).

ICAEW, a global professional body for chartered accountants, has been vocal in its frustration over the 2025 government funding policy change, stating that apprenticeships work, with the number of school leavers entering accountancy doubling since the introduction of the levy in 2017.

But the average starting age of a Level 7 ICAEW apprentice is 22 not 21. The ICAEW (2025) has warned that the withdrawal of funding for this cohort is likely to produce unintended and far-reaching consequences for firms, the professional skills pipeline, and the broader economy.

Evidence from outsourcing specialists AdvanceTrack (AAT, 2024) further highlights the issue, with nearly half (45%) of accounting firms surveyed reporting they are 'severely' or 'significantly' affected by skills shortages

– challenges exacerbated by an ageing workforce and the retirement of baby boomers. Disruptions to the talent pipeline are therefore expected to generate substantial and lasting impacts.

John Chase, Unit Accountant, Leeds Teaching Hospitals NHS Trust, Leeds (John, 2025) agrees:

> *From an employers' perspective 21 and below would seem too low and would have excluded many of our current apprentices...One of the biggest benefits of the level 7 apprenticeship is the diversity of people it brings in. It opens the door for people from all sorts of backgrounds, many of whom wouldn't have been able to afford a higher-level qualification otherwise. This means we can attract a more varied and diverse group of individuals, which makes our workforce stronger and more reflective of the population we serve.*

It remains to be seen how this plays out, but the government is keen for employers to pay for Level 7 study programmes themselves. This would free up the new Growth and Skills Levy (Gov.UK, 2024) to pivot towards young people through new foundation apprenticeships, designed for 16–21-year-olds, or up to age 24 for apprentices who were in care, in prison or with an education, health and care plan (Chowen, 2025b) (Table 17.1).

But the Accountancy and Taxation Professional is the most popular of all the Level 7 apprenticeships:

While larger firms may be able to absorb the additional costs associated with the withdrawal of funding, smaller practices are unlikely to match the current levels of financial support. Rob Alder, ACCA's Head of Apprenticeships and Relationships (Johnson, 2025), agrees:

Table 17.1 Most popular apprenticeships between September 2022 and 2024

Top 20 most popular Level 7 apprenticeships	Starts between September 2022 and so far in 2024
Accountancy or taxation professional	17585
Senior leader	11814
Advanced clinical practitioner (Integrated Degree)	2709
Solicitor	2090

Source: Camden (2025)

Training accountants isn't cheap, so many organisations have used level 7 funding, particularly given already-under-pressure training budgets. Nowhere will this be felt more keenly than in the public sector and small to medium-sized practices.

Gavin Spencer of Beach Accountants (Hattersley, 2025) observes that the introduction of HMRC's *Making Tax Digital* (GOV.UK, n.d.), combined with the ongoing departure of traditional accountants from the profession, has created a critical skills gap. Spencer questions the policy shift, asking: "Why would the government remove the incentive for accountancy practices to train young accountants to fill this void?"

Looking to the future for business and management H&DAs

The landscape of Business and Management Level 5, 6 and 7 apprenticeships in England is undergoing profound transformation. Once a growing and vibrant route to high-level skills development, particularly through Level 7 standards such as the Senior Leader and Accountancy and Taxation Professional apprenticeships, the government's 2025 decision to withdraw apprenticeship levy funding for most Level 7 programmes signals a pivotal policy shift. While the stated intention is to rebalance investment towards younger learners and entry-level skills, this change risks undermining the significant gains made in upskilling the existing workforce, widening access to higher education, and supporting social mobility.

With nearly 95,000 new starts in 2023/2024 within the Business, Administration, and Law subject group, and well over half of those in Business and Management subject areas, these apprenticeships remain both popular and impactful. Such apprenticeships continue to demonstrate their ability to attract talent, support professional development, and respond effectively to employer needs.

The case studies included in this chapter on the Chartered Manager Degree Apprenticeship (CMDA) and the Accounting and Finance Degree Apprenticeship (AFDA) highlight the breadth and adaptability of these programmes. They show how degree apprenticeships serve both large corporations and SMEs by embedding job-specific learning, improving management and technical competencies, and supporting inclusive recruitment strategies.

While the government encourages employers to fund Level 7 provision independently, this may only be feasible for larger organisations. Small and medium-sized enterprises, which often lack the financial resources to support such training, could be disproportionately affected, weakening the broader professional ecosystem. These developments are particularly concerning in sectors like accountancy, where skills shortages are already acute and experienced professionals are retiring in growing numbers.

Despite these challenges, DAs at Level 6 and below continue to offer a robust, flexible, and impactful model for talent development. Programmes like the CMDA – soon to be replaced by the Leadership and Management Professional Apprenticeship (LaMP) – demonstrate how curriculum innovation, employer involvement, and sector-specific tailoring can continue to drive engagement and success. The inclusion of emerging themes such as artificial intelligence, sustainability, and ethical leadership signals a forward-looking approach that is well-aligned with industry needs.

Looking ahead, the success of Business and Management apprenticeships will depend on maintaining their appeal, accessibility, and employer relevance. Ensuring that funding, policy, and practice remain responsive to the needs of learners and industry alike will be critical to sustaining their role as a cornerstone of workforce development and economic resilience.

References

AAT. (2024, October 18). *Worcestershire County Council: A Case Study in Running a Successful AAT Apprenticeship*. https://www.aatcomment.org.uk/audience/employers/worcestershire-county-council-a-case-study-in-running-a-successful-aat-apprenticeship/

Ascentant Accountancy. (2024, September 2). Accountancy apprenticeship – Employer case study [Video]. *YouTube*. https://www.youtube.com/watch?v=EVs8iHpkhh4

Camden, B. (2025, June 3). *Phillipson: Scrapping Level 7 Apprenticeships Won't Harm Skills Supply*. FE Week. https://feweek.co.uk/phillipson-scrapping-level-7-apprenticeships-wont-harm-skills-supply/

Chowen, S. (2025a, May 27). *Level 7 Apprenticeship Funding to be Axed from January 2026*. https://feweek.co.uk/level-7-apprenticeship-funding-to-be-axed-from-january-2026/

Chowen, S. (2025b, May 28). *Nine in Ten Level 7 Apprentices Will Be Ineligible for Funding, New Figures Reveal*. https://feweek.co.uk/nine-in-ten-level-7-apprentices-will-be-ineligible-for-funding-new-figures-reveal/

Department for Education, (n.d.). *Apprenticeships Summary*. https://app.powerbi.com/view?r=eyJrIjoiYzJjYjgxYjMtOWNmNS00NGM1LWFmMzEtODg5MzRiODBlODUzIiwidCI6ImZhZDI3N2M5LWM2MGEtNGRhMS1iNWYzLWIzYjhiMzRhODJmOSIsImMiOjh9

FE Week. (2025, July 26). *Level 7 Apprenticeship Cuts Are Death Blow for HE and Social Mobility*. https://feweek.co.uk/level-7-apprenticeship-cuts-are-death-blow-for-he-and-social-mobility/

GOV.UK. (2024). https://www.gov.uk/government/news/prime-minister-overhauls-apprenticeships-to-support-opportunity

GOV.UK. (2025, May 27). https://www.gov.uk/government/news/next-generation-of-builders-and-carers-set-to-rebuild-britain

GOV.UK. (n.d.). https://www.gov.uk/guidance/use-making-tax-digital-for-income-tax

Hattersley, R. (2025, May, 27). *Cut to Level 7 Funding Will Hit Accountants*. https://www.accountingweb.co.uk/practice/people/cut-to-level-7-funding-will-hit-accountants

Horackova, C., Bloomfield, S., Periera, C., & Mutwarasibo, M. (2023). Delivering the chartered manager degree apprenticeship: what are the challenges and implications for good practice? *Higher Education, Skills and Work-Based Learning*, 2042–3896. https://doi.org/10.1108/HESWBL-09-2023-0262

ICAEW. (2025, May 27). *Cuts to Apprenticeship Funding a 'Major Blow'*. https://www.icaew.com/insights/viewpoints-on-the-news/2025/may-2025/cuts-to-apprenticeship-funding-a-major-blow

Jeffreys, B. (2025, May 27). *Higher-Level Apprenticeship Funding to be Scrapped as Focus Shifts to under-22s*. https://www.bbc.co.uk/news/articles/c9vgd8zmpe3o#:~:text=From%20January%2C%20only%2016%20to,completely%20paid%20for%20by%20employers

John, G. (2025, May 27). Employers Urge Government to Extend Level 7. *Apprenticeship Funding Beyond Age*, 21. https://www.fenews.co.uk/exclusive/employers-urge-government-to-extend-level-7-apprenticeship-funding-beyond-age-21/

Johnson, N. (2025, March). *The Case for Apprenticeships*. https://abmagazine.accaglobal.com/global/articles/2025/mar/practice/the-case-for-apprenticeships.html

Mayne, M. (2025, May 28). *Government's £3bn Apprenticeship Overhaul Could Have 'Unintended Consequences', Experts Warn*. https://www.peoplemanagement.co.uk/article/1919608/governments-3bn-apprenticeship-overhaul-unintended-consequences-experts-warn

Mellor, J. (2025, August 11). NHS to save Level 7 apprenticeships from funding axe. *FE Week*. https://feweek.co.uk/nhs-to-save-level-7-apprenticeships-from-funding-axe/

Moss, R. (2025, May 27). *Scrapping Level 7 Apprenticeship Funding is a 'Major Blow'*. https://www.personneltoday.com/hr/scrapping-level-7-apprenticeship-funding/

Nawaz, R., Edifor, E., Holland, S., Cao, Q., & Liu, L. (2022). The impact of Degree Apprenticeships: Analysis, insights and policy recommendations. *Transforming Government: People, Process and Policy*, 17 (3), 372–386. https://doi.org/10.1108/TG-07-2022-0105

People Management. (2024, September 20). *Inclusive Workplaces can Solve the Hospitality Sector's Staffing Problems*. https://www.peoplemanagement.co.uk/article/1889408/inclusive-workplaces-solve-hospitality-sectors-staffing-problems

Prospects. (2025, June). *Level 7 Apprenticeships: Funding Cuts Explained*. https://www.prospects.ac.uk/the-topic/level-7-apprenticeships-funding-cuts-explained

Skills England. (n.d.-a). *Chartered Manager (Degree)*. https://skillsengland.education.gov.uk/apprenticeships/st0272-v1-1

Skills England. (n.d.-c). *Accounting Finance Manager*. https://skillsengland.education.gov.uk/apprenticeships/st1303-v1-0

Trailblazers. (2025). *Leadership and Management Professional Apprenticeship Insight Session 15th January 2025*. The Leadership and Management Trailblazer Group 15th January 2025. [webinar]

UVAC. (2024). *Degree Apprenticeship: Voices from the Front Line*. https://uvac.ac.uk/degree-apprenticeship-voices-from-the-frontline/#:~:text=The%20report%20Degree%20Apprenticeship%3A%20Voices,be%20crucial%20for%20programme%20sustainability

18 Engineering
Criticality and misalignments

Beverley Gibbs

The importance of engineering apprenticeships

Engineering apprenticeships play a vital role in the national skills landscape. The engineering sector employs 19% of the total UK workforce, with engineering and technology roles predicted to grow faster than other occupations in all UK regions over the next five years. Engineering skills are particularly critical to net zero ambitions, and the last five years have seen a 55% increase in jobs that service this aim (Engineering UK, 2024). The manufacturing sector is a key driver in economic growth, and advanced manufacturing – encompassing digital technologies, automation, and advanced materials – is a critical enabler to increasing productivity. Productivity is a key measure of efficiency in the economy and one which can lead to lower prices, improved wages, lower environmental impact, and increased tax yield (DBT, 2023).

Recent governments have promoted degree apprenticeships as having an important role to play in addressing engineering and digital skills shortages (Edge Foundation, 2024). Universities are reported as having recognised that engineering degree apprenticeships are an important route for employers in the recruitment and development of high-quality staff, and in supporting the development of technicians into more advanced engineering roles (Lester & Bravenboer, 2020). Engineering and digital skills (alongside management) were identified as the disciplines driving growth in the degree apprenticeship model introduced in 2015 (University UK, 2017). However, by the 2022/2023 session, there were only 34,000 advanced and higher apprentices in engineering and manufacturing, 13% of the total number of apprentices at these levels. Therefore, the scale of apprenticeships in this sector and at these

DOI: 10.4324/9781003567844-20

levels is mismatched with the sector's size and importance. In part, this is the consequence of a decline in engineering apprenticeships that began in the COVID-19 pandemic and which is showing slow signs of recovery (GOV.UK, 2024).

Delivery of Higher and Degree Apprenticeships in engineering

Engineering involves designing, testing and building machines, structures and processes using mathematical techniques and scientific concepts. Descriptions of engineering skills and occupations usually differentiate between 'craft' and 'technical' roles. Craft roles are akin to trades such as drinks dispensing technician or autocare technician and emphasise hands-on expertise. Technical roles such as railway signalling engineer or power engineer typically mobilise calculations and complex technical design (e.g. Humphries-Smith, Hunt & White, 2019). This distinction is important because, despite having comparable entry requirements, the choice of a technical qualification sets a learner on a path towards advanced and degree-level opportunities, but a craft qualification does not and will typically be truncated at Level 4.

Higher and Degree Apprenticeships are commonly delivered by further education colleges and higher education institutes such as universities. Apprenticeship qualifications are often adapted from existing qualification pathways, which is considered a valid and cost-effective approach. Universities, in particular, draw on existing extensive employer involvement and collaborations, and engineering degrees are generally broad enough to be able to accommodate specific apprenticeship pathway needs within existing programme structures (Bishop & Hordern, 2017). However, compared to full-time undergraduates, individual apprentices may begin their studies with important differences in experience and prior attainment. In particular, apprentices can require significant additional mathematics support if they do not have Mathematics A-level, an almost-ubiquitous requirement for admittance to an engineering degree (EPC, 2017; Lester & Bravenboer, 2020).

Joining this landscape of provision have been Institutes of Technology (IoT), of which there are now 21 regional hubs across England. Introduced from 2019 to deliver higher technical education, and supported by £300 million of capital funding, IoTs are collaborations between industry employers, universities and FE colleges. They support the development of 'place-based skills' and are thus important to the idea of economic levelling-up. IoTs specialise in technical qualifications and draw on effective collaboration to offer a range of courses from T-levels to master's degree, often with clear pathways through these levels. Apprenticeship offers and part-time courses are offered side-by-side to provide maximum flexibility to learners.

Distinctive features of engineering apprenticeships

Engineering and manufacturing roles are unusually broad and includes many specialist areas, illustrated in the 39 different professional engineering institutions that are licensed by the Engineering Council to register professional engineers and accredit academic programmes. These institutions reflect specific professions (e.g. the Institution of Railway Signal Engineers), specific areas of technology (e.g. the Energy Institute), or specific parts of the engineering process (e.g. the Institution of Engineering Designers).

The accreditation of educational programmes in engineering ensures that students who successfully complete them are eligible, or have an easier route to demonstrate compliance with, requirements for professional accreditation such as Engineering Technician (for advanced apprenticeships), Incorporated Engineer (bachelor's degrees), and Chartered Engineer (master's degrees). This accreditation framework, known as Accreditation of Higher Education Programmes (AHEP) 4 (Engineering Council, 2020a) facilitates international standardisation of engineering education and supports the global mobility of engineers. Accreditation is realised through a philosophy of threshold competence in five domains, which provides some consensus on the knowledge areas an engineer should possess:

- Science and mathematics
- Engineering analysis
- Design and innovation
- The engineer and society
- Engineering practice

The AHEP framework can be applied to academic programmes for the full range of modes of study (full-time, part-time, modular, distance, apprenticeship) for academic qualifications at Levels 6, 7 or 8. Apprenticeships not at degree level are supported by an additional standard (AAQA) which supports non-degree learning that is not covered in AHEP4 (Engineering Council, 2020b). The Approval and Accreditation of Qualifications and Apprenticeships (AAQA) is structured around the same subject areas as AHEP4, with threshold descriptors adjusted appropriately. Accreditation is a process that is pursued by educational providers at their discretion and, because 'engineer' is not a protected occupational title in the UK, it is not mandatory for qualifications or schemes using the word 'engineering' in their title. Education providers may pursue accreditation or approval for a range of reasons: where they believe that it will serve to bolster student recruitment, in recognition of the enhanced employability of graduates, in response to employer demand, or where the educational provider is keen to benchmark against external quality frameworks.

Engineering apprenticeships are also characterised by the intensity of specialist equipment, for example from high-performance computers through to proprietary simulation software and five-axis machining. Such equipment supports the development of in-depth technical skills on industry-standard equipment and software (Bishop & Hordern, 2017). Courses need to be up-to-date, relevant and forward-thinking in a sector that is characterised by accelerated development and innovation. The need for specialist equipment was recognised by government in the capital investment that supported the launch of Institutes of Technology, but all education providers need to make strategic decisions about which facilities will add most value to most learners whilst acknowledging that the equipment an individual apprentice will use in the workplace might be more advanced than that which can be realised in the educational environment (Lester & Bravenboer, 2020). This is an example of where the work-based apprenticeship training can be more advanced than the educational programme being followed.

This need for advanced equipment, as well as educational staff with advanced knowledge, leads to delivery costs that are higher than many other subject areas, and which increase as level of study increases. The Engineering Professors' Council has advocated for degree apprenticeships being adequately resourced, highlighting that the cost of delivery outstrips income, and calling for an increase in engineering degree apprenticeship fees or catalyst funding to support the development of programmes (EPC, 2017). Development funding was subsequently made available to accompany the introduction of Institutes of Technology, from 2019.

A final differentiator of engineering apprenticeships is the attributes of learners. Engineering is a challenging and rewarding subject that draws on an unusually wide range of skills – cognitive, practical, interpersonal. It attracts candidates of high academic calibre, who are frequently expected to demonstrate academic strengths in mathematics and physics. These relatively demanding entry criteria can increase barriers for those who wish to switch to engineering after time in another career. Since the inception of engineering degree apprenticeships, and despite the aims of universities who offer them, they have largely functioned as a tool of attraction into the profession rather than as a development platform for established practitioners (Bishop & Hordern, 2017; Edge Foundation, 2024).

Contemporary debates in engineering apprenticeships

Amongst the contemporary debates that surround engineering apprenticeships, one of the most significant relates to the apprenticeship standards that structure learning. In this chapter we have seen that engineering apprenticeships cover a broad range of activities, each of which reaches significant depth, and which are overseen by an unusually wide number of professional institutions. Many of the apprenticeship standards in this subject reflect sector-specific roles, such as space systems engineer, robotics engineer, food and drink engineer, rail and rail systems engineer, and there are 41 different standards approved for delivery across Levels 5, 6, and 7. A number of sectoral perspectives have remarked that apprenticeship standards are becoming overly narrow and short-term in orientation, focussing on specific job roles rather than looking more broadly at transferable skills within professions or occupational fields (Policy Connect/HEC, 2019).

This is particularly true in engineering, which raises the question of whether apprentices would be better served by following standards that are relevant to multiple employers. This is feasible given well-developed and respected accreditation and approval frameworks overseen by the Engineering Council. However, standards development takes place in employer-led groups, often from a common sector, whose priority is (naturally) their specific skills needs rather than accreditation frameworks that would support apprentice mobility. There can be significant gaps between occupational standards and accreditation frameworks; these gaps offer the opportunity to optimise alignment between the two (EPC, 2017). In addition to employers who resist alignment, there is what is described as politicised resistance from policy sponsors who are, '...determined to explicitly link a degree apprenticeship with 'mastery of a specific occupation' (Bishop & Hordern, 2017).

Engineering small and medium-sized enterprises (SMEs) constitute a particularly large proportion of the sector in some regions, especially areas of socio-economic disadvantage (Bridge Group, 2022), but the interests of SMEs are not always well-represented in apprenticeship development and delivery. Large companies are particularly prevalent in the development of occupational standards which, as well as leading to limited appeal to the wider sector, is thought to embed unduly high standards that SMEs struggle to support. If academic content in a standard becomes overly demanding, more study time is required which takes apprentices away from their work tasks, and admissions requirements must rise to ensure learners can be successful academically.

SMEs can find it challenging to recruit the highest-calibre applicants, who may be more attracted to the well-known brands associated with large companies (Bishop & Hordern, 2017). To support the uptake of apprenticeships amongst SMEs, the Department for Education (DfE) launched an SME Brokerage Pathfinder programme – prioritising manufacturing – in four regions of the North of England. This programme supports SMEs that have not had an apprentice in the past two years to do so and offers assistance in navigating the apprenticeship landscape (DfE, 2024; DBT, 2023). Thus, there has been some modest support for SMEs, but this only tackles challenges of access rather than any fundamental mismatch between apprenticeship standards and SME requirements.

The role of the End-Point Assessment (EPA) in degree apprenticeships has been questioned in both engineering (EPC, 2017) and nursing. In both fields, the degree is required for, or contributes to, professional registration, and the additional value of completing an EPA is not clear. This step can be perceived as a burden by apprentices (Mulkeen et al., 2017) and can further erode the financial viability of educational providers given that a portion of the fee is retained for EPA. Where an apprentice achieves their academic qualification and meets the requirements of the professional body, but fails to pass the EPA, the final tranche of funding would be withheld (Lester & Bravenboer, 2020). A focus on the EPA is also driving a transition away from on-programme assessment of work-based skills that was characteristic of the NVQ approach in engineering. Instead, learning strategies are seen to focus on professional behaviours moving towards an EPA (Crawford-Lee & Moorwood, 2019). The ongoing transition towards integrated degree standards (where work, academic study, and EPA are 'hard-linked' together) will better incentivise apprentices towards successfully completing all parts of their course.

A fourth topic of discussion in engineering degree apprenticeships relates to the diversity of apprentice cohorts. Engineering has a longstanding gender disparity that spans students, graduates and employees. Apprentices are no exception, where the proportion of women (8%) is even lower than the proportion of women studying engineering at university in mainstream courses (18%) (Institution of Mechanical Engineers, 2018; Engineering UK, 2023). Apprenticeships are commonly imagined to be an effective vehicle for learners from more disadvantaged socio-economic backgrounds to access advanced and higher education. Unfortunately, within the engineering pipeline, apprentices from lower socio-economic backgrounds are much less likely to be studying technical qualifications that can lead to progression to higher education than those apprentices from middle-class and upwards socio-economic backgrounds. They are more likely to be undertaking craft subjects, which do not have the same forward trajectory. Given that the entry requirements for Level 2 craft and technical qualifications are almost identical, this is thought to be an outcome of careers advice rather than admission thresholds. The proliferation of standards with their specialist terminology and wide variety in pathway potential may well be related to the difficulties careers advisors have in helping young people navigate their opportunities for long-term career success. Students following technical (rather than craft) pathways within engineering are more likely to have parents with Class 1 or 2 occupations (Humphries-Smith, White, & Hunt, 2017).

The final question relating to engineering apprentices is the perceptions of the Learners themselves. Of all applicants interested in pursuing engineering undergraduate studies, only 28% are reported as being interested in apprenticeship pathway, the lowest amongst the subject domains reported. In contrast, the proportion of current apprentices who would recommend an apprenticeship route is particularly high in engineering and technology, at 73% (Sutton Trust & UCAS, 2023). Whilst degree apprenticeships in general are increasingly recognised as having a parity of esteem with mainstream degrees (Laczik et al., 2024 citing UUK, 2019), this does not seem to be the case in engineering, where vocational pathways are often held in lower esteem than traditional academic routes and are reported to carry connotations of low status with young people and their influencers (EPC, 2017).

Concluding remarks

Engineering and manufacturing are critical economic activities that support employment and provide the foundation from which to achieve important societal goals. There is a well-established shortage of skills in this area, and also long-term unfilled job vacancies. For a sector that values practical skill, commercial awareness, technical capability, and application of knowledge, higher and degree apprenticeships have the potential to make a meaningful contribution to this skills gap. And yet this model of education is not reaching its potential in the engineering sector and is not proving as disruptive as many have hoped. The model has not resolved longstanding challenges in the low diversity of learner cohorts, and it has not transformed the public perception of engineering. Rather, the confusion between professional engineering and craft occupations remains, with relatively poor transferability between these two domains.

Institutes of Technology have been an innovative step in this landscape, and are closely bound up with advanced and degree apprenticeships. These new employer-education collaborations appear to be more effective than other arrangements in building pathways from T-levels through advanced and degree apprenticeships, offered in regional clusters of providers. This joined-up thinking is refreshing and does important work in communicating short and long-term prospects to prospective apprentices.

Larger employers are able to influence occupational standards to secure a pipeline of carefully defined roles, exactly as policymakers imagined. SMEs do not fare so well and have multiple difficulties. It is challenging for them to navigate the apprenticeship landscape, to release apprentices for highly demanding programmes of study, and to compete for talented applicants against larger, well-known companies. Standards that are shaped by employers can also be dissonant with engineering accreditation requirements, and it is left to education providers to try and reconcile these two frameworks if they wish. Where this is resolved successfully, providers are left wondering what the role of the EPA is in this already burdensome context. For courses where this remains unreconciled, learners are undertaking unaccredited courses which will increase the difficulty of achieving professional recognition such as Incorporated Engineer (IEng).

Policy interventions to ensure all engineering standards are aligned with accreditation requirements would resolve this dissonance and make a tangible step towards breadth and commonality in what is a single subject field.

In turn, this would increase the mobility of apprentices as they could more easily move between sectors if their qualification was underpinned by a framework that had multi-occupation recognition.

The poor uptake of apprenticeships by established engineers who are developing into specialist roles, or wish to refresh or reorient their skills, needs a different approach. Here, Level 7 qualifications become critical given the technical specialism needed in much technical engineering work. The changes to Level 7 apprenticeship funding announced in May 2025 (GOV.UK, 2025) will greatly limit the ways in which on-the-job master's-level engineering education can be delivered. In turn, this will reduce opportunities to increase the supply of qualified and experienced people for critical roles, such as process engineering, defence and security, infrastructure asset management, AI data, and digital technology strategy. These are key technologies which underpin half of the sectors identified as 'growth drivers' in the UK government's ten year Industrial Strategy. This exemplifies a further misalignment, this time between national economic policy and skills policy. A concerted effort to address these many misalignments will be key to ensuring higher and advanced engineering apprenticeships make their fullest, much-needed contribution to the UK economy and society.

Suggested further reading

EPC. (2018). *Experience enhanced: Improving engineering degree apprenticeships*. Engineering Professors' Council.

IMechE. (2018). *Never Too Late: Profiling female engineering apprentices*. Gatsby Foundation.

Lester, S., & Bravenboer, D. (2020). *Sustainable degree apprenticeships*. Centre for Degree Apprenticeships.

References

Bishop, D., & Hordern, J. (2017). *Degree apprenticeships: Higher technical or technical higher (education)*. Bath Spa University, Institute for Education.

Bridge Group. (2022). *Bridging the Gap: Socio-economic diversity in the engineering sector: Access, pay and progression*. The Bridge Group.

Crawford-Lee, M., & Moorwood, S. (2019). Degree apprenticeships: Delivering quality and social mobility? *Higher Education, Skills and Work-Based Learning*, 9(2), 134–140.

DBT: Department for Business and Trade. (2023). *Advanced Manufacturing Plan*, 6th December 2023.

DfE: Department for Education. (2024). *Apprenticeship SME brokerage pathfinder: Early evaluation research report.*

Edge Foundation. (2024). *Widening participation and degree apprenticeships.*

Engineering Council (2020a). *The accreditation of higher education programmes (AHEP)* (4th ed). Engineering Council.

Engineering Council. (2020b). *The approval and accreditation of qualifications and apprenticeships (AAQA)* (1st ed). Engineering Council.

Engineering UK. (2023). *From A levels to engineering: Exploring the gender gap in higher education.* https://www.engineeringuk.com/media/mxxjczpv/engineering-in-higher-education_report_engineeringuk_march-23.pdf [Accessed 23rd January 2024].

Engineering UK. (2024). *Key stats infographic.* https://www.engineeringuk.com/media/jw3fcykh/facts-and-stats-engineeringuk-dec-24.pdf [Accessed 7 February 2025].

GOV.UK. (2024). *Apprenticeships and traineeships: Academic year 2022/23. UK Government Education Statistics.* https://explore-education-statistics.service.gov.uk/find-statistics/apprenticeships-and-traineeships [Accessed 3 February 2024].

GOV.UK. (2025). Changes to funding for level 7 apprenticeships. *UK Government.* https://help.apprenticeships.education.gov.uk/hc/en-gb/articles/24002145831954-Changes-to-funding-for-level-7-apprenticeships [Accessed 27 June 2025].

Humphries-Smith, T. M., White, M., & Hunt, C. (2017). Engineering design, apprenticeships & diversity. In *DS 88: Proceedings of the 19th international conference on engineering and product design education (E&PDE). Building community: Design education for a sustainable future*, Oslo, Norway, 7 & 8 September 2017 (pp. 236–241).

Humphries-Smith, T., Hunt, C., & White, M. (2019, September). *Unpicking the barriers to diversity in engineering apprenticeships*. The Design Society.

Laczik, A., Patel, J., Emms, K., Hordern, J., Orr, K., Dabbous, D., Polding, E., Wormald, J., James Relly, S., Newton, O., & Quyoum, A. (2024). *Degree apprenticeships in England: What can we learn from the experiences of apprentices, employers, and education and training providers?* The Edge Foundation.

EPC. (2017). *Designing apprenticeships for success: A discussion document on engineering degree apprenticeships*. Engineering Professors' Council.

Institution of Mechanical Engineers (2018). *Never too late: Profiling female engineering apprentices*. London: Institution of Mechanical Engineers. Available at: https://www.imeche.org/policy-and-press/reports/detail/never-too-late-profiling-female-engineering-apprentices (Accessed: 24 November 2025).

Mulkeen, J., Abdou, H. A., Leigh, J., & Ward, P. (2017). Degree and Higher Level Apprenticeships: an empirical investigation of stakeholder perceptions of challenges and opportunities. *Studies in Higher Education*, 44(2), 333–346. https://doi.org/10.1080/03075079.2017.1365357

Policy Connect/Higher Education Commission (2019). *Apprenticeship standards: professional and technical routes in higher education*. London: Policy Connect.

Sutton Trust., & UCAS. (2023). *Where Next? What influences the choices of would-be apprentices?* https://www.suttontrust.com/wp-content/uploads/2023/07/Where-next-What-influences-the-choices-of-would-be-apprentices.pdf [Accessed 27 February 2025].

Universities UK. (2017). *The future growth of degree apprenticeships*. Universities UK.

19

Computing

Shaping tomorrow's technologists, challenges, and opportunities

Jordan Allison

Introduction

As a course leader for an apprenticeship within the computing discipline, specifically the Level 6 Digital Technology Solutions Professional Degree Apprenticeship (Institute for Apprenticeships and Technical Education, 2024), I have had the privilege of witnessing the intersection of academic study and real-world industry experience. Each year a new cohort of apprentices bring a diverse range of experiences, aspirations, and challenges. As a course leader and lecturer, my role is not just to deliver academic content and ensure course currency, it is to ensure these students navigate the complex landscape of balancing study with full-time work, all while developing the technical and soft skills that will prepare them for successful careers in the tech industry.

Despite the many advantages of degree apprenticeships within computing, there remain significant challenges that need to be addressed if these programmes are to fully achieve their aim of bridging the gap between academic knowledge and industry skills, improving employability, and addressing skills shortages in the sector. Throughout this chapter, I will share insights from my perspective as a course leader and lecturer, reflecting on both the successes and the challenges of computing degree apprenticeships. I will explore the complexities of learner disparity, the issues surrounding access to essential technical tools, and the difficulties in finding appropriate projects for apprentices to complete their End-Point Assessments (EPAs). By weaving together personal reflections from my own experience with apprenticeship-related literature, this chapter aims to provide a deeper

DOI: 10.4324/9781003567844-21

understanding of how these programmes function operationally. I will also offer suggestions for how educators and employers can work together to overcome these challenges and create a more effective, equitable computing apprenticeship experience for all involved.

Learner disparity

Learner disparity represents a significant challenge within computing education, where there is a broad diversity of learner backgrounds and preconceived expectations for what computing education should look like (Allison, 2021). This challenge is even more evident within computing degree apprenticeships. Apprentices often arrive with vastly different educational and technical backgrounds. Some candidates may have completed A-levels in computing or vocational qualifications, while others may have little to no experience in the field. However, employers might recognise potential in young school leavers or seek to strengthen their computing and IT teams by upskilling employees from non-technical roles. Equally, some computing apprentices may be in a software development role and have been in that position for a couple of years, whereas others may be new to the organisation, and have no experience at all with programming. These differences create a divide in learning disparity, with a learning environment where one size does *not* fit all, requiring universities and employers to tailor their support. Due to this disparity, some training providers have even developed summer schools for computing degree apprentices to ensure all apprentices start with more similar baseline expertise (Somerville, Cutts, Barr, and Parkinson, 2020). During my time as a course leader, finding the balance in terms of level of course content, managing accreditation requirements, mapping to Knowledge, Skills, and Behaviours (KSBs), or subject benchmark statements is a continually evolving task, and challenged by some students indicating how the content is too simplistic, and others stating how it is far too difficult.

> *I keep asking myself, 'Are we doing enough to support these apprentices, or are we just adding to their stress by expecting too much?'*
>
> Jordan, Course Leader

This comment reflects a growing concern among academic staff about the balance between academic expectations and pastoral care in degree apprenticeship programmes. It highlights the ethical tension educators face when managing both institutional demands and the well-being of learners who often juggle employment and study. Apprentices with less technical experience may find it difficult to keep pace with both academic and workplace expectations. This mismatch can lead to frustration, underachievement, and, ultimately, stress. Additionally, balancing full-time work and academic study exacerbates disparities, particularly when workplace demands limit the time apprentices can dedicate to learning. Employers may unintentionally widen this gap by assigning tasks that do not align with the apprentice's academic development, leaving less-experienced learners struggling to connect theory with practice (Taylor-Smith, Smith, and Smith, 2019).

> *I often find myself asking my apprentices where they are on a continuum of challenged and overwhelmed. We need to find the sweet spot and recognise when corrective action is needed.*
>
> Helen, Computing Learner Review Coach

This observation underscores the importance of responsive pedagogy in degree apprenticeships, where monitoring learner well-being is not peripheral but central to effective programme delivery. Therefore, clear expectations from the start of the programme with all parties, clear communication, and early identification of issues are key. Due to the technical and evolving nature of content, successful stakeholder management and collaboration is even more important for computing apprenticeships, and the Learner disparity coming into the programme. Universities and employers working together to identify individual needs and provide targeted support can reduce problems and enhance outcomes (Parkinson and Dziallas, 2024).

On the positive side, the diversity of both educational and professional experience among apprentices can enrich the learning experience, as they all bring their own unique practical experience and can support one another (Taylor-Smith, Smith, and Smith, 2019). Those with strong foundational knowledge might mentor less-experienced peers, fostering collaboration and peer-supported learning. Indeed, I have experienced a junior software developer of 20 years old mentor other apprentices who are in managerial roles with regards to programming. Pair-programming is common in the computing industry, and encouraging learners to do so in class can help mitigate these disparities. Similarly, the more experienced apprentices have often mentored the younger apprentices in terms of navigating workplace dynamics. This dynamic exchange of knowledge not only enhances individual learning but also cultivates a collaborative culture that mirrors real-world industry practices. By leveraging the strengths of a diverse apprentice cohort, degree apprenticeship programmes can create a more inclusive and supportive learning environment that benefits all participants.

Software red tape

Another form of disparity arises when apprentices have unequal access to the technical software required for their programme, a challenge faced by their employer and/or the educational institution delivering the computing apprenticeship (Allison, 2022). Advanced tools for programming, data analysis, network simulation, and system design are integral to the computing curriculum (Kumar et al., 2024) and apprenticeship standards, but they can be costly and may not align with the tools and software which employers use. This disconnect can hinder apprentices who lack access to the software required for module assessments. For example, I have experienced data analyst apprentices who have found themselves unable to use Python at work due to IT restrictions, such as not having administrative access to install software on their devices, even though it is a key tool in their academic curriculum, and indeed commonly used for Data Science (Gottipati, Shim and Sahoo, 2021). Without workplace support for tools such as this, they may struggle to practice and apply their academic learning effectively. Similarly, students studying cyber security frequently encounter difficulties using virtual machines (VMs) on their work-based devices. These tools are essential for simulating and analysing secure environments but often require lengthy approval processes or are outright blocked due to organisational policies or IT infrastructure limitations. Therefore, collaborative discussions during the onboarding process between the training provider and employer regarding software expectations can potentially help alleviate these issues before the Learner begins their apprenticeship.

If not addressed, these technical constraints create a noticeable gap between academic and practical learning. In my experience, it is perhaps surprising that it is the apprentices in larger organisations who struggle more than those in smaller ones. In larger organisations, the presence of extensive structures and organisational policies can lead to bureaucratic practices creating ICT-related red tape. While these regulations are often intended to ensure security and standardisation, they can inadvertently restrict apprentices' access to essential software, tools, or systems, making it more difficult for them to complete coursework and develop the hands-on skills needed for their roles. In these cases, apprentices are often left to bridge the gap independently, which can add stress and delay their progress. It is easy for a university to say that the students have all the equipment available on campus should they need it, but apprentices cannot necessarily access the university as frequently as other students due to the nature of apprenticeship working.

> *One apprentice waited over a year for approval to use virtual machines on their work device, but by then the module was long over.*
>
> Paula, Employer Early Careers Lead

This example illustrates the often slow-moving nature of organisational processes, which can inadvertently undermine the pedagogical intentions of the degree apprenticeship model. It highlights the misalignment that can occur between academic timetables and workplace bureaucracy, revealing how operational delays risk compromising apprentices' ability to engage meaningfully with technical content in a timely manner. However, limited software access can also lead to resourcefulness and adaptability, key skills for technology professionals (Bowers and Sabin, 2022). Apprentices often navigate these challenges by seeking open-source alternatives or leveraging personal devices to work outside the organisational IT ecosystem. These approaches can enhance problem-solving skills and expose apprentices to a wider array of tools, fostering versatility. For example, an apprentice who cannot use an organisation approved Python environment might learn to deploy their projects in alternative online environments, such as on Jupyter Notebooks. However, using alternative environments may limit apprentices' exposure to the specific tools and workflows used in their workplace. While this approach fosters adaptability, it can also create challenges when transitioning to industry-approved systems, as apprentices may not gain direct experience with the exact platforms and processes required by their employers.

From the Employer side, this challenge can act as a catalyst for growth. Apprentices may often bring back to the workplace different tools and methods from their academic study that can encourage employers to adopt.

For example, I recall when students were studying Agile Methods in their second year and were introduced to tools such as Jira, a popular project management tool (Garcia et al., 2020). After speaking to the line manager of two apprentices taking this module, they informed me how they are now adopting Jira into their own practice, as the apprentices had shared the benefits they experienced using it for their academic study in the module.

Nevertheless, overcoming these challenges requires a collaborative effort. Apprenticeship providers could negotiate software licenses for apprentices or provide remote access to campus computing environments that support tools like Python and VMs. Equally, employers could allocate resources to approve and implement the software needed for apprenticeships, viewing it as an investment in both their workforce and the organisation's innovation. Collaborative discussions between universities and employers before the apprenticeship begins can also help align workplace tools with academic requirements, ensuring that apprentices can fully integrate their learning into their professional roles. However, this creates additional administrative overhead, and the effort and communication required to manage employer relationships present a challenge for many training providers of computing-related apprenticeships (Parkinson and Dziallas, 2024).

Sourcing technical projects for End-Point Assessments

A similar challenge to software access which emerges is sourcing appropriate technical projects for computing EPAs (Parkinson and Dziallas, 2024). This can be a complex process when considering organisational systems and software requirements. Of course, for an employer, the EPA provides a structured opportunity to address real-world challenges using the apprentice's skills. For example, an apprentice designing a data management system for their EPA might simultaneously solve a persistent organisational need.

Challenges arise, however, when employers cannot provide projects that meet the EPA's technical and academic standards. For those in smaller organisations, they may lack the resources or scope for a large technical project for EPA. In organisations like this, apprentices are often required to wear multiple hats, taking on a wide range of responsibilities that might include software development, network administration, and even customer support. This can be demanding for the apprentice learner when trying to fit in a larger project alongside other business as usual commitments. Furthermore, apprentices in these situations may lack access to the same level of mentorship or specialised training as their peers in larger companies. In a small IT team, for instance, there may not be an experienced software engineer available to provide in-depth guidance on complex coding challenges. Hence, apprentices must be resourceful, and resilient to the demands placed on them.

> *One apprentice I worked with is one of only three software engineers in their entire company. This meant they had to be more independent, but also meant they had more influence on what should be prioritised.*
>
> Steve, Computing Learner Review Coach

This account highlights the dual-edged nature of small-team environments within degree apprenticeships, where apprentices may experience accelerated professional growth through autonomy and responsibility, yet also face heightened pressures due to limited peer support. For students in larger organisations, sourcing technical projects for EPA can still be challenging, particularly when they may be in rotational schemes. Rotational schemes provide the benefit of broad exposure to different aspects of computing. By working in diverse departments, apprentices gain a well-rounded understanding of how various functions within a business interconnect. For example, an apprentice might begin in IT support, where they develop a strong foundation in troubleshooting and systems management, before rotating into a project management or software development team. This breadth of experience enhances the apprentice's skill set but also in identifying areas of specialisation they may wish to pursue after completing the apprenticeship. However, when identifying projects for EPA or other work-based modules, rotational schemes may not align with the timelines of academic study, with students unable to plan what projects they may undertake until they are in the next rotation. I've seen this at first hand when a group was introduced to a project in September but didn't rotate into the relevant team until late November. In fields like software development or big data projects, losing two months of project planning and execution can severely impact their ability to meet academic requirements, especially when they need time to grasp complex technical content and deliver results.

To address the issue of identifying suitable projects, training providers and employers could adopt a more proactive approach. This might involve identifying potential projects early in the apprenticeship, ensuring they align with the apprentice's learning outcomes and timing of the EPA. Ongoing collaborative discussions between the Employer and training provider on apprenticeship expectations are therefore vital to ensure sufficient planning and to mitigate EPA project concerns. More flexible EPA frameworks that accommodate a range of project types and scales could also help, allowing apprentices in diverse work environments to demonstrate their competencies. However, for the computing domain, there are often also issues regarding the necessity of maintaining confidentiality and adhering to data protection regulations. Many computing projects involve company systems and sensitive data, such as customer records or proprietary business information, which cannot be shared publicly due to privacy laws like General Data Protection Regulation (GDPR). This creates a tension when apprentices must demonstrate their competencies through university assignments, as they often need to showcase their work in a detailed and transparent way. For example, in data analysis, apprentices may be required to analyse real-world data sets and present their findings, but using actual company data may violate confidentiality agreements. Similarly, in cyber security, apprentices tasked with penetration testing or vulnerability assessments may encounter situations where they are unable to openly share the systems or vulnerabilities they have worked on for their assignments.

> *I've had several conversations with apprentices and employers on meeting the balance of confidentiality whilst showcasing their work and projects. Sometimes there needs to be discussions on NDAs, particularly with cyber or defence companies.*
>
> Omar, Course Leader

As illustrated above, there can be a recurring tension in degree apprenticeships between academic assessment requirements and the constraints of commercial confidentiality. To overcome this, the training provider, apprentice, and employer may need to enter into a non-disclosure agreement (NDA) to ensure data protection (Barr and Parkinson, 2019), and aspects of the project may need to be abstracted or anonymised for academic submission. This means that while apprentices can still meet the technical requirements of their EPA, they may face significant challenges in demonstrating the depth of their work without compromising confidentiality. The interplay between academic expectations and confidentiality concerns requires careful navigation to ensure that the integrity of both the project and the assignment is preserved.

> *During the technical discussion or presentation aspects of EPA, apprentices have sometimes had their line manager present, not for moral support, but so they can double check whether they are allowed to speak about certain aspects of their work.*
>
> Daniel, Course Leader

The presence of a line manager not as a supporter but as a gatekeeper reflects the layered accountability apprentices face, and highlights the importance of clear communication protocols between universities, employers, and apprentices to avoid compromising assessment integrity.

Constant technological innovation

The computing industry is defined by constant technological change and computing degree apprenticeships are often developed in response to these changes (Azmat, Ahmed, Colombo, and Harrison, 2020). Innovations in fields like artificial intelligence, cloud computing, cyber security, and data science emerge rapidly. However, the tools, programming languages, and methodologies that are state-of-the-art today can become obsolete in just a few years. This relentless pace of innovation poses a challenge for computing degree apprenticeships, where apprentices, universities, and employers must continuously adapt to ensure that skills and knowledge remain relevant, and each may be at different stages for different aspects of technology adoption. For instance, there is the issue of curriculum lag (Barr and Parkinson, 2019), where degree programmes may not be able to keep pace with industry in terms of the latest technologies. Meanwhile some companies are very innovative and use the latest technologies whereas I have encountered several that are using legacy systems and outdated tools. Again, there is a disparity, which relates to the issue of 'access to software'. Here, though, the problem is finding the balance in terms of what content is useful for the current cohort of apprentices, whilst also ensuring the programme itself keeps pace with industry trends. For apprentices, this means that the curriculum delivered by universities and the work experience provided by employers must strike a delicate balance: grounding apprentices in foundational computing principles relevant to their workplace, while exposing them to emerging trends (Barr and Parkinson, 2019).

Apprentices often tell me that certain modules don't seem relevant to their work. However, these modules contribute to their broader knowledge base that will be essential for their technological development for the future, even if not directly applicable to their current role.

Joanna, Employer HR Manager

This comment demonstrates that while apprentices may seek direct applicability, the curriculum is designed to foster transferable knowledge and skills. Ensuring apprentices realise they are going to have to continually learn beyond their degree apprenticeship is a key skill, as lifelong learning is imperative in the computing profession (Duan, Exter, Tagare, and Sabin, 2022). The industry's dynamic nature means that even seasoned professionals must continually upskill. Computing apprentices, by virtue of navigating both academic and professional environments, often learn how to identify technological knowledge gaps and seek out resources to fill them, whether through online courses, university resources, or workplace training. These habits, cultivated early in an apprentice's career, become invaluable as they advance into senior roles that require staying ahead of technological trends.

However, we must be mindful that balancing the demands of an apprenticeship alongside a full-time job can create multiple, competing priorities, potentially leaving students feeling stressed. Hence, students often want the university curriculum to be directly aligned to their workplace for maximum synergy. This is particularly the case if there are competing deadlines, as there is a clear tension between prioritising activities that offer short-term benefits and engaging with content that provides long-term advantages for future learning. Once more, clear communication between all parties is key.

Conclusion

Computing degree apprenticeships offer a unique opportunity to connect academic learning with real-world industry experience, preparing apprentices for dynamic and challenging careers in the tech sector. However, their success relies on addressing several key challenges: learner disparity, access to essential technical tools, sourcing appropriate End-Point Assessment projects, and keeping pace with rapid technological changes. Therefore, employers and universities must work closely to co-design apprenticeship programmes that not only respond to industry developments but also provide immediate value in the workplace.

By fostering effective collaboration between training providers, employers, and apprentices, these obstacles can be converted into opportunities for growth for all involved. Aligning curriculum and workplace demands, ensuring access to necessary resources, and maintaining open communication are crucial for creating a supportive and effective learning environment. If these measures are put into place, computing degree apprenticeships can continue to thrive, equipping apprentices with the skills, adaptability, and resilience needed to excel in a constantly evolving industry, while simultaneously creating a pipeline of talent that is proficient in current technologies and agile enough to adapt to future disruptions.

References

Allison, J. (2021). The importance of context: Assessing the challenges of K-12 computing education through the lens of Biggs 3P model. In *Proceedings of the 21st Koli Calling International Conference on Computing Education Research (Koli Calling '21)* (Article 15, pp. 1–10). Association for Computing Machinery. https://doi.org/10.1145/3488042.3488043

Allison, J. (2022). The who, how and why of choosing post-16 computing curricula: a case study of English further education colleges. *Journal of Further and Higher Education*, 46(10), 1447–1464. https://doi.org/10.1080/0309877X.2022.2088269

Azmat, F., Ahmed, B., Colombo, W., & Harrison, R. (2020). Closing the skills gap in the era of industrial digitalisation. In *2020 IEEE Conference on Industrial Cyberphysical Systems (ICPS)* (pp. 365–370). IEEE. https://doi.org/10.1109/ICPS48405.2020.9274788

Barr, M., & Parkinson, J. (2019). Developing a work-based software engineering degree in collaboration with industry. In *Proceedings of the 2019 Conference on United Kingdom & Ireland Computing Education Research (UKICER '19)* (Article 9, pp. 1–7). Association for Computing Machinery. https://doi.org/10.1145/3351287.3351292

Bowers, D., & Sabin, M. (2022). Using a professional skills framework to support the assessment of dispositions in IT education. In *Proceedings of the 23rd Annual Conference on Information Technology Education (SIGITE '22)* (pp. 103–109). Association for Computing Machinery. https://doi.org/10.1145/3537674.3554747

Duan, S., Exter, M., Tagare, D., & Sabin, M. (2022). Managerial and professional skills and dispositions from professionals' interviews. In *Proceedings of the 23rd Annual Conference on Information Technology Education (SIGITE '22)* (pp. 1–8). Association for Computing Machinery. https://doi.org/10.1145/3537674.3554751

Garcia, A. L., Miguel, I. da R., Eugênio, J. B., Vilela, M. da S., & Marcondes, G. A. B. (2020). Scrum-based application for agile project management. *Jsoftware*, 15(4), 106–113. https://doi.org/10.17706/jsw.15.4.106-113

Gottipati, S., Shim, K. J., & Sahoo, S. (2021). Glassdoor job description analytics – Analyzing data science professional roles and skills. In *2021 IEEE Global Engineering Education Conference (EDUCON)* (pp. 1329–1336). https://doi.org/10.1109/EDUCON46332.2021.9453931

Institute for Apprenticeships and Technical Education. (2024). Digital and technology solutions professional. Retrieved December 8, 2024, from https://www.instituteforapprenticeships.org/apprenticeship-standards/digital-and-technology-solutions-professional-v1-2

Kumar, A. N., Raj, R. K., Aly, S. G., Anderson, M. D., Becker, B. A., Blumenthal, R. L., Eaton, E., Epstein, S. L., Goldweber, M., Jalote, P., Lea, D., Oudshoorn, M., Pias, M., Reiser, S., Servin, C., Simha, R., Winters, T., & Xiang, Q. (2024). *Computer Science Curricula 2023*. ACM Press, IEEE Computer Society Press and AAAI Press. https://doi.org/10.1145/3664191

Parkinson, J., & Dziallas, S. (2024). Institutional perspectives on formal work-based learning programs in the UK. In *Proceedings of the 55th ACM Technical Symposium on Computer Science Education V. 1 (SIGCSE 2024)* (pp. 1028–1034). Association for Computing Machinery. https://doi.org/10.1145/3626252.3630879

Somerville, D., Cutts, Q., Barr, M., & Parkinson, J. (2020). Addressing mixed levels of prior knowledge by individualising learning pathways in a degree apprenticeship summer school. In *Proceedings of the 4th Conference on Computing Education Practice (CEP '20)* (Article 14, pp. 1–5). Association for Computing Machinery. https://doi.org/10.1145/3372356.3372370

Taylor-Smith, E., Smith, S., & Smith, C. (2019). Identity and belonging for graduate apprenticeships in computing: The experience of first cohort degree apprentices in Scotland. In *Proceedings of the 2019 ACM Conference on Innovation and Technology in Computer Science Education (ITiCSE '19)* (pp. 2–8). Association for Computing Machinery. https://doi.org/10.1145/3304221.3319753

Index

For Product Safety Concerns and Information please contact our EU representative GPSR@taylorandfrancis.com Taylor & Francis Verlag GmbH, Kaufingerstraße 24, 80331 München, Germany